THE NEW KEY TO BELIZE

THE NEW KEY TO BELIZE

STACY RITZ

GLENN KIM
Illustrator

DOUG PERRINE
Photographer

ULYSSES PRESS

Published by: Ulysses Press
3286 Adeline Street, Suite 1
Berkeley, CA 94703

Library of Congress Catalog Card Number 93-60746
ISBN 0-915233-93-2

Printed in the U.S.A. by the George Banta Company

10 9 8 7 6 5 4 3 2 1

Publishers: Ray Riegert, Leslie Henriques
Editor: Joanna Pearlman
Contributing Editor: Richard Harris
Managing Editor: Claire Chun
Editorial Associates: Lee Micheaux, Andrea Orvik, William Kiester, Per Casey
Maps: Phil Gardner, Claire Chun
Cover Designer: Bonnie Smetts
Indexer: Sayre Van Young
Color Separations: Twin Age Limited, Hong Kong

Cover illustration by Deidre Hyde

Distributed in the United States by Publishers Group West, in Canada by Raincoast Books, and in Great Britain and Europe by World Leisure Marketing

Printed on recycled paper

The authors and publisher have made every effort to ensure the accuracy of information contained in *The New Key to Belize*, but can accept no liability for any loss, injury or inconvenience sustained by any traveler as a result of information or advice contained in this guide.

For Judith Kahn, who showed me the way

Acknowledgments

No one deserves more thanks than my traveling companion, photographer and best friend, David Ritz, who also happens to be my husband. His unfailing patience, objectivity and ability to spot a silver lining will never be forgotten.

This book would of course never have been written without Ray Riegert, who in early 1992 asked that momentous questions: "What do you know about Belize?" During ensuing months, he supplied guidance, support and good judgment. Leslie Henriques oversaw the project while lending her invaluable skills as diplomat, mediator and graphics organizer. As always, Claire Chun performed tirelessly as manager, map maker and listener. Joanna Pearlman did an outstanding job of editing and organizing. Lee Micheaux, Andrea Orvik, William Kiester and Per Casey deserve credit for proofreading. Doug Perrine captured the best of Belize in the photos found in this book, while Glenn Kim is responsible for the compelling illustrations. Thanks also to Richard Harris for his thorough and enthusiastic coverage of Guatemala and Copán, and to Beatrice Blake for welcoming us into her best-selling "New Key" series.

For their hospitality and insights into Belize, I owe thanks to George and Corol Bevier, Tom and Josie Harding, Mick and Lucy Fleming, Rosita Arvigo and Sharon Matola, who also extended friendship. Special recognition goes to Michelle Gabourel at the Belize Tourist Board for answering the thousandth question. Thanks to Elena Malliaris for a highly memorable day in Cayo, and to Fiona van Riesen for the same in Cockscomb. And last but foremost, I am indebted to the truly remarkable people of Belize for their enduring warmth and wit, and exemplary passion for the environment.

The New Key To Belize Green Rating

It is unlikely that you will encounter a place so conscious of the environment as Belize. No matter who you meet—taxi drivers, restaurant cooks, bank tellers—they will have some opinion on how their country can be preserved, especially now in the face of increasing tourism.

Among those who deserve special recognition for environmental efforts are lodge owners, who every day must weigh the immediate value of guest receipts against the value and future of their surroundings. *The New Key To Belize* recognizes and recommends those lodges that strive to follow the principles of ecotourism, including protecting local habitats and wildlife, conserving energy and employing local residents. Throughout the text, these lodges are distinguished by a special Green Rating (❂).

To obtain information about Belize lodges, I personally visited each one, interviewing owners and staff as well as guests and former guests. I also mailed an Ecotourism Questionnaire to most of the lodges highlighted in *The New Key To Belize* (those that I observed violating ecotourism principles were omitted), inquiring about numerous issues such as water and sewage disposal, use of biodegradable soap, conservation training for employees and guests, support for local environmental organizations, and what impact the lodge had on the environment during construction.

Of the 60 lodges that were sent questionnaires, 30 responded. The majority of those 30 received the Green Rating. Best of all, many lodge owners have gone well beyond the call to ecotourism. One dive lodge, for instance, prints a special brochure warning guests about damaging the precious coral reef, mangroves and turtle grass. A jungle lodge uses local Maya talent for everything from employee uniforms and nightly dinners to room furnishings and guided tours. And a fishing lodge forbids anglers to hold their fish vertically when posing for pictures, since it may injure the fish before it is released.

This is all good news for Belize, and for travelers seeking to experience a *real* place taking pains to protect its natural treasures. At these lodges, guests can immerse themselves in the beauty and history of the region. And they can get to know Belizeans and their wonderfully diverse culture.

When booking a room, remember that these lodges, by their very nature, are not fancy but rather comfortably charming and altogether Belizean. Some are beachside bungalows whose windward architecture catches lots of sea breezes, while others are jungle huts with wild monkeys just outside the thatched door. Of course, no matter where you stay in Belize, remember to be an ecotourist.

LODGES RECEIVING GREEN RATINGS

(Please note that I did not list towns or geographic areas for places that are isolated and far from any town.)

THE CAYES

Ambergris Caye: Victoria House (page 85); Caribbean Villas (page 85); El Pescador (page 87)

Caye Caulker: Vega Inn and Gardens (page 92)

St. George's Caye: Cottage Colony (pages 95–96)

The Atolls: Turneffe Island Lodge (page 98); Manta Resort (page 99)

BELIZE CITY

Colton House (pages 107–108)

NORTHERN BELIZE

Maruba Resort & Jungle Spa (page 122); Adventure Inn (page 127)

WESTERN BELIZE

Warrie Head Ranch (page 133); Caesar's Place (page 137); Mida's Resort (page 138); Maya Mountain Lodge (page 138); Chaa Creek Cottages (page 138–39); duPlooy's (page 139); Black Rock Lodge (page 139); Windy Hill Cottages (page 139); Hidden Valley Inn (page 150); Pine Ridge Lodge (page 150); Blancaneaux Lodge (pages 150–51); Chan Chich Lodge (page 153)

SOUTHERN BELIZE

Dangriga: Pelican Beach Resort (page 159)

Placencia: Turtle Inn (page 164); Rum Point Inn (page 164–65)

"The land is one great wild, untidy luxuriant hothouse, made by nature for herself."
—Charles Darwin, Voyage of the Beagle

Introduction

THE ADVENTURE COAST

There are places in Belize where no human has ever laid foot, at least not in the last 1000 years, not since the time when the ancient Maya ruled these jungles from their lofty pyramids. Most regions that have been explored are still wild and rugged, possessed by beautiful beasts and birds, by silky green seas overflowing with life and palm-speckled shores reveling in seclusion, by mountains wrapped in colossal trees and forests carpeted with flamboyant flowers and emerald greenery, luxuriating, as it were, in nature's own hothouse.

How nature has reigned so long here, and how Belize has come to be so undiscovered, is due at least in part to its secret location. Indeed, the tiny country is but a blink on the map of Central America, wedged between formidable Guatemala and Mexico's vast Yucatán Peninsula, a mite-sized piece of jungle confronting two giants. Facing the Caribbean, Belize seems ready to break from land and fling itself out to sea.

But packed into this country the size of Massachusetts is an array of natural wonders, including the world's second-longest barrier reef (behind Australia's), where a thread of unspoiled isles are washed by the Caribbean Sea. Here also is the world's only jaguar preserve, the longest chain of caves in the Western Hemisphere, and the seventh-highest waterfall in the world.

Wild animals come in a splendorous array of shapes, sizes and names, from spiny anteaters, spider monkeys and red-eyed tree frogs to kinkajou bears, hawksbill turtles and bare-throated tiger herons. Fishing and scuba diving are so outstanding, their praises are whispered so as not to spoil their secrets.

Beyond the natural wonders is a lost manmade world slowly waking from its jungle slumber. Entire Maya cities, some only discovered in the last 40 years, are being resurrected by teams of archaeologists. Each day's excavations reveal marvels offering few explanations and many mysteries, beckoning outsiders to come ponder Belize's ancient treasures. Toothy pyramids loom on mountain ridges, and three-story-high masks stare out from jungle haunts. Elaborate networks of reservoirs, causeways and *sacbes*, or ancient roads, link age-old cities sprinkled down the length of this Adventure Coast.

Here are five distinct regions—the Cayes, Belize City, northern Belize, western Belize and southern Belize. Of course, the Cayes actually extend off the coast, forming a thread of islands trimmed in coral rock and mangroves. Only about two dozen of the islands are inhabited and only two, Ambergris Caye and Caye Caulker, possess villages. Right on the coast, covering a finger of land, is Belize City. Belize's only real city, it is the country's center of business.

North of Belize City, northern Belize presents a lush, lonely landscape harboring the powerful ancient ceremonial center of Lamanai and the peaceful Altun Ha, where fantastic jade artifacts have been found. Here, too, are vast sanctuaries for birds, butterflies and baboons, the Belizean name for howler monkeys. Western Belize attracts chic adventurers who stay in charming jungle lodges and explore Maya medicine trails, the popular ruins at Xunantunich and the cool, shady depths of the Mountain Pine Ridge forest. The west is also home to the great Caracol, a Maya city swallowed in jungle, hours from civilization, and home to the tallest building in Belize.

Southern Belize is a far-flung outback where hard-core explorers go to see what few travelers have seen: primitive Maya and Garifuna villages and the profound ruins at Lubaantun and Nim Li Punit. Along the southern coast is an anomaly called Placencia, whose pure white beaches and sun-dappled waters are attracting a coterie of young travelers. Inland, impermeable cloud forests cover much of the region, protecting an extraordinary web of life, including the world's densest population of jaguars, who reside at Cockscomb Basin Wildlife Sanctuary.

For those who would adventure beyond Belize's borders, thrilling side trips await to the west and south. Guatemala's Petén, North America's largest rainforest, sprawls across Belize's western border, thrilling travelers with the exquisite and daunting Maya city of Tikal. Southward from Belize is Guatemala's Río Dulce River, the picturesque "Sweet River" that leads to relaxing, time-locked villages. And then there is Copán, just across the Honduras border and enveloped in banana plantations, the site of unequaled Maya stone sculpture and hieroglyphic carvings.

Throughout these regions, travelers will find few creature comforts. Instead, they will discover a land that still belongs to the rainforest and to the sea, not to the frills of tourism. For unlike the money-driven throngs of "developed" countries, the residents of Belize have chosen to stay undeveloped, preferring the old, natural ways to the new, glitzy ones, opting to build a simple thatched lodge instead of a seaside highrise, to make nature and culture, not some contrived theme park, the big attractions.

And therein lies the reason for Belize's decided allure, and for the traveler's compulsion to go back once she has returned home, an affliction known as the "Belize Factor." Belize holds boundless opportunities for adventure, beckoning around every turn of a wornout jungle road, calling from every mountaintop washed in sun-dappled haze, waiting deep in a sea set with brilliant coral.

There is a certain innocence in Belize, a simple existence where the rigors of life have not yet slipped in. Events here often seem surreal: rabbits hop around a restaurant floor, a monkey joins you for breakfast, and toucans fill the garden where you're having a jungle massage. Women wash their clothes in the rivers and cook iguanas on their wood-fired stoves. No one wears shoes on the islands, but why should they, since the streets are made of sand.

After awhile, when you begin thinking Belize might be a little too primitive, too far out there, something Belizean happens. Like a destitute farmer donating his land to save the animals. Or a Maya villager taking time to show a stranger how to grind corn. Or a wild dolphin taking you for a swim off an isolated island. And then you fall in love with Belize all over again.

Belize is just like that. In no time, it burrows deep into your consciousness. And before you know it, you find yourself humming a Garifuna tune, listening for the howl of a monkey, searching the horizon for the familiar site of a Maya village.

Table of Contents

Belize

MEXICO

307

186

Chetumal

SANTA RITA

Corozal

CERRO MAYA

Orange Walk Town

Ambergris Caye

San Pedro

Hol Chan Marine Reserve

N

Caye Caulker

LAMANAI

ALTUN HA

Northern Highway

Old Northern Highway

Crooked Tree Wildlife Sanctuary

St. George's Caye

Belize City

Lighthouse Reef

Turneffe Islands

Blue Hole

Half Moon Caye Natural Monument

Belize Zoo

Spanish Lookout

Western Highway

Belmopan

XUNANTUNICH

San Ignacio

Blue Hole and St. Herman's Cave National Park

Hummingbird Highway

Dangriga

Tobacco Caye

Mountain Pine Ridge Forest Reserve

Glover's Reef

CARACOL

Cockscomb Basin Wildlife Sanctuary

South Water Caye

Placencia

Southern Highway

NIM LI PUNIT

LUBAANTUN

San Antonio

Punta Gorda

BARRIER REEF

CARIBBEAN SEA

GUATEMALA

CAMPECHE

QUINTANA ROO

0   25 kilometers

25 miles

ONE

Belize: History and Culture

Three thousand years ago, in the verdant, sun-drenched land that is now Belize, the Maya created a civilization that knew no equal. Appearing mysteriously like early-morning fog, they built magnificent cities, developed extensive trade routes and fashioned ceremonial centers that arched toward the heavens. Today, two of their temples remain the tallest buildings in Belize. For a traveler searching for historical truth, their lofty limestone summits are a haunting reminder of a civilization far grander than anything before or since in Belize history.

In fact, some legends tell that local human history began with the Maya. According to stories of the Quiché Maya, the great gods Tepeu and Gucumatz first made men from mud, but the rains came and washed them away. Then they honed them from trees, but the wooden men were mindless, so they made them of flesh and blood. These were the worst men, filled with cunning and wickedness, and had to be destroyed in a flood. Finally, Tepeu and Gucumatz pulled out some maize dough and molded the first "real men" of the world—Quiché Maya men.

Archaeologists' stories are just as vague and not nearly as entertaining, since there is little evidence of human life here before the Maya. Some speculate that primal hunters roamed the area from Mexico south through Central and South America about 13,000 years ago until the Pleistocene, or Ice Age, in 7500 B.C. Sometime during the next 3500 years, it is believed that Asians set out across the Bering Straits, perhaps even boatloads of Asians over several generations, all ending up on this part of the continent. In Belize, they probably subdued patches of swamp and jungle to grow rice, hunted the bounteous hot forests, caught plenty of fish in the rivers and seas, and laid the foundation for a society that would become the mighty Maya.

How the Maya became so mighty and so sophisticated over the next 2000 years, paralleling and even surpassing the other great thinkers of their time, is truly a mystery. What is known for sure is that it all started in the earliest, Preclassic days, from about 2000 B.C. to 250 A.D., when the Maya borrowed

1

a calendar from neighboring Olmec tribes and learned how to calculate time. They planted fields of maize and tomatoes and cacao beans, and fashioned temples for the gods of sun and rain. And they spoke a language that became the root for all modern Maya dialects.

But it was the Classic Period, from 250 to 900 A.D., when Maya life sky-rocketed into a golden age of exquisitely painted and ornamented temples and palaces and pyramids, fantastic works of art, astonishing achievements in math, science and astronomy, and a writing system more sophisticated than any other ever conceived in the Western Hemisphere. Colossal stelae, or carved stone monuments, were inscribed with fanciful text and dramatic stories of war and peace and just everyday life. Belize's greatest ceremonial centers— Caracol, Xunantunich, Altun Ha, Lamanai—were built during the Classic Period, though Lamanai's architecture extends well before and after this time, amazingly spanning some 3000 years.

And though the Maya world stretched from Mexico's Yucatán Peninsula all the way south to El Salvador, recent findings point to Belize as the heart of that world, the crossroads of economic and cultural exchange, the "in" place to live. Part of it was Belize's coveted locale: a subtropical seacoast whose waters were speckled with lovely coral isles and whose interior was covered in flourishing rainforest, majestic mountains and fertile valleys. Discoveries in 1993 even revealed a rich mineral belt in southern Belize where the Maya were likely mining hematite, pyrite, granite and other valuables crucial to their economy.

Like the Morocco of the Western Hemisphere, Classic Period Belize overflowed with sophisticated trade and profound culture, mystical religions and mighty kingdoms. Great rulers and priests lived here, and so did artists, writers and aristocrats. There were peasants and farmers and also middle class families, whose spacious thousand-year-old homes boasted big "king-size" bed slabs and ornate burial tombs, and a location convenient to reservoirs and "downtown" shopping areas. From the downtown, *sacbes*, or ancient limestone roads, ran out for miles around like spokes on a wheel, to Belize's first— and only—suburbs. (Today's sparsely populated Belize has no real suburbs, unless you count Hattieville, which grew from a temporary hurricane camp to a primitive village outside Belize City.) In fact, it is hard to imagine that one single ancient Maya city, the jungle-veiled Caracol, boasted nearly 190,000 residents—as many as live in all of Belize today. In 562 A.D., Caracol crushed its big neighbor, Tikal, Guatemala, and ruled the Maya world for more than 100 years.

And then something happened. Just as the Maya empire had mysteriously blossomed beyond belief, it mysteriously collapsed. The beginning of the end was around 900 A.D., when the Maya suddenly started abandoning their cities. This Postclassic Period of decline lasted over 600 years, during which time archaeologists theorize there may have been earthquakes, wars, famines, disease and massive peasant uprising. Any or all of these could have caused the Maya downfall, or perhaps the Maya simply evolved away from an elite society into a farming one. For the Maya are by no means gone; indeed, some four million Maya still thrive throughout Belize and the surrounding countries in an area known today as *La Ruta Maya*, or The Maya Route.

This 1500-mile-long Maya Route runs down the length of Mexico's Yucatán Peninsula, crosses the jungles and mountains of Guatemala, Honduras and El Salvador, and loops through lush Belize—a perfect place for today's travelers to begin a *La Ruta Maya* odyssey. Along the way, there are hulking temples and steep pyramids that rise above the jungle canopies, thousands of stone dwellings and *sacbes*, intricate Maya sculptures and stelae and, greatest of all, a fascinating society of proud Maya people who live much as their Classic ancestors did. From thatched-hut villages stashed deep in the jungle, tucked along rushing rivers and parked atop hills, they grow their maize and beans and rice on *milpa* farms, in an ancient endless cycle inspired by gods of sun and rain and by the beasts of the jungle. In the heat of the day, Belize's Maya women squat for hours over wood set ablaze on their dirt floors, grilling corn tortillas on a *comal*, or griddle stone, for tortillas are the staple of modern Maya life, much as they were 2000 years ago.

The Maya were no doubt tending their corn fields when the Spanish arrived in the early 1500s. Explorers Vicente Yáñez Pinzón and Juan Díaz de Solís sailed up the coast from Honduras to Yucatán around 1506 and claimed everything they saw, including Belize, for the Spanish empire. Soon missionaries made their way down from Yucatán to Lamanai in northern Belize. The Maya at Lamanai were friendly to their uninvited guests until the guests built a church and told the Maya they had to attend. Angry, the Maya burned the church. Several years later, more missionaries fashioned a second, sturdier church at Lamanai, but the Maya burned it down, too.

Other than the Lamanai incidents, the Spanish strangely did little to bother the Maya in Belize. Instead, they concentrated their efforts in neighboring Guatemala and in Yucatán, where Hernando Cortez and a small army combed the land for slaves.

While on the outs with the Spanish government, Cortez and his 11 ships and 600 troops snuck away from Cuba to the Mexican shore in 1519 and over the next few years slaughtered thousands of Maya who refused to be enslaved. Cortez' tyranny laid the groundwork for nearly 400 years of Maya oppression in the Yucatán, during which a stream of Maya and *Mestizo* (Spanish-Maya) refugees flowed into neighboring Belize. The most profound Yucatán war was the War of the Castes, from 1848 to 1858, when the Maya slaves rose against their Spanish masters. It was a bloody decade, and those who could escaped south to Belize. Many settled on Ambergris Caye and Caye Caulker, just south of the Yucatán border, and today those islands are thriving *Mestizo* communities.

Just as refugees and former slaves helped give today's Belize its frontier veneer, so did the pirates and loggers who latched on to its shores in the early

1600s. The pirates found Belize's sheltered cayes a prime vantage point for raiding and plundering Spanish galleons gorged with gold and silver. Belize's treacherous barrier reef helped out, too, laying open the bowels of many a ship carrying treasure. The pirates particularly loved tiny St. George's Caye, where they would catch large sea turtles and smoke their meat over mangrove fires on large racks called "boucans"—hence the name buccaneers. They sold the meat to passing loggers, privateers and other pirates, and began what would become Belize's most lucrative fishing business through the late 1800s.

As for the loggers, many were driven south from Yucatán and north from Honduras by Spanish harassment, and they, too, settled on the Belize shores, building meager thatched huts on a muddy bank near the mouth of what is now the Belize River. By the mid-1600s, as logwood became prized in Europe for its black, blue and purple dyes, many pirates made a career change to logwood cutting. They soon became known as the Baymen, for they would haul the logs across the Bay of Honduras, though it was too romantic a name for such a disgraceful lot who regularly drank themselves to the bottom of rum bottles and tormented the Puritans who had migrated from Nicaragua and Honduras. One 1705 report to the British Trade Council called the Belize settlement a "River of Bullys." In fact it is said that ship's captains used to mark the spot on their maps with an "obelize" to signify a place of corruption, and then the word itself was eventually corrupted into "Belize." Others say

Margay

Belize got its name from Scottish buccaneer Peter Wallace, who established a community at the river's mouth in 1638, and whose name was pronounced Wal-EEZ. Still others claim the roots of the word go deeper in history, back to the ancient Maya word *belikin*, meaning "toward the east," as Belize faces east out to sea. No one can tell you the real truth, but most everyone in Belize can tell you that Belikin is the name of their good-tasting national beer.

By the 18th century, the logwood and mahogany business was flourishing and so was the lawless society of British Baymen, who hacked away at the forests and fought off frequent attacks by the Spanish. Spain still claimed the land, despite a 1763 agreement in which it gave England the "right" to cut logwood. Of course, it wasn't the English who did the actual cutting, but slaves who were imported by the Baymen. Most slaves were West Africans brought over via Jamaica and Bermuda, or Indian slaves from the Mosquito Tribes of Nicaragua. Many were women forced to care for the Baymen, primarily as sex slaves, though a number of Baymen did free their commonlaw wives— a custom that set the tone for a future ethnic-rich Belize. In fact, the beautiful, tan-skinned children of the Baymen and slaves would be the first of many generations of Creoles, who are today Belize's foremost ethnic group. The West African slaves also fused the growing settlement with their pulsing dances, drum-driven music—the first "goombay" sounds in Belize—and *obeah* black magic; their celebrations in the swamps outside their huts lasted all night, with the obeah man or woman appealing to dead ancestors to free them from the shackles of their white masters.

It was not obeah but the British government that finally freed the slaves in 1807, though many Belizean landowners refused to give up their free labor. In 1812, slaves laid the cornerstone for Belize's first church, St. John's in Belize City, then spent 14 grueling years building the cathedral brick by brick. A few years after the church was finished, church fathers held a little ceremony for the slaves to celebrate their "emancipation."

While the 19th century heralded the beginnings of freedom for slaves, it also ended the pesky attacks by the Spanish. The attack that ended it all was in 1798, near St. George's Caye, then the capital of the colony. Recorded history recalls a great cannon battle between Spanish and British ships, though many say it was no more than a few Spanish galleons retreating after being threatened by a ragtag band of Baymen. Whatever the truth, the Battle of St. George's Caye officially ended Spanish claims and secured British dominion, though it was not until 1862 that the colony formally became British Honduras. Today, a national holiday commemorates the Battle of St. George's Caye, though some political and cultural independents do not join the festivities, believing that the day commemorates British rule and not Belizean freedom.

Freedom was the reason thousands of new immigrants arrived during the 1800s. From the north came the Maya and *Mestizos* escaping Yucatan's Caste War and settling in northern Belize and on outlying cayes. In northern areas, where the terrain had been stripped by logging, they planted sugar cane—and thus began the industry now number-one in Belize. They also flavored this northern area with Spanish-Maya culture, and travelers today who drive through the towns of Corozal, Santa Clara and Santa Elena Concepción will be met by pueblo and mission architecture.

The 1800s also saw a stream of new residents from Honduras in the south. The Garifuna, oddly enough, came to Belize to escape British oppression. Their story is one of great intrigue and mystery, as their history is woven with both true and questionable tales. What is certain is that in the 1600s, a ship carrying West African slaves ran aground on the Caribbean island of St. Vincent. The survivors either became slaves or citizens, or perhaps both, and eventually intermarried with the native Carib Indians and created the Garifuna. From these haphazard beginnings, they founded a culture on freedom— freedom to play their driving, soulful music now known as *punta rock*; freedom to farm their simple plots of earth; freedom to practice their obscure religion, which revolves around the *dugu* ceremony of calling to dead ancestors; and, most importantly, freedom of self-rule. But the British wouldn't allow it, and drove the Garifuna from St. Vincent when they refused to colonize. Most were banished to the deserted but paradisaic island of Roatan in the Bay of Honduras. From there, they made their way to mainland Honduras, Guatemala and Belize.

In southern Belize the Garifuna established outposts along the coast and began reviving their close-knit society. Over the years, the colonial government sought to suppress their religion and force the Garifuna into Catholicism, but the Garifuna simply pacified the British by adding a few Catholic practices to their own ceremonies. As late as the 1950s and 1960s, *dugus* were held in secret so as not to incite local magistrates. Today, however, Belize's 15,000 Garifuna worship freely and in recent years have even begun allowing outside observers. In the southern Belize towns of Dangriga and Punta Gorda, artists' canvases dramatically recreate scenes from dugus and from the Garifunas' voyage from St. Vincent to Honduras and Belize.

While the colony broadened culturally during the 1800s, it struggled economically. The logging industry went boom and bust several times, and by the late 19th century large accessible forests were nearly wiped out. Sugar cane did reasonably well in northern Belize and bananas were planted in southern regions. By the turn of the century, sapodilla trees were surrendering their precious sap for the chicle business, which peaked at the height of World War II with Chiclets chewing gum.

But the 1900s brought many setbacks, not the least of which was a nameless 1931 hurricane that nearly blew away Belize City, killing ten percent of the capital's 15,000 residents. In 1949, when colonial magistrates devalued local currency and raised the cost of living, British Hondurans formed a People's Committee to protest. A year later, the grassroots committee had strengthened and, changing its name to the People's United Party (or PUP, as it's called today), began rallying for Belize independence.

In 1950, Belizeans elected five party members to the Belize City Council to form a majority, and over the next decade worked toward national democracy. In 1965, Great Britain gave its blessing to the new nation but Belize stopped short of declaring independence because of Guatemala. Like Spanish conquerors of earlier centuries, big-neighbor Guatemala had long laid claim to the colony. And since Belizeans had been pushing for independence, Guatemala had begun pushing to take over Belize. So Belize waited 16 more years, until 1981, to officially become Belize. At the time, Belize struck a deal whereby British troops could train in the Belize jungles if they'd keep a show of force against Guatemala. Today, you'll see British battalions at the international airport, in the cayes and along the Belize-Guatemala border. And you can't miss the Brits, as Belizeans call the boisterous rank and file, tossing back Belikins across the land.

Like every other walk of Belizean life, the Brits only add to the tropical spice. In fact, Belize's 190,000 residents are a truly diverse phenomenon, an improbable blend of Creoles and Maya, Mennonites and Chinese, Arabs and *Mestizos*, Germans and Garifuna, and of course, British. English is the country's first language, but there are five other major languages, including Maya.

It is this kaleidoscope of humanity, of music and art and dress, of triumphs and defeats and expectations, all joined by a determination to exist free, that makes Belize so unusual. Born of Maya brilliance, baptized by raucous pirates and Spanish outlaws, ignited by African rhythms and only slightly refined by British gentility, Belize is branded with a tenacious pioneer mentality. That same mentality is what ensures travelers of a great adventure on this tropical coast.

WHITE IBIS

TWO

The Ecological Picture

ECOTOURISM

It is hard to imagine that in just two centuries, more than 80 percent of Latin America's tropical forests have been erased from the planet. Population explosions, frenetic development, widespread logging and slash-and-burn farming—where forests are burned to grow crops and raise cattle—are mainly to blame. Much has been written about the destruction, but little has been done until recently, with the advent of a concept called ecotourism. The basic idea behind ecotourism is that visitors to a place can contribute to the environment and support the people who live in that environment. If villagers can make a living from tourism, it is reasoned, then there's no need to burn off the forest for food or hunt endangered animals for the price of their skins.

But ecotourism means much more than that. In fact, this catchword of the '90s has come to mean setting aside vast forests as sanctuaries and preserves and controlling tourism to those areas. It means fighting destruction of virgin lands planned for resorts, and encouraging reforestation in decimated areas. It means giving someone tempted to loot a Maya ruin a job as a tour guide to those ruins. It means convincing a family who doesn't know where their next meal is coming from to preserve the forest that provides that meal. And for a traveler, it means safeguarding the areas you visit as if they were your own backyard. If you must leave something behind, let it be footprints.

Among Central American countries, Belize is a paradigm of ecotourism. Indeed, this tiny country, where the per capita income is only $1100 a year, is waging an intense campaign to save its environment. More than 25 wildlife and archaeological preserves have been set aside, including the 100,000-acre Cockscomb Basin, the world's only jaguar sanctuary. Jaguars have been wiped out of other parts of Central America, where rainforests are ravaged every day. Belizeans point to this devastation, as well as to overdevelopment in Florida and the Caribbean, in the crusade to save their country. Bumper stickers proclaim Belizeans' love for wild animals, and local gossip is laced with the latest ecotourism news.

9

Every day, new ecotourism programs are being created. Numerous environmental organizations, as well as the Belize government, are working together to promote ecotourism. In 1992, Belize welcomed countries from around the world to an ecotourism "congress," which addressed the earth's environmental problems and needs. Environmentalists, government officials, developers, tour operators, hoteliers and others in the tourist industry met for intense discussions. The congress included field seminars where participants learned about such subjects as recycling and eco-sensitive diving and sportfishing.

Of course, ecotourism can only work if it is supported by tourists. To help visitors better enjoy and contribute to the environment of Belize, we've compiled a short environmental code of ethics:

1. **Do not disturb wildlife and natural habitats.** Stay on the trails, avoid using machetes and collecting plants or wildlife. Coral reefs are especially sensitive, and should never be touched. Even a slight brush with your fin can cause disease in the reef. Bird nests should be viewed from a safe distance with binoculars, and nesting sea turtles should be observed only with a trained guide. Do not feed monkeys and other wild animals, because it alters their diets and behaviors. Raccoons, who normally live alone, become pack animals when fed and spread diseases that kill them.

2. **Do not litter.** If you'll be in remote areas, take along a sack to carry out your garbage.

3. **Be conscious of helping local communities.** Use native tour guides—they *are* the best—and patronize locally owned inns and restaurants. Buy souvenirs from native crafts people; the Maya villagers make marvelous handicrafts.

4. **Be culturally sensitive.** Remember that you are a guest in a country. Make an effort to learn basic local customs and follow them. Don't judge Belize by your hometown. On one jungle tour, two travelers from Texas constantly compared everything to "how it is back home." Somehow, I couldn't imagine the Maya guide being interested in a four-hour litany on how things are done in Texas.

ECOSYSTEMS

GEOGRAPHY

Few regions as small as Belize are so physically diverse. Where else, in a space the size of Massachusetts, do you find cool pine forests and saunalike jungle, luscious green islands and parched brown savannah, majestic mountains and flat muddy swamps? There are hushed coastal lagoons and fizzing streams, thundering waterfalls and shadowy rivers cocooned in jungle. And then there is the emerald sea, which stretches to the horizon where it blends into sky. Everywhere there is wild landscape, but few people.

Offshore, many of the untamed and mostly uninhabited cayes are actually peaks of the Maya Mountain Range. These coral rock islets peek up from a shallow underwater valley, called the Inner Channel, that runs from the Belize coast out to a great barrier reef. The reef, in turn, stretches some 180 miles from the Gulf of Honduras to the Bay of Chetumal in southern Yucatán. Formed over thousands of years, and second in scope only to Australia's Great Barrier Reef, Belize's reef system is complex beyond imagination: millions of life forms interacting and depending, yet so fragile that humans could obliterate them in a few years.

If coral rock defines the reef, then limestone is the trademark of northern Belize. In fact, the northern region is the end of a great limestone shelf that reaches down from the Yucatán Peninsula. From the air, you can see the vast flat shelf poking out into the frothy green Caribbean Sea. A thin layer of soil covers much of the limestone, and is fertile enough to support a healthy sugar business. In the winter, farmers burn underbrush from the cane fields, and dark smoke clings to the skies.

But most of northern Belize still belongs to the forests—mangrove along the coast, pine and palmetto along a central plain, and luxurious broadleaf rainforests in the west. Ponds, lagoons and swamps decorate the forests, as do abandoned logging camps—testaments to centuries when mowing down trees was the biggest business in Belize. Today, many camps lie within reserves where selective logging is practiced.

The land across central and western Belize is rippled with hills and valleys and terraced fields, and spidery rivers that nourish the fields. Out in the district known as Cayo, broadleaf jungle is interspersed with great forests of slash pines, where the soil is a mix of sand and clay, and waterfalls and bubbling streams create vistas of stunning beauty. The limestone here is ancient, probably of the Cretaceous Age, and eons of percolating water have created vast sinkholes and caves and underground streams.

The Maya Mountains form a spine of granite down southern Belize. Most prominent of all Belize's natural features, they are marked by deep canyons and shallow valleys, snaking rivers and ebbing ridges, which eventually rise to Victoria Peak, Belize's highest at 3675 feet. But mostly the area is solid jungle, with areas so dense and remote they have yet to be visited by modern-day humans. Southern Belize boasts true "cloud forests," tropical rainforests high enough to enjoy thick mists and rains most every day. Here there are double canopies of trees, with cohune palms that reach five stories high, and deep webs of bromeliads and mosses that thrive in perpetual dampness.

FLORA

Seeing the jungle for the first time is exhilarating, indeed overwhelming. Take just one tree. Soaring like an ancient column, its limbs drip with perfumed orchids and lacy mosses, its branches offer refuge to both a hawk's nest and a nest of yellow wasps, its trunk bears the scrapings of a jaguar along with the scars of a human machete. Vines and epiphytes—aerial roots—creep and curl around the tree in orderly fashion, then slither away on the jungle floor. Wildly colored fungi cling to its wood and leaves, and ferns blanket its feet. On this, a single tree, the intricate web of life is nearly beyond comprehension.

Yet this one tree is but a blink in the Belizean florascape. In fact, it would take volumes of books to do justice to the flora of Belize. Within this fabulously diverse region are more than 4000 species of flowering plants, including 250 different orchids and 700 types of trees. There are heart-shaped anthuriums and paddle-shaped heliconia, flaming bromeliads and purple passion flowers. And there is much beauty that does not bloom—water-gorged jungle plants and cathedrals of pine trees, island palms burdened with coconuts and grand old cedar and mahogany trees that somehow eluded the logger's axe. There are strangler figs that can fell a 100-foot oak tree, and vines that will wound with their thorns and heal that wound with their leaves. And there are jungles so unimaginably dense they have buried whole cities for thousands of years.

Here, in Eden-like settings, bromeliads and orchids grow as big as tree trunks and trees grow as tall as skyscrapers. Guanacaste trees, which can reach 400 feet high, are decorated with flowering air plants—making them nature's own Christmas trees. The bookut also grows tall and wide, with a canopy spanning about 40 feet. Howler monkeys love to eat its seed pods, though the pods' musky smell gives the tree its nickname of "stinking toe."

Ocelot

The black oozing sap from the poisonwood tree inflicts angry blisters that last up to two weeks. The antidote, used since the time of the Maya, is to apply sap from the gumbo limbo. Near every poisonwood tree there's always a gumbo limbo tree.

The sap from the sapodilla tree fueled the country's largest industry during the first half of this century. Chicling, or the harvest of sapodilla sap, was accomplished by *chicleros*, rugged bushmen who would climb 40 to 60 feet up a sapodilla tree, then, working their way back down, use a machete to slash deep zigzags along the trunk. Chicle was used as a base for chewing gum (remember Chiclets?). Today, Belize forests are filled with sapodilla trees, though rare is the one that does not bear the scars of a *chiclero*.

But it is the cohune palm, with its thick trunk and elegant plumed fronds, that has come to symbolize Belize's jungles. Preferring to grow in deep, rich, well-drained soil, cohunes have been an integral part of local life since the time of the Maya. Virtually every part of this exquisite tree can be used—the sturdy fronds for making thatched roofs; the tender hearts, as a culinary delicacy; the tiny, coconutlike nuts, for making charcoal and oil. During World War II, the U.S. Air Force used the husks of cohune palms to make charcoal filter masks for its pilots. Today, Maya villagers boil the nuts to extract their oil, which is bottled in a glass jar, corked with a corn cob and sold at the markets. Surely no Belize sight is more mystical than that of cohune palms dripping in the foggy aftermath of a forest rain, looking like wispy giants of the jungle.

Riverbanks play host to dense webs of spiny bamboo, whose love of water makes it amenable to floods. The bamboo protects the banks from erosion, and protects itself with sharp barbs that can reach four inches long. Few trees can protect themselves from the strangler fig, which slowly and methodically kills its prey. The strangler wraps its roots around a tree trunk until, after a few years, the roots grow and fuse and choke the tree to death. The trunk falls and becomes hollow, providing shelter for a variety of animals. Bats particularly love the damp, dark space where they can escape the light of day.

The jungles are also thick with tropical fungi that bloom with brilliant color and take on exotic shapes. Ferns cool the forest with their double ceiling canopies and provide food for many animals. In less dense areas, ferns also form soft green carpets that make openings in the forest.

Out of the jungle and along the Caribbean coast, the flora resembles many people's idea of tropical paradise: shade-giving papaya, mango and breadfruit trees; rambling bougainvillea and hibiscus bursting with brilliant color; and wind-blown palms, heavy with coconuts. Exotic flowers, such as red ginger and birds of paradise, grow wild. Here, too, are the mangroves, propped along the shore, looking like bushes on stilts. Mangroves are crucial to the environment, as they provide nurseries for birds and animals and protect the shore from erosion.

FAUNA

It is a feat of nature that a place as small as Belize should possess such a mind-boggling array of exotic animals. Here among the Maya mysteries live mysterious creatures like spiny anteaters and kinkajou bears, long-nosed bats and portly tapirs, scaly iguanas and gangly Jesus Christ lizards—who actually *can* walk on water.

These enchanting animals thrive in Belize's amazing range of environments, from pine forests, dry savannahs and moist jungle and rainforest to offshore islands, low coastal plains and swamplands. However, as their homes quickly succumb to farming and development, many face extinction. During recent years, Belize has set aside protected sanctuaries where animals can flourish and people can view their worlds. With a little time and patience, one soon learns how easy it is to witness this wonderful wildlife.

JAGUARS   "God decided to make man because the jaguar already existed," begins a Maya folktale, related in the book *Jaguar*. The jaguar was in fact a god to the ancient Maya, steeped in mystery and worshipped from a distance. Today's Maya still revere, and fear, this king of carnivores they call *balum*.

Jaguars are brooding creatures who prefer a solitary life and lots of room—a male will roam over a 100-square-mile area. They are massive, weighing as much as 300 pounds, and cloaked in downy soft coats with spots that are sometimes shaped like flowers and butterflies. Despite their reputation for aggression, jaguars rarely attack people unless provoked. A caged jaguar, however, will hypnotize you with his eyes; one flinch and he will charge his fence.

The jaguar is a night lover, using the cool blackness of the jungle underbrush to pursue its favorite meal—prickly, piglike peccaries. When a jaguar attacks, it is lightning-fast: one swipe to the neck with its massive paw, then a head-crushing blow with knifelike teeth. But he is not a picky eater, and will feast on whatever mammals come around: monkeys, deer, otters, birds, and even iguana and fish. During the day, he dozes on a bed of leaves or on fallen tree trunks.

Jaguars are rare throughout their range—Mexico to Argentina—though thanks to recent conservation efforts, Belize is thought to have the world's greatest concentration of the hulking spotted cats. The world's only jaguar preserve, the Cockscomb Basin Wildlife Sanctuary, lies in southern Belize, the very area where just ten years ago it was common for wealthy, rifle-toting Americans to hunt for "trophy jaguar." Poaching still occurs in Belize and perhaps will until people no longer feel compelled to display the animals' stuffed skulls and skins.

OTHER CATS   The Belize jungles are also home to other exotic cats—pumas, ocelots, margays and jaguarundis—who, like the jaguar, are threatened by poaching. Pumas are in fact quite rare, having been nearly obliterated by hunters, and it is doubtful you will see one in the wild. Known also as cougars or mountain lions, they love the mountains as well as low forests and savannah. Pumas are slightly smaller than jaguars, weighing up to 200 pounds, and have wild, piercing eyes and fur the color of honey.

Ocelots are much smaller, less than 35 pounds, and margays are the size of big housecats. Both are slender and dainty, and exquisitely garbed in velvety coats with spots and stripes that run together like watercolors. Sadly, it is their gorgeous coats that make them more valuable dead than alive.

Jaguarundis do not look like cats as much as weasels, with long, barrel-shaped bodies, stumpy legs and snaking tails. Most common of all wild cats, with coats that are dark brown to black, they prefer to live in savannahs and scrub forests, foraging the ground for small prey.

TAPIRS   Belize's national animal may also be its homeliest, growing as large as 650 pounds, sporting a long upper lip and splayed toes, covered with hairless ashen skin, and boasting characteristics of both the pig and cow. It is, in fact, a relative of the rhinoceros and the horse, though its nickname is mountain cow. Tapirs will live anywhere there are tasty plants and fruit, from dry savannah to swampy mangroves to dense rainforest, but they never pass up a chance to wallow in a mudhole.

Belize's most famous tapir, April, lives at the Belize Zoo. Every April, school children from around the country gather to celebrate her birthday and watch April gulp down a two-foot-tall cake of horse chow, bananas and carrots. Don't miss a chance to visit April; it will probably be your only encounter with a tapir. The bright animals are shy, having been hunted to near extinction in every Latin American country but Belize. Though they are not particularly good to eat, tapirs are thought to be cattle killers (which they're not), and local myths say they cast spells on people. Baby tapirs, which have spots and stripes, are especially feared. Unfortunately, some people shoot tapirs just for the sport of it, leaving them to die in the forest with bullet wounds.

MONKEYS   Two types of monkeys live in Belize: the spider monkey and the black howler. It takes a watchful eye to spy either species scrambling through the treetops, though if you spend even a few days in the Belize jungle, you will likely see many monkeys.

Spider monkeys are found only in Belize and Mexico's Yucatán Peninsula; they were nearly wiped out by yellow fever in the mid-1900s. They have lanky arms and legs and tails as long as their body. Their hands are thumbless—all the better for zipping gracefully from branch to branch.

Nearly twice as big as spider monkeys, weighing up to 22 pounds, black howlers have a slightly wider range that includes Guatemala. Called baboons in Belize, they have faces that are hauntingly human, and a male and female will hold hands while resting. When they are ready to mate, the pair will lock eyes, then flick their tongues at each other and lick tails, before the male approaches from behind, clinging with his tail to a tree limb for support.

Howlers howl to defend a troop's territory, or sometimes before a rain or if frightened. If you are ever awakened by the jackhammer scream of a howler at night, you may well think an angry lion is bearing down on your door.

OTHER MAMMALS   Few jungle inhabitants seem so well equipped as the anteater, whose long slithery tongue is fitted with tiny prongs that keep the ants marching in the right direction—toward its stomach, where a special muscle crushes insect exoskeletons. An anteater spends its waking hours poking its uninvited nose into termite nests, where ants inhabit the outer compartments. Its front claws are curled and strong, useful for digging deep into nests. Anteaters are common, though their telltale signs—raided termite nests—are commoner still.

Like the anteater, a kinkajou makes its home in a hollow tree, preferring to snooze during the day. At night, it emerges to feed, flicking its long tongue in the honey pot of a bee's nest or the nectar pouch of a flower. Chestnut colored and rippled with soft fur, it is also called honey bear or nightwalker, although it is a relative of the raccoon. Kinkajous are so appealing they are frequently stolen from the jungle and turned into pets, though they make lousy ones, refusing to be housebroken and staying up all night wrecking one's house.

Coatimundis, also known as coatis or quash, look even more like their relative the raccoon, with their snouty masked face and tail of black rings. Found throughout the Belize forests, they have a wide diet, feasting on everything from lizards and snakes to mice and fruit. Tayras, or bushdogs, are lean and mean creatures a little smaller than coatimundis, but with the same culinary penchants. A member of the weasel family, the tayra isn't particularly dangerous but extremely territorial, and will snarl at anyone who encroaches on its homestead.

You will know a peccary is near even before you see him, since the odor that precedes him is not unlike that of a dairy farm. The smell radiates from the animal's back and actually entices other peccaries, who will rub their head in it, though it would seem painful, since pecarries are covered with bristly spines.

Peccaries look and taste a lot like wild pigs, and are the favorite meal of jaguars and many other jungle predators. There are two types of peccaries in Belize: collared, who have bands of white hair around their necks; and white-lipped, with white whiskers. Both move in herds, and a herd of 100 or more white-lipped peccaries has been known to charge people who stumble upon them in the rainforest. Researcher John C. Kricher advises that "climbing a tree is the best escape route, though the peccaries may wait around beneath the tree for a while."

Rare is the visitor who encounters a paca, a handsome, intensely shy little rodent who leaves his hole only at night. Hunters, however, chase the furry creatures from their holes and shoot them, for their white flesh is prized throughout Belize. Paca is also known as gibnut and royal rat, the latter name being bestowed upon it several years ago when the queen of England ate stewed paca in Belize. Less tasty but still killed for its meat, agouti is another common rodent that's smaller and furrier than the paca.

White-tailed deer and brocket deer have been hunted incessantly, though sightings in Belize are more frequent now that reserves provide some protection. White-tailed deer grow to 200 pounds, though they average about 60 pounds in Belize. They have an elegant, lustrous body sheathed in peppery brown to whitish brown fur, and a fluffy white tail, which they hide when attempting to elude a predator. Brocket deer are diminutive, usually weighing less than 40 pounds, and have a silky auburn coat that blends nicely into the rainforest.

FROGS, LIZARDS AND TURTLES   Belize has numerous frogs and also toads, but the most dazzling is the red-eyed tree frog, whose ruby gelatinous eyes are like night beacons of the jungle. As the frog perches on an emerald leaf, attached firmly by rubbery, neon-orange hands and feet, its eyes bulge out from its metallic green body, which is splashed with white dots and blue patches. All in all, it makes quite a spectacle.

Not nearly as resplendent as the tree frog but immensely entertaining, the basilisk lizard sprints on two hind legs right across the top of a river. Nicknamed the Jesus Christ lizard, he's a comical sight, really, a miniature dinosaur constantly on the run with nothing chasing him and nowhere in particular to go. The basilisk's lizard opposite is the iguana, who prefers to bask lethargically all day on a riverbank. Iguanas seem to be everywhere—including restaurant menus, where they're often listed as "bamboo chicken."

Hickatees have all but disappeared from the rivers, victims of relentless hunting and pollution and their inability to lay many eggs. Unlike sea turtles, who

Green turtle

lay over 100 eggs at a time, these Central American river turtles may lay as few as a dozen eggs, depositing them under a canopy of floating vegetation or along a sheltered riverbank. If an egg is not snatched by a wood rail or otter, it will become a baby turtle hunted by crocodiles and raccoons. If it survives to adulthood, it will probably meet its fate at the end of an oar—the preferred weapon of human hunters, who whack the brownish green turtles as they float along the river's surface, snoozing the day away.

Amazingly, hickatee hunting is still legal in Belize, as is sea turtle hunting. Belize's three types of sea turtles—the green, the loggerhead and the hawksbill—are all endangered for countless reasons, including hunting, coastal development (which eliminates the turtles' eating and nesting grounds) and fishing nets that entangle and drown them.

Green turtles graze on sea grass, which turns their fat green and gives them their name. Unfortunately, as more seabeds are dredged, the turtles have fewer places to feed. Green turtles used to grow as large as four feet and weigh over 600 pounds, but thanks to humans, they no longer make it to such a ripe old age.

Loggerhead turtles have big heads, stocky necks and reddish shells shaped like hearts. The female returns each year to the same beach to lay her eggs, abandoning the safety of her sea home and swimming through dark waters toward a familiar shore, hauling her 300-pound body awkwardly across the sand and digging a giant pit, laboring for hours in the moonlight. Then, one by one, she painfully deposits her eggs—up to 100 of them—covers them with sand, and lumbers back to sea before dawn. For all her hard work, poachers will soon come and steal most of her eggs. The few they leave will hatch and wait for night, then scurry toward the surf, only to be picked off by birds, lizards and crabs. Today, fewer than five percent of baby loggerheads will grow to become adults, when they become eligible to be hunted. And which is why tomorrow there may be no more loggerheads.

Hawksbill turtles have peculiar-looking, sharp-hooked beaks, but are also gloriously adorned with shells of golden brown and orange shingles. Their shells have been their doom, fetching big bucks in markets around the world for many years now.

POISONOUS SNAKES   When you walk in the jungle, your thoughts (and possibly fears) will eventually turn to poisonous snakes. Travelers worry more about snakes than they should, since the vast majority are neither aggressive nor poisonous. Those few that are venomous fall into two categories: rear-fanged and front-fanged. Venom from rear-fanged snakes is dangerous only to the snakes' small prey, such as lizards and toads, but is *not harmful to humans.*

Front-fanged snakes are a different story. The coral snake, also called a bead-and-coral snake, is a front-fanged snake whose venom attacks the nervous system, causing paralysis and sometimes death. Fortunately, the coral snake is rarely aggressive and an excellent coral snake antivenin is widely available.

The front-fanged snake Belizeans fear most is the fer-de-lance, a pit viper also known as a yellow-jawed tommygoff for the yellow jaws and throat that accentuate its brown body. The most poisonous snake in Central America and one of the most common, it has unusually long, spiked fangs that resemble inverted tusks. Mice are its main prey, so the fer-de-lance spends much of its time on the ground and around barns and wells and other places mice enjoy. It has a reputation for aggressiveness, but truth is it would rather flee than strike a human, if given the chance. Even when it does strike, the bite is not always fatal, since the snake rarely disgorges all its venom on something too large to eat.

If you encounter any snake, retreat as quietly as possible. If you are bitten by a poisonous snake, go immediately to a hospital or other emergency facility. Every public hospital and clinic in Belize stocks antivenin. Contrary to local bush practice, you should not cut the wound to make it bleed (you might cut a blood vessel or nerve, causing more harm than the snakebite) nor drink alcohol, which only speeds the flow of blood and therefore venom.

BIRDS   Belize's islands and coastal marshes are filled with beautiful and bizarre birds such as the red-footed booby, which has golden white feathers and outlandish red webbed feet. Its name comes from a lack of fear—sailors to the New World used to walk right up and strike it on the head. Much less friendly is the frigate bird, whose gaunt, black silhouette gives it an ominous appearance. Despite its penchant for fish, the frigate refuses to get wet, and so is adept at swiping flying fish in midair. The cinnamon-colored jacana bird, which lives in marshes, ponds and rivers, is nicknamed the lily pad trotter—it gracefully hops across each pad with pencil thin legs.

But the most famous of all Belize water birds is the jabiru stork. The largest flying bird in the Western Hemisphere, it reaches human proportions, growing as tall as five feet with an astounding wing span of up to ten feet. Unfortunately, it is greatly endangered, as fewer than 300 birds are thought to still be alive.

Inland, birds are flamboyantly colorful. The tiny hummingbird shimmers in iridescent colors as it hovers motionless sucking out flower nectar. Its incredibly high metabolism forces it to feed from dawn to dusk. The turkey-like curassow, who mates for life, boasts lacy crests and lustrous black or crimson feathers. Male curassows are extremely protective of females, and will risk their lives to keep others from getting near their mates.

The bird probably most associated with the Belize jungle is the keel-billed toucan, who sports a crayola-yellow bib and a fantastic, rainbow-hued bill fashioned like a capsized boat. It flies with the bill up and out, as if trying to keep up with the huge apparatus, though in fact the beak is quite light. The national bird of Belize, toucans are best seen in deep rainforest, far away from the people who want to trap them to sell as pets.

Woodpeckers are the jackhammers of the forest, spending hours drilling into tree trunks at unimaginable speeds. The hammering is so constant and tireless that one wonders how the bird's pointy little beak manages not to be mangled by day's end. There are many species of woodpeckers, ranging in color from black to red to green and richly embellished with stripes or streaks. All woodpeckers have tough-as-nails tails to prop them against trees while they do their jackhammering.

Oftentimes, woodpeckers will drill their nest hole only to have them stolen by woodcreepers. Though similar in appearance, woodpeckers and woodcreepers are not closely related, and woodcreepers do not drill holes but probe them. The most intriguing woodcreeper is the scythebill, whose beak resembles a long, sharp upside-down scythe.

One reason birdwatchers come to Belize is for a glimpse of a blue-crowned motmot, distinguished by a tiara of shimmering blue feathers and a racquet-shaped, blue-green tail that's half as long as its body. There's no mistaking its call, either, a series of delicate *hoot-hoots* that echo through the forest. Montezuma oropendolas are also sought by bird lovers, though it is their nests, draped from trees like elaborate baskets, that are most fascinating. Montezuma oropendolas are blackish-brown and have the silhouette of a crow, their close relative.

INSECTS   Some of the jungle's most ingenious and industrious creatures are not much bigger than a pinhead. Take leaf cutter ants, who work all day and all night chopping leaves and shuttling them in perfect lines to piles that reach six feet high. Each leaf is lifted by a tiny ant who seems to have the strength of Hercules. Another ant pilots the leaf, sending codes to ants in the back of the parade to watch out for that stump, rock—or anteater.

The ants' leaf piles turn into deep, rich soil that trees love. In fact, it's not uncommon to see a cohune palm towering ten feet above surrounding cohune palms that were not lucky enough to grow in leaf cutter compost. What do the ants get out of it? They crave a fungus that grows on the cut leaves, kind of like ant caviar.

Termites are everywhere, as evidenced by their gray spun nests fastened to trees of all varieties. The nests, many larger than basketballs, are made of a papery glue formed by digested wood and termite feces. The obese queen, burdened by a yellow, pouchlike abdomen and hardly able to move, is hidden deep in the nest and is tended to (and impregnated) by zillions of worker termites. The workers are blind, making their way around the nest by sniffing chemical trails laid by other workers. Soldier termites defend the nest from invaders by discharging a sticky, musky liquid.

When termites eat wood, they expel chemical gases. Considering the size of a termite, this would seem inconsequential until you consider how many termites there are in the world. Some researchers believe the gases may contribute to global warming. John C. Kricher, quoting the studies of P.R. Zimmerman, suggests that the termites' "combined digestive abilities produce significant quantities of atmospheric methane, carbon dioxide and molecular hydrogen."

The forest-floor millipede spews its own chemicals, though they are harmless to humans and used strictly for self-defense. At the first hint of danger, the yellow-orange, many-legged creatures tuck themselves into a tight ball and squirt a liquid up to a foot away.

Above the forest floor, butterflies color the air with extraordinary poise and beauty. Most elusive and naturally most sought after by butterfly collectors is the blue morpho, or in Belize, the Belizean Blue. For several years, British naturalist Charles Wright has been living in the deep jungles of southern Belize studying blue morphos. About his subject, he writes that "this butterfly cruises the light and shadow pattern along a forest trail, electric flashes of turquoise blue accompany its passage. It is indeed something to remember."

Similarly fascinating, and cloaked in many Maya myths, is the lantern fly. Looking like a miniature crocodile with wings, it soars through the air toting a toothy, woody-brown snout, resembling some shrunken beast escaped from a Japanese horror movie.

Actually, the tiny creatures are quite benign; indeed they spend most of their time eluding predators. However, Maya folktales say they glow in the dark, which they don't, and that if a girl is bitten by a lantern fly, she must have sex with her boyfriend within 24 hours or she will perish. No doubt the tale was concocted by someone's frustrated boyfriend.

MEDICINAL PLANTS AND NATURAL HEALING

For thousands of years, Belize's rainforests have yielded plants, trees and shrubs prized for their medicinal value. These "healing" plants and their uses are carefully guarded secrets, passed down through generations of Maya bush doctors, though today many Maya villagers use the jungle as their backyard medicine cabinets. The leaves of the wild pineapple plant, for instance, can be heated and formed into a cast to set injured bones. The seeds from the custard apple are a sure cure for head lice, and the sinewy, water-gorged grapevine supplies water so pure the Maya used it to cleanse newborn babies—a practice that continues today. The prickly "give and take" vine stabs with its spikes, then stops the blood flow with its leaves. And the gnarly bullhoof vine, when boiled and consumed as a liquid, will stop internal bleeding.

One tree, the negrito, is nicknamed the dysentery bark tree for its ability to cure the oft-fatal disease. In the days of New World exploration, the tree's bark saved European sailors suffering from severe cases of dysentery and diarrhea. They promptly named it dysentery bark, and began shipping it to Europe, where it was worth its weight in gold for over 200 years.

For stomach problems experienced by many of today's travelers, there is jackass bitters, also known as *tres puntas*. The boiled leaves, turned into a tea or wine tincture, are a powerful antidote to parasites, amoebas, giardia and even malaria. The taste is so bitter, however, than some have trouble keeping it down.

Of course, there are hundreds, perhaps thousands, of other healing plants residing in the jungle. It is impossible to recognize them without some training. Several places around Belize offer jungle tours that explain basic medicinal plants. The best is the Panti Mayan Medicine Trail near San Ignacio, where Americans Rosita Arvigo and Gregory Shropshire are conducting research on natural cures for cancer, AIDS and other diseases. Grants from several U.S. organizations are funding their work, including the National Cancer Research Institute and U.S. A.I.D.

The trail is named for Don Eligio Panti, Arvigo's mentor and one of Central America's most revered bush doctors. Though in his late 90s and nearly blind, he continues his 60-year-old natural healing practice from a remote Belize village, treating dozens of patients each week, some of whom travel for days on foot from neighboring Mexico, Guatemala and Honduras.

Bottled herbal treatments, labeled Rainforest Remedies, and herb packets are available at the trail, or by mail by writing to Dr. Rosita Arvigo, Ix Chel Tropical Research Centre, San Ignacio, Cayo, Belize, Central America. Among the potions are:

Blood Tonic Tea, for anemia, rheumatism, arthritis and fatigue. High in iron and minerals, and made with wild yams and China root.

Balsam Bark Tea, for kidney, bladder and liver problems. Made with balsam bark.

Party Punch, a smooth-tasting pick-me-up, made with lemon grass, rose petals, mint leaves and orange peel.

Billy Webb Bark Tea, for diabetes, hypoglycemia and dry coughs.

Jackass Bitters Tea, a bitter-tasting brew for internal parasites, amoebas, malaria, ringworm and yeast infections.

Bellyache Tea, a mild sedative for indigestion, gastritis and constipation. Made with man vine.

Female Tonic Tea, for menstrual cramps or irregularities. Made with man vine, contribo, guaco and copalchi.

Male Tonic, for impotence and kidney and bladder problems. Made with balsam bark, corn silk, man vine root and cane alcohol water.

ENVIRONMENTAL EXPEDITIONS

Many tour companies specialize in environment-oriented expeditions across Belize. A few of the best include:

Great Trips, 1616 West 139th Street, Burnsville, MN 55337; (612) 890-4405.

Sea and Explore, 1809 Carol Sue Avenue, Suite E, Gretna, LA 70056; (504) 366-9985.

Chaa Creek Inland and Jungle Expeditions, P.O. Box 53, San Ignacio, Cayo, Belize; 92-2037.

Float Belize, P.O. Box 48, San Ignacio, Cayo, Belize; 92-2188.

Mayaworld Safaris, P.O. Box 997, West Landivar, Belize City, Belize; 2-31063.

Native Guide System, P.O. Box 1045, 1 Water Lane, Belize City, Belize; 2-75819.

HOW TO HELP

For information on environmental programs, contact one of these organizations:

Belize Audubon Society, 29 Regent Street, P.O. Box 1001, Belize City, Belize; 2-77369.

Belize Zoo And Tropical Education Center, P.O. Box 1787, Belize City, Belize (no phone).

Programme for Belize, 1 King Street, Belize City, Belize; 2-75616.

Belize Center for Environmental Studies, P.O. Box 666, Belize City, Belize; 2-45739.

La Ruta Maya Conservation Foundation, 209 Seneca Road, Great Falls, VA 22066; (703) 450-4160.

Mundo Maya Organization, 7A Avenida 14-44 Zona 9, Eddiferi La Galeria, Local 35, Guatemala; 2-340323.

Iguana

THREE

Planning Your Trip

WHEN TO GO

CLIMATE AND SEASONS

Located in a subtropical rainforest region, Belize has just two seasons: rainy and dry. Generally, rain falls and temperatures rise during summer and autumn months, from June through October. Daily rains can soak inland jungle roads, creating sludge trails that are impassable without four-wheel-drive vehicles.

Summer rains increase dramatically in Belize as you head from north to south. Northern Corozal, for instance, averages 50 inches of annual rain, while Punta Gorda, only 200 miles to the south, gets an incredible 170 inches a year. During the rainy season, afternoon showers give life to the forests and a welcome drop in temperatures for those who reside there. Temperatures along the coast and inland rainforests, however, often reach 95 degrees by midday during summer months.

Late summer and early fall can also mean hurricane season, particularly along the Caribbean coast. It's not likely that you'll encounter one—they blow in every decade or so—but if you should, take it seriously: hurricanes are monsters that take lives and leave paths of destruction. In October, "northers" usually set in, bringing persistent winds from the north of 15 to 25 knots. Northers are the lower fringe of cold fronts that swirl down from North America.

During the dry season, from November through March, the thermometer registers in the comfortable low 80s. In the mountains of inland Belize, the mercury drops into the 50s at night during winter, with perfect daytime weather in the 70s. During winter, some lodges, particularly in the cayes, raise their prices as much as 30 percent in response to visitors arriving to enjoy the idyllic weather.

Springtime creates crystalline waters in the offshore cayes, with visibility reaching an amazing 100 feet in some dive spots. However, the months of April and May enjoy neither winter trade winds nor cooling afternoon rains, and can be intensely hot—in the 100s—and suffocatingly humid. May is when

25

many Belizeans living inland head to the cayes for heat relief. This author, despite being a native Floridian accustomed to the tropics, finds an air-conditioned room a necessity in Belize during April and May.

All that said, visitors should know that those who follow Belize's weather say it is entirely unpredictable. For instance, during the "rainy" season, there may be many days with overcast skies but little rain. And in the dry season, there may be several days of drizzling or even torrential rains. George Bevier, an American entomologist living in southern Belize, has recorded the daily weather for more than 20 years, only to find that there are absolutely no consistent patterns!

HOLIDAYS

You may want to plan your Belize visit around a certain holiday or festival and join in the local spirit. Make your reservations at least three to four months in advance, because hotels fill up fast during special events.

During major holidays, rum and island music flow freely through towns and villages, and locals celebrate with jumpup street dances that can last until sunup. Remember that because of the festivities, everything else practically shuts down, including government agencies, businesses and professional offices. In other words, if there's a holiday, forget about business and join the party!

Here are the most important events in Belize:

JANUARY-FEBRUARY

New Year's Day is celebrated on January 1 as a national holiday, complete with parades and fireworks.

MARCH-APRIL

Holy Week—the week leading up to Easter—rivals the Christmas season as the biggest holiday of the year. Businesses close for **Good Friday, Holy Saturday, Easter Sunday** and the following Monday so locals can celebrate at home. On March 9, **Baron Bliss Day** pays homage to the man who left his $2 million fortune to the tiny country. Belizeans remember him with a day of fishing and sailing, an apt remembrance since the baron was devoted to both pursuits.

MAY

Belizeans take a break from work every May 1, which is **Labour Day**. Kite contests, bicycling and horse races, and a harbor regatta are featured. On May 24, they pay respects to the British Commonwealth on **Commonwealth Day**. Also in May, the residents of Crooked Tree Village in northern Belize celebrate the cashew harvest season. Their **Crooked Tree Cashew Festival** features storytelling and Caribbean folklore performances, Belizean cuisine, nature walks, river trips and expeditions to local Maya ruins.

JUNE

June 29 is the **Feast Day of Saint Peter**, patron saint of San Pedro, Ambergris Caye. Residents celebrate the 1848 founding of their village with merrymaking and a parade of fishing boats that are blessed in the town harbor.

JULY–AUGUST

Mexico, Guatemala, El Salvador and Honduras join Belize in the **International Sea & Air Festival,** held the third week of July in San Pedro, Ambergris Caye. Showcasing myriads of ethnic dances and cuisines, costumes and crafts, the festival is a celebration of the countries' cooperation and work together on the Mundo Maya (Maya World) tourism project.

SEPTEMBER

September means virtual nonstop celebrating in Belize. One of the biggest, most joyous national holidays, the **Battle of St. George's Caye** remembers the September 10, 1798, victory of the British over the Spanish. Every town joins in with a week of parades, jumpup street dancing and community-wide feasting. The British eventually gave Belize its independence on September 21, 1981, and Belizeans celebrate with **National Independence Day**. The whole country is like a carnival, and streets are filled with artisans, musicians, dancers, actors and delicious local food.

OCTOBER

Back-to-back holidays mean twice as much celebrating. October 12 brings **Columbus Day,** while October 13 is **Pan American Day**. Big events are horse races, boat racing and cross-country cycling competitions.

NOVEMBER

Pulsing drums and punta rock music signal the start of **Garifuna Day** in southern Belize. The November 19 festivities, centered in the Toledo District, mark the 1823 arrival of the Garifunas (African Indians).

DECEMBER

Christmas festivities begin on Christmas Eve, when Belizeans light the yule log and exchange presents. December 26 marks **Boxing Day**, a national holiday.

COMING AND GOING

ENTRY REQUIREMENTS

All visitors to Belize must have valid passports. Besides clearing immigration, you will need to show your passport when renting a car, cashing traveler's checks or, in many cases, checking into a hotel.

Belize does not require visas (except for visitors from Cuba, Hong Kong and parts of Africa and the Middle East). Visitors who plan to stay longer than 30 days in Belize, however, should obtain an extension from the Belize Immigration Office (115 Barrack Road, Belize City; 2-33505). Visa extensions cost US$12.50.

Visitors who plan a side trip to Guatemala must have either a visa (free, obtained in advance from any Guatemalan consulate in the United States or Mexico) or a tourist card (US$5, issued upon entry into Guatemala). Visitors who drive motor vehicles into Guatemala need visas. So do citizens of certain foreign nations.

To cross over to the great Maya ruins at Copán in Honduras, you need only your passport. Visitors staying 12 hours or less can get a special tourist card that does not cancel their Guatemalan visa or tourist card. If you stay longer than 12 hours, you are supposed to wait 72 hours before reentering Guatemala and must pay a new US$5 tourist card fee.

If you want to travel deeper into Honduras or El Salvador, where there are a few minor Maya ruins, entry requirements can range from a visa to a tourist card to just a passport, depending on who you ask. If you are flying there directly, check with the nearest consulate at least two weeks before your departure and obtain either a visa or an official letter waiving any visa requirement. Many airlines require one or the other.

CUSTOMS REGULATIONS

Belize customs regulations are liberal to tourists. However, they are notoriously slow at the Belize City international airport. This is especially true on Monday mornings, when Belizeans returning from weekend shopping sprees in Miami must itemize their purchases and pay duties. Customs officials literally check every corner of every suitcase. Twice, I waited nearly two hours in the boiling heat to clear customs. If you find yourself in this waiting-forever situation, slow down and remember—this is the tropics!

If you take your boat to Belize, the following documents must be presented to the customs officer who will board your vessel upon its arrival: (1) the boat's certificate of registration; (2) proof of clearance from your last port of call; (3) four copies of your crew and passenger list; (4) four copies of your stores list; and finally, (5) four copies of your cargo manifest, if you are transporting cargo.

Guatemala's customs regulations, as they apply to tourists, are minimal and somewhat vague. As a practical matter, instead of physically inspecting your luggage, Guatemalan *Aduana* officials prefer to charge a small fee per bag for a tag certifying that they have inspected it.

U.S. CUSTOMS REGULATIONS

Even if you live there, the United States can be harder to enter than Central American countries. When returning home, United States residents may bring $400 worth of purchases duty-free. Anything over this amount is subject to a ten percent tax on the next $1000 worth of items. In case customs officials question the values you declare, save the purchase receipts for goods you buy in retail stores and record your marketplace and street vendor purchases neatly in a notebook. Persons over 21 years of age are allowed one liter (or quart) of liquor duty-free.

Fruits, vegetables and many other fresh foods are not allowed into the United States and will be confiscated. Fish, shrimp and any seafood that can be legally caught in Belize can be brought across the border. However, conservation-minded travelers will catch only what they can eat in Belize. There's nothing more embarrassing than an American tourist lugging a cooler full of lobsters from a country where many children don't get enough to eat.

All items made from any part of an endangered species—such as the sea turtle, crocodile, black coral or ocelot—are prohibited in the United States and will be confiscated. Vendors of such items usually will not warn you that you can't take them home.

Ancient relics, such as Maya artifacts or pre-Columbian art, cannot be taken from their country of origin and will be confiscated if found in your possession. All archaeological finds are considered national treasures and the property of the country in which they were found.

For more details, write **U.S. Customs** (1301 Constitution Avenue, Washington, DC 20229; 202-566-8195); the **U.S. Fish and Wildlife Service** (Department of the Interior, Mailstop 430, Arlington Square, 1849 C Street Northwest, Washington, DC 20240; 202-208-5634); and **TRAFFIC, World Wildlife Fund and the Conservation Foundation** (1250 24th Street Northwest, Washington, DC 20037; 202-293-4800).

To avoid confiscation of prescribed drugs, label them carefully and bring along a doctor's certificate of prescription. As for contraband drugs, there's a war on. Smart travelers remain neutral.

Customs checks at the U.S. border can be stringent or swift, depending on how suspicious you look. To avoid any problems, dress neatly and declare your purchases.

TRANSPORTATION

AIRLINES SERVING BELIZE

By far the best way to get to Belize is to fly. Commercial airlines fly daily between the United States and Canada and the international airport in Belize City. The Honduras-based **Sahsa Airlines** has daily nonstop flights, and also offers an excellent "Maya World Fare," which allows unlimited stops in Belize, Guatemala and Honduras for $399 round-trip from Miami, New Orleans or Houston. Other airline carriers serving Belize include **TACA, American** and **Continental.**

Baggage allowances on international flights are generally the same as on U.S. domestic flights—two carry-on items small enough to fit under the seat or in an overhead rack, plus two pieces of check-through luggage. In addition, some Latin American airlines have a weight limitation—typically 40 kilograms (88 pounds)—on check-through luggage. All airlines allow considerably more baggage than you would want to carry around on this trip.

During special events, holidays and the November-to-April high season, make flight reservations at least two weeks to a month in advance. Air delays are common. So are flight cancellations—be sure to confirm your flight 48 hours before departure. Canceled flights seem to be a particular problem between Belize City and Flores (the airport for Guatemala's Tikal National Park), where the next flight out may not be for several days.

Visitors leaving Belize's international airport are required to pay a departure tax equivalent to US$10, paid in Belize dollars, at the time they check in.

When booking your international airline tickets, if you will be taking a connecting flight on your return trip, be sure to allow plenty of time. At the hub airport where you first land in the United States—probably Miami, New Orleans or Houston—you will have to wait for and claim your baggage, clear U.S. Customs, and recheck your bags before boarding your onward flight. Allow one-and-a-half to two hours.

DRIVING TO BELIZE

Traveling from the United States to Belize by car is a challenging and time-consuming adventure. Not that it's particularly dangerous—just demanding. The drive to Belize from Brownsville, Texas, through Mexico, is almost 1400 miles. It can be done in roughly 55 hours of actual driving time. To make the journey comfortably, without arriving in Belize exhausted, allow at least a week. Most Mexican highways are two-lane roads, not limited-access freeways, and driving takes longer than you would expect.

If you are driving to Belize from the U.S. border, plan well ahead for refueling and evening stops. Gas stations in Mexico are a government monopoly, and in much of the country they are few and far between. Never pass up an opportunity to fill your vehicle's tank. Driving after dark can be dangerous (the most common hazards are vehicles stopped in the traffic lane without lights and vehicles traveling without lights well after dusk—sometimes considered a display of Mexican machismo).

Note: One of the most important things you should know is that unleaded gas is not available in Belize. But then, there are not many cars in Belize. Leaded fuel is sold by the gallon at slightly more than the price of gas in the United States.

MOTOR VEHICLE REQUIREMENTS   For driving in Belize, your current driver's license is valid. If you're bringing your own car via Mexico, you'll need a Mexican car permit and Mexican auto insurance. To obtain a car permit (a special stamp on the owner's tourist card, issued for up to 180 days), you need proof of ownership—a current registration certificate and title. If the title shows a lien against the vehicle or if it is registered in another person's name or a company name, you need a notarized letter from the lienholder or owner authorizing you to take the vehicle to Mexico for a specified time. The owner or driver who has the car permit stamp on his or her tourist card *must* be in the car whenever it is being driven.

Anyone bringing a motor vehicle into Mexico must show either a major credit card or a collision/comprehensive insurance policy valid for the duration of the stay. Otherwise, the owner can be required to post a cash bond guaranteeing that he or she will return with the vehicle to the United States. At the same time, the Mexican government has promised to simplify procedures for temporarily importing vehicles. For current requirements, contact a Mexican consulate in the United States or the **U.S. Embassy in Mexico City** (Paseo de Reforma No. 305, Mexico City, 60500 Mexico, D.F.; 5-211-0042).

Auto insurance policies issued in the United States are not valid in Belize or Mexico. Purchase motor vehicle liability insurance (and, if you wish, collision/comprehensive) before crossing into Mexico. Insurance is sold by agencies on the U.S. side at all border crossings. Causing an auto accident is a crime under Mexican law, which presumes defendants guilty until proven innocent. This means that if you are involved in an accident that causes property damage, your vehicle will be impounded until you pay the damage and a fine. If any person is injured in the accident, you will go to jail.

The documentation you need to take your vehicle into Mexico is more than sufficient to bring it into Belize. However, Belize requires local liability insurance, which can be fairly expensive.

PACKING

Pack light! A camera plus whatever else you can fit in a large duffel bag and a backpack would be perfect. For a two-week trip, I carry a canvas French Army backpack and a sturdy, woven Guatemalan bag (available in Belize for about US$20) packed light enough to tote on successive boat and commuter plane trips. There is nothing like lugging 75 pounds of suitcases around the jungle to make one feel absurdly materialistic.

When choosing your clothing, remember that Belize is far from fashion conscious. In fact, both women and men dress in a practical, unpretentious manner. Flaunting a new pair of Nike Air Jordans around Belize City is not only in poor taste, it's an invitation to petty thieves. Keep your clothing modest and sensible, as befitting a country where wildlife and forests are held in higher regard than the latest styles.

Bring along a minimum of sporty, summery clothing, T-shirts, shorts and a swimsuit, as well as a rain poncho and a pair of polarized sunglasses (essential for spotting fish). Cotton shirts breathe better and wick away perspiration. For treks to the Maya ruins and wildlife reserves, you'll need a sturdy but lightweight pair of hiking boots, a comfortable pair of slacks—I like loose-fitting cotton fatigues—and socks to protect your ankles from insects. A long-sleeve cotton shirt protects against bugs and brambly bush, while a light jacket will keep you warm on winter nights. Leave your blue jeans at home. Not only are they extremely hot, they get heavy when wet.

A walk in the jungle is like a walk in the dark, unless you take a good pair of binoculars. Binoculars help you find the hundreds of tiny critters that hide out in the dense foliage all around. The best binoculars are those with high

Blue-crowned Motmot

magnification that let in plenty of light—all the better for seeing in the dim, shadowy forest. Many birdwatchers recommend Zeiss or Leitz 10 x 40 lenses.

A flashlight with extra batteries is a must for exploring caves and for those nights when hotel generators shut down early. I take a lighter and a couple of votive candles for reading at night. And don't forget to take a roll of toilet paper for the long forays into the jungle.

You should definitely pack a first-aid kit. Include a good insect repellent, aspirin, band-aids, cold capsules, vitamins, motion sickness tablets, prescription drugs you use, iodine or alcohol for disinfecting wounds, antibiotic ointment, water purification tablets, sunscreen with at least a 15 SPF, lip balm and diarrhea medicine. For insect bites and jellyfish stings, carry a bottle of calamine lotion, a tube of Benadryl ointment, and a bottle of Benadryl pills. When you're covered with itchy red welts that keep you up all night, nothing gives relief like Benadryl.

Anyone with a medical condition should consider wearing a medic alert identification tag that identifies the problem and gives a phone number to call for more information. Contact **Medic Alert Foundation International** (P.O. Box 1009, Turlock, CA 95381; 800-344-3226).

Belize, filled as it is with quirky humanity, ancient crumbling cities and travel poster islands, is a photographer's dream. At virtually every turn, you will find the makings of a great picture. But, be aware that the Adventure Coast can be tough on camera equipment, so unless you're competing in a photo contest, consider bringing something compact and inexpensive. Pocket-sized instamatic cameras hold up well, and are easy to tote around the jungle in a backpack. Disposable cameras are also practical because you don't have to worry about carrying rolls of film. I use an underwater camera that also takes decent above-water photos, and won't succumb to the Belize humidity.

The best way to protect your equipment is to keep it in a padded, zippered camera bag. Remember that if you tour on the mainland, you will be bouncing down rocky roads for hours on end. Belize's rains also wreak havoc on cameras, so keep a couple of ziplocked bags handy for sudden showers.

Definitely bring plenty of film; in Belize, film costs double and triple what it does in the U.S., and it's tough to find. Slide film is virtually unheard of. It's also wise to bring an extra camera battery and, if you're using a 35mm camera, a couple of clear lens filters. The jungle has a way of leaving its mark (scratches and dents) on camera lenses.

When it comes to toiletries, most towns in Belize carry everything you'll find in the United States, though usually at higher prices: toothpaste, deodorant, shampoo, soap, insect repellent, skin creams, shaving cream and batteries (buy the expensive ones; the cheapest kind often don't work). Imported items like tampons and suntan lotions are also widely available in larger towns, though they cost a lot more than in the United States.

Scuba divers should check with their lodge about available equipment. Few dive resorts carry enough for everyone, so plan to bring your own mask, snorkel, booties and fins, BC (buoyancy control device), regulator, weights and, of course, your certification card. Tanks are normally provided. Always pack your dive gear in a suitcase; a dive bag checked alone is a prime target for thieves—in the U.S., not Belize. Make sure your dive knife is in your suitcase, checked with the rest of your gear. I know of a foolish diver who, attempting to carry his knife on the plane, had to surrender it at a Miami departure gate.

Likewise, anglers staying at fishing lodges will want to bring along their rods and tackle. Check with your individual lodge about what it has on hand.

Take along some good paperbacks (hard covers don't hold up well in the jungle). However, in English-speaking Belize, where the literacy rate is over 90 percent, you'll have no trouble finding good books on all subjects. Many innkeepers stock superb libraries on Belizean and Maya history and culture and are happy to loan books while you're a guest. In archaeological areas, you will find English-language books about the ancient Maya civilization that are not available in the United States. In areas of Belize where American expatriates congregate, such as San Ignacio and Placencia, English-language novels are recycled endlessly. There are used-book or trade-in racks full of paperback potboilers left over from decades past at bookstores, hotels and restaurants where foreign visitors gather. No matter where you plan to travel, don't forget to bring your copy of *The New Key to Belize!*

ELECTRICITY

You'll likely stay in places without electricity, but those that do have it carry current the same as in the United States—110 volt, 60 cycles. If you need to convert appliances from other countries, bring your own adapters.

TRAVELING EXPENSES

Travelers accustomed to low prices in Guatemala and Mexico may be surprised to find their next-door neighbor more expensive. Belize is in fact on par with Caribbean destinations such as Jamaica, St. Thomas and Grand Cayman when it comes to lodging, restaurant and tour prices. A three-star hotel that's US$5 a night in Guatemala will be US$40 a night across the border in Belize. The best jungle lodges and beach hotels charge over US$100 a night, and dinner at a "better" restaurant costs about US$30 a person. Not that you can't find acceptable lodging at lower prices. During the winter, when air conditioning is not as essential, it is possible to find clean, suitable rooms with shared bath for under US$20 in most towns. If you prefer a little more comfort and charm, plan to spend at least US$40.

If you're staying in remote areas, it will be necessary to have all your meals at your lodge. Expect to pay from US$30 to US$60 per person per day for these meals. While I have found the meals at some of these "all-inclusive" lodges to be exceptional and well worth the price, others have been marginal and overpriced. Throughout this book, lodges are critiqued on the quality and value of their meals.

Sightseeing tours are expensive. This is partly due to the horrid condition of the roads, which can destroy tour vehicles in a matter of months. What else makes them so expensive, I have not been able to ascertain. Expect to pay from US$100 to US$250, for one to four people, for a day trip to a Maya ruin or nature reserve. Travel agencies in Belize City and Ambergris Caye sometimes arrange less expensive tours by organizing larger groups. In remote areas, however, your chances of joining a large group are slim. Single travelers will find tour prices exorbitant. Traveling alone, I have paid as much as US$200 for a six-hour tour to a ruin.

Groceries cost more (from 10 to 100 percent more) than those in the United States, particularly convenience foods and toiletries. Bus transportation is inexpensive, costing about US 25 cents to travel around Belize City and only US$4 to travel from Belize City west all the way to the Guatemala border.

Stick to local beer and rum. A bottle of Belize beer, a mild, tasty brew called Belikin, sells for US$1 to US$2 and is consumed by locals and tourists alike. Cocktails made with Belize's Caribbean White Rum are about US$2.50. Imported brands will run you two to three times that price.

INOCULATIONS

No inoculations are required to enter Belize. Cases of hepatitis, malaria, typhoid, cholera, dengue fever and other tropical diseases do occur but seldom afflict travelers. If you are planning to visit remote areas, your doctor may recommend yellow fever, tetanus, typhoid and gamma globulin (for hepatitis) shots and/or malaria pills.

LODGING IN BELIZE

After you have stayed awhile in Belize, you will become accustomed to (and endeared to) the country's funky style of accommodations. A Belize City guesthouse, for instance, may offer drapes made of seashells and battered furniture painted every primary color. Decor in your seaside motel may include a lava lamp, a vinyl '50s-era chair and a boat oar parked on the wall, but hey, the room's got character! Lodge owners often furnish rooms with the same care and Belizean quirkiness they use in their own houses. Before long, you'll feel right at home.

Cabanas, made of stucco, wood or bamboo and crowned with palm thatching, are ubiquitous in Belize. They range from elegant bedrooms with glossy teakwood floors, mahogany furniture and canopy beds to basic round shelters with concrete floors and curtained closet doors. If you're staying in the jungle, make sure your room is properly protected from bugs by screens and other devices. During certain times of the year, insects migrate and can literally invade your room if it's not bug-proofed. I had this experience, and it is not one I wish to repeat.

Most towns and islands have at least one motel or lodge that offers electricity and, thus, air conditioning. However, you will pay a premium for cold air, often twice as much as a room without air conditioning—but worth it on suffocatingly hot days. Many lodges, particularly in the jungle, out islands and remote villages, receive their electricity from gasoline-powered generators. In some instances, electricity is rationed to a few hours after dusk. But their location makes the experience of staying there special enough to justify any mild inconveniences you might encounter. Indeed, I have found these jungle lodges to be some of the most memorable places in Belize.

During the November to April high season, and around major holidays like Christmas, Easter and National Independence Day, many hotels raise their rates and sell out weeks in advance. Reservations for these times of the year should be made at least two months ahead of time.

This book's lodging listings range from budget to very expensive, with an emphasis on unique or special midrange to upper midrange establishments. All price ranges are based on double occupancy, and *do not* include a five percent government tax. Lodging is rated as follows: *budget* facilities have rooms for less than $35 a night for two people; *moderate* hotels are priced between $35 and $70; *expensive* facilities offer rates from $70 to $100; and *very expensive* have accommodations at prices above $100.

Be aware that, except for a few chain hotels in Belize City (such as the Radisson Fort George and Ramada Royal Reef), most "expensive" and "very expensive" lodges will be neither fancy nor elegant. Rather, they will assure comfort and charm, picturesque surroundings and excellent meals, and plenty of assistance with local excursions.

Note that many Belizean hotels charge an additional five percent if you pay for your room with a credit card. Some resorts also add a service charge of 10 to 15 percent to their rates.

NOTES FOR WOMEN TRAVELERS

Belize is quite liberated when it comes to women's issues. Women traveling here can expect at least the same freedom and respect they enjoy in the United States, if not more. Belize women are hard-working, independent individuals who are often family breadwinners. It is not uncommon to hear a Belize man complaining that his girlfriend is "too busy with her career" to settle down. After traveling around Belize for three months, the only sexual harassment I experienced was from American men!

NOTES FOR TRAVELING WITH CHILDREN

Should you bring the kids to Belize? That depends. If you plan to spend a lot of time in the cayes and other resort areas, then by all means, take them along. As you move into remote jungle areas of Belize, you may want to consider taking only older children. The jungle does hold limitless fascination for older children; they adore hiking through mysterious forests and exploring on horseback and in canoes. In archaeological areas, ancient temples and pyramids are great for climbing and poking into secret passageways, and the mysteries of a vanished civilization the ruins present can tantalize young minds for weeks on end. Belizeans love children and are very family oriented. Numerous lodges across the country are owned by families, and children often join the guests at mealtime. Many travelers find it easy to enjoy both worlds— parenting and adventuring.

Remember to get a tourist card for each child. Children traveling with only one parent must have notarized permission from the other parent (or, if applicable, divorce papers, guardianship document or death certificate). Minors traveling alone must have a notarized letter of permission signed by both parents or guardians.

Prepare a junior first-aid kit with baby aspirin, thermometer, vitamins, diarrhea medicine, sun block, bug repellent, tissues and cold medicine. Parents traveling with infants will want to pack cloth diapers, plastic bags for dirty diapers, and a wraparound or papoose-style baby carrier. Strollers aren't practical on Belize's crumbling city roads and island sand streets.

Disposable diapers, baby food and medicines are available in larger towns. Outside Belize City and Ambergris Caye, few lodges have cribs or babysitting services. However, some lodge owners will help you find a local babysitter.

Belize restaurants are plenty casual for children, but the fare may not please picky eaters. You might want to bring some rolls, peanut butter and jelly, toaster pastries and other easy-to-pack munchies. In the meantime, encourage your child to try local foods. You'd be surprised how quickly they adapt to stewed chicken and beans and rice.

Go ahead and splurge on a rental car. Traveling with children, especially young ones, on public buses could be one too many stressors. If you tour by car with an infant, bring a portable car seat. For children of any age, be sure to pack toys, books and art supplies to drive away boredom during long trips.

Pace your trip so your child has time to adapt to changes. Don't plan exhausting whirlwind tours, and keep travel time to a minimum. Seek out beaches, parks, plazas and short excursions to amuse your child. The Belize Zoo is a wonderful place for children; thousands of local children visit each year. While you're there, pick up a copy of *Hoodwink the Owl*, a warm-hearted tale that introduces children to Belize's fascinating animals.

NOTES FOR SENIOR TRAVELERS

Belize has much to offer seniors, including adventures tailored to individual strength and endurance. In other words, not every trek to the ruins has to last 12 hours. Older travelers will find companionship everywhere, from the fishing and jungle lodges to tiny beach motels. They will also discover that Belize seniors are often in astoundingly good shape; I met several Maya bushmen who looked (and acted) much younger than their years.

There is, however, no organized senior travel to Belize, mainly because modern tourism facilities, including transportation and roadways, are still developing. A good travel agent can recommend accommodations and sights to suit your needs.

Be extra careful about health matters. Bring any medications you use, along with the prescriptions. Consider carrying a medical record with you—including your current medical status, medical history, your doctor's name, phone number and address. If possible, include a summary of your medical status and history. Check to see that your health insurance covers you while traveling in Belize.

NOTES FOR TRAVELERS WITH DISABILITIES

There are few sidewalks in Belize, and town roads tend to be narrow and bumpy. In the cayes, the streets are all sand. Most establishments and transportation systems do not provide special amenities, such as wheelchair access, for people with disabilities. You may want to get help from a good travel agent to track down facilities to suit your situation.

You may also wish to contact one of the following organizations: the **Society for the Advancement of Travel for the Handicapped** (SATH) (26 Court Street, Brooklyn, NY 11242; 718-858-5483); **Travel Information Center** (Moss Rehabilitation Hospital, 1200 West Tabor Road, Philadelphia, PA 19141; 215-329-5715); **Mobility International USA** (P.O. Box 3551, Eugene, OR 97403; 503-343-1284); or **Flying Wheels Travel** (143 West Bridge Street, P.O. Box 382, Owatonna, MN 55060; 800-535-6790). **Travelin' Talk** (P.O. Box 3534, Clarksville, TN 37043; 615-552-6670), a networking organization, provides useful information.

NOTES FOR STUDENT TRAVELERS

While there are few organized student tours to Belize, the country is well-suited to young people traveling on a budget.

Numerous lodges across Belize are popular with students from the United States, Europe and Latin America, and the public bus system is extensive and inexpensive. And, Belize's abundant outdoor experiences appeal to vigorous young travelers.

You'll find budget-priced rates and fellow students at the following lodges:

On Ambergris Caye, at **Lily's** (Barrier Reef Drive, San Pedro; 26-2059). On Caye Caulker, at **Vega Inn and Gardens** (located seafront, near the middle of town; 22-2142).

In Belize City, at the **Seaside Guest House** (3 Prince Street; 2-78339), **Mom's Triangle Inn** (11 Handyside Street; 2-45523) and **Fort Street Guest House** (4 Fort Street; 2-30116).

In western Belize, at **Maya Mountain Lodge** (Cristo Rey Road, near San Ignacio; 92-2164) and **Venus Hotel** (29 Burns Avenue, San Ignacio; 92-2186). Maya Mountain Lodge even offers educational programs on natural history, archaeology and social science.

In Placencia, southern Belize, at the **Sea Spray Hotel** (on the beach in Placencia village; 6-23148).

NOTES FOR TRAVELING WITH PETS

If you want to bring a pet into Belize, you must have an International Health Certificate for Dogs and Cats (Form 77-043) signed by a U.S. veterinarian verifying that the animal is in good health, as well as a separate certification that it has been immunized against distemper and rabies within the last six months. Belize also requires an import permit, available from the Veterinarian Office in Belize City (2-45230).

VISITOR INFORMATION

Because mainstream tourism is still relatively new to Belize, its only stateside tourist office can't provide much assistance, and is incapable of answering even routine questions about the country. However, it will send out a prepared list of Belizean hotels and tour operators. Contact the **Belize Tourist Board** (415 Seventh Avenue, New York, NY 10001; 800-624-0686 or 212-268-8798).

The best resource for travelers is in Belize City at the **Belize Tourist Board** (83 North Front Street; 2-77213, fax: 2-77490). For information on ecotourism in Belize, contact the **Belize Audubon Society** (Box 282, Belize City,

Belize; 2-77369); the **Programme for Belize** (1 King Street, Belize City, Belize; 2-75616); or the **Belize Zoo and Tropical Education Center** (Box 474, Belize City, Belize).

SAMPLE ITINERARIES

Belize may be small, but getting around takes a lot more time than you would imagine. Most of the country is still covered by forest, and paved roads are few. Towns and sights are spread out, sometimes separated by hours-long drives down rocky roads. Likewise offshore, many cayes are reached by boat trips that take two to four hours, depending on the height of the seas.

To get the most out of Belize, you should spend at least a week. Two weeks will give you a taste of every region, though you could return for two more weeks and still not experience all the best Belize has to offer.

First-time travelers to Belize who have only a few days usually spend them on Ambergris Caye, with maybe a day trip to a Maya ruin. It's not bad for a tight schedule, but then again, you won't get a real sense of the country. For those who have more time, I recommend the following itineraries:

ONE WEEK

Day 1   Fly to Belize City, rent a car and drive to San Ignacio in western Belize. Overnight in San Ignacio.

Day 2   Drive to Caracol for a morning tour, then explore Mountain Pine Ridge in the afternoon. Overnight in San Ignacio.

Day 3   Visit the Panti Medicine Trail and the ruins at Xunan-tunich in your rental car. Cool off in the late afternoon with a swim in the Macal River. Overnight in San Ignacio.

Day 4   Drive from San Ignacio to Belize City, stopping at Guanacaste National Park and the Belize Zoo along the way. Catch a late afternoon flight to San Pedro, Ambergris Caye. Overnight on Ambergris Caye.

Days 5 & 6 Relax, fish or dive at Ambergris Caye. One morning or afternoon, take a 15-minute launch over to Caye Caulker and explore the small, neighboring island. Overnight on Ambergris Caye.

Day 7   Fly from Ambergris Caye to Belize City, then fly home.

TWO WEEKS

Days 1–3   Spend your time in San Ignacio, as described in the one-week itinerary above.

Day 4   Drive from San Ignacio to Belize City, then fly to Flores, Guatemala. Overnight in Flores or at nearby Tikal.

Days 5 & 6   Spend the day exploring the magnificent ruins of Tikal. Overnight in Flores or Tikal.

Day 7   Fly from Flores to Belize City, then take the short flight to Placencia in southern Belize. Overnight in Placencia. (*Note:* If there are no connecting flights to Placencia, spend the night in Belize City, then take a flight the next morning.)

Day 8   Relax on the beach at Placencia, or take a trip to nearby cayes for snorkeling and lunch. Overnight in Placencia.

Day 9   Take a guided tour to the Cockscomb Basin Wildlife Sanctuary. Overnight in Placencia.

Day 10   Fly from Placencia to Belize City, then fly to San Pedro, Ambergris Caye. Overnight on Ambergris Caye.

Days 11–13   Relax, dive or fish around Ambergris Caye. Spend a day exploring neighboring Caye Caulker. Overnight on Ambergris Caye.

Day 14   Fly from Ambergris Caye to Belize City, then fly home.

If you prefer to spend all your time on the mainland, consider using days ten through thirteen to visit northern Belize. Take one day trip to Lamanai, and another to Altun Ha and the Community Baboon Sanctuary.

On the other hand, if you're a hard-core island person, think about spending one of your weeks at an out island. Lighthouse Reef, Turneffe Islands, St. George's Caye and South Water Caye offer splendid week-long, all inclusive packages.

SPECIAL WAYS TO VISIT BELIZE

To truly understand and appreciate Belize, it must be explored and then savored, like an exotic food one learns to enjoy. One way to experience the country's complex, multifaceted terrain and culture is to take a specialty tour. Specialty expeditions offer unusual insights into people, wildlife and places few travelers have seen, and encounters with a world virtually unchanged over centuries.

Most unusual among specialty tours are the **Back-A-Bush Expeditions** offered by **Mountain Equestrian Trails** (8-22149, fax: 8-23235), near San Ignacio in western Belize. The three-day camping tours are limited to six people, who journey through the dense Chiquibul Forest in a four-ton Mercedes Unimog, the Superman of off-road vehicles. Among the forest's treasures are the Puente Natural Bridge, home to the rare and lyrical Solitaire bird, and the Las Cuevas caves, filled with Maya glyphs and relics.

Mountain Equestrian Trails will also take you on a **River Cave Float Trip**, an inner-tube ride through caves of dazzling limestone and warm water clear as air. The Nohoch Sayab river cave, with its labyrinth of underground streams, is the trip's highlight. Another unusual adventure offered by the equestrian trails is a five-day **horseback excursion to Caracol**, the fantastic, little known Maya ruins hidden deep in southwestern Belize.

The educational field station at **Maya Mountain Lodge** (92-2164) near San Ignacio is the starting point for **Archaeology and Natural History Tours** across western Belize. Two popular tours are the five-day **Ruta Maya Experience** and three-day **Rainforest Ecology Tour**. Also near San Ignacio, **Chaa Creek Cottages** (92-2037, fax: 92-2501) provides an array of nature and archaeological expeditions ranging from two to four days.

Paradise Bicycle Tours (P.O. Box 1726, Evergreen, CO 80439; 800-626-8271 or 303-670-1842) combines biking and hiking with snorkeling and a trip to the ruins at Tikal. The eight-day tour, offered several times a year, is called **"Belize Rainforest, Reef and Ruins."**

International Expeditions (One Environs Park, Helena, AL 35080; 800-633-4734 or 205-428-1700), widely regarded as one of the best stateside organizers of specialty tours to Belize, offers several unique expeditions:

> An 11-day **Naturalist's Quest** that takes in nearly a dozen reserves, parks and sanctuaries, as well as the great Maya city of Tikal, Guatemala.

> An 11-day **Maya Heartland** expedition that traces the Maya Route from southern Yucatán south through northern and western Belize, climaxing in Guatemala at Tikal.

> An eight-day **Wildlife Contact Experience**, featuring encounters with exotic birds and beasts of the jungle. Among those usually sighted: endangered orange-breasted falcons, American swallow-tailed kites, king vultures, ocellated turkeys, manatees, black howler monkeys, margays, ocelots and the jungle's king, the jaguar.

> A four-day **Safari Tour** through Mountain Pine Ridge in western Belize, including visits to magnificent Caracol and numerous minor Maya ruins.

> The eight- or ten-day **Crooked Tree Cashew Festival Tour**, offered every May during the celebration of the cashew harvest at Crooked

Tree Village in northern Belize. A splendid opportunity to experience the spiritual side of Belize culture.

An eight-day **Barrier Reef Snorkel Experience,** including the out islands of St. George's Caye, Sergeant's Caye, Water Caye and Turneffe Islands.

Perhaps the most exhilarating way to explore Belize's hidden cayes is to kayak them. The Utah-based **Slickrock Adventures** (P.O. Box 1400, Moab, UT 84532; 801-259-6996) organizes **kayak tours** that leave from Glover's Reef and take in a scattering of palmy, sand-fringed southern cayes, most uninhabited. Every night, the tour group camps on a different island, dining on the day's catch around a campfire and sleeping in hammocks. Slickrock owner Cully Erdman, a Vermont native who has kayaked for 20 years, is one of several experienced guides who leads the expeditions. To join the trip, kayaking experience is not necessary. However, hours of daily paddling can be strenuous, so the tour is recommended for those who don't mind a workout with their vacation.

If you prefer to relax and rejuvenate your body, opt for a **jungle spa.** In northern Belize, **Maruba Resort & Jungle Spa** (3-22199, or 713-799-2031 in Texas) uses rainforest petals, leaves and bark to make soothing potions for massages, body wraps and packs, manicures and pedicures. A five-night package includes numerous body treatments, jungle safaris and trips to surrounding Maya ruins—some of Belize's best.

A typical Belizean hut

This idyllic beach on Northern Two Cayes is in the Lighthouse Reef Atoll.

Above: Blue Hole, in Lighthouse Reef, descends 480 feet and is lined with intricate limestone formations.

Below: Aerial view of San Pedro, a sleepy town of sand streets, wobbly piers and shallow blue waters.

Above: Belize City is a collection of colonial buildings, tin-roof shanties and white-washed houses.

Above: The easy life at Turneffe Island Lodge on Turneffe Island.

Left: The Garcia sisters carve faithful replicas of Maya friezes on slate.

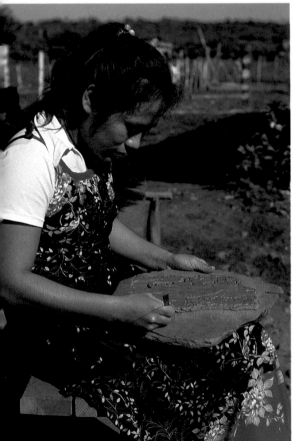

Right: A Belize City fish market, where snapper and other local fish comprise the catch of the day.

Below: Dugout fishing canoes at Half Moon Caye.

Above: Swimmers and divers in Belize often find themselves sharing the ocean with dolphins.

Top: The red-footed booby is an extremely rare sight except at Half Moon Caye Natural Monument, where about 4000 of the birds reside.

Middle left: Two manatees move lazily through shallow Belizean waters.

Middle right: An ocelot casts a wary look.

Right: A howler monkey performs a balancing act on a palm frond.

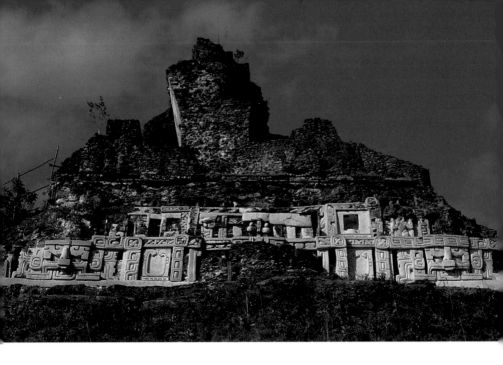

Above: The Maya ruins of Xunantunich, including 130-foot-high El Castillo, rise from the dense jungle.

Below: Altun Ha, an ancient Maya ceremonial center, consists of 13 buildings and two plazas.

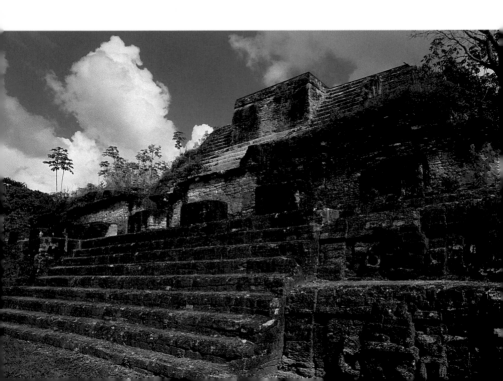

FOUR

Once You Arrive:
Getting Around In Belize

THE LANGUAGE

While English is Belize's first language, don't expect everyone to speak your brand of English. Belizeans speak with a variety of accents, and may have just as much trouble understanding your English as you do theirs. In villages and areas near the Guatemala and Mexican borders, Spanish, Maya and other languages are spoken. If you know a little Spanish, or are good with body language, you'll have no problem communicating. Belizeans are gregarious people who enjoy making new friends.

MONEY MATTERS

CURRENCY

Belize currency, measured in Belize Dollars (BZE$), is extremely stable. For the last few years, the exchange rate has stayed steady at BZE$2 to US$1. You'll have no trouble using U.S. dollars throughout Belize; in fact, many places now post their prices in U.S. currency to make them seem less expensive (which they rarely are). Foreigners, however, being respectful of where they are, should change their money and use Belize dollars. If you have any doubts about the issue, consider how you would like it if Belizeans insisted on using Belize dollars in the United States.

CHANGING MONEY

Be smart and protect your vacation by carrying traveler's checks. Even though you will get a slightly lower exchange rate, it's worth safeguarding your money. Well-known brands, especially American Express, are easiest to cash. You will need your passport to cash them. Canadian and European traveler's checks and currency can pose problems; some banks will not cash them.

Keep in mind that most villages have no banks, and it is usually impossible to cash traveler's checks there. On market days, there are often moneychangers around. At other times, only small-denomination local currency will work.

Most banks are open 8:00 a.m. to 1:00 p.m., Monday through Thursday. On Friday, hours are from 8:00 a.m. to 1:00 p.m. and 3:00 to 6:00 p.m. Banks often have specified hours for exchanging foreign money, which vary from bank to bank and day to day.

CREDIT CARDS

Credit cards are accepted at most lodges but only a few restaurants and shops, mainly those in Belize City. Many hotels add a surcharge if you pay by credit card. Mastercard, Visa and Discover are the most widely accepted cards; American Express cards are sometimes frowned upon because of their stiff fees to merchants.

If you need a financial transfusion while in Belize, most banks will provide a cash advance on your credit card. The transaction can take up to several hours, and there is usually a fee of three to five percent of the withdrawal amount. Money transfers can also be made via Western Union (*usually* taking one day) or via any big bank at home through one of its Belizean affiliates (which can take as long as three working days). Check before you leave home to see whether your bank offers this service.

TIPPING

Belizeans are not as gratuity-oriented as Americans, but they do appreciate a tip for good service. In general, follow the same customs on tipping as you would back home. Tip taxi drivers and chambermaids five to ten percent; restaurant waiters and waitresses, 15 percent; and airport porters, US 50 cents per bag. Some hotels and restaurants include a service charge, so check your bill before tipping. Tour guides are some of the most knowledgeable, patient workers in Belize and deserve a generous tip when they do a good job.

LOCAL TRANSPORTATION

FROM THE AIRPORT

Taxis charge about US$15 for the nine-mile trip from Philip S.W. Goldson International Airport, in Ladyville, to Belize City. That's the maximum fare allowed by the government, so don't pay more. Public buses run every hour during the day between the airport and city, but they're hot, crowded and slow, and don't have room for a lot of luggage. However, the price is right: US 75 cents.

TAXIS

The Belize government sets maximum fares for regular taxi routes around the country. Reputable drivers will have the fare schedule posted in their cars

The prices are high by U.S. standards, but considering the condition of Belize roads and the price of gas, they're actually quite reasonable. One driver who frequently travels to southern Belize, the land of rugged roads, replaces his car every year.

A few sample one-way fares from Belize City: north to Corozal, US$97; west to San Ignacio, US$85; south to Punta Gorda—a hellacious 202-mile ride on bumpy roads—nearly US$200. If you're going all the way to Punta Gorda, forget taxis; a 30-minute plane flight costs only US$50.

Most taxi drivers are good public relations for Belize: They're friendly, knowledgeable and in a hurry when you need them to be. Otherwise, they'll admonish you to slow way down, reminding that you are, after all, in Belize.

Indeed, some of the most memorable Belize experiences are in taxis. One American woman recalls how, in the middle of a trip, a driver asked for part of his fare in advance to buy his wife a chicken for dinner. After a brief stop at the market, the woman spent the rest of the trip in the back seat with a clucking, flapping chicken.

CARS FOR HIRE

Almost all taxi drivers double as tour guides, and will customize an itinerary and negotiate a fair fee. Many specialize in certain Maya ruins and wildlife reserves, and will act as bush guides. If you enjoy your tour, a tip of 10 to 15 percent is in order. Ask your hotel about qualified drivers, or check with the **Belize Tourist Board** (89 North Front Street, Belize City; 2-77213).

HITCHHIKING

Because bus service is widely available, there's really no need to hitchhike. Anyway, Belize is so small that if you do need a short ride, someone usually knows someone willing to give you a lift.

BUSES

There's only one class of bus in Belize, and it's closer to a school bus than a Greyhound bus. However, service is extensive and usually on time, and the fares are cheap. The express bus from Belize City to Corozal, near the Mexican border, is only US$3.75. To San Ignacio in the west, the fare is US$2. Be advised that if you're traveling during "rush" hour on a popular route, like the one between Belize City and Belmopan, get there early or you may not get a seat.

The **Z-Line** (Venus Bus Terminal, Magazine Road, Belize City; 2-73937) runs from Belize City to Belmopan, Dangriga and Punta Gorda, and points in between. **Novelos** (West Collet Canal, Belize City; 2-77372) services western Belize all the way to the Guatemala border. **Batty Brothers** (15 Mosul Street, Belize City; 2-72025), which offers similar routes through western Belize, will also take you to major points in northern Belize. Batty also has an express run from Belize City to Chetumal, Mexico. **Venus** (7th Avenue, Corozal; 4-22132) offers service in northern Belize.

Current schedules and fares are available from the **Belize Tourist Board** (89 North Front Street, Belize City; 2-77213).

PLANES

Flying is by far the quickest, least tiring way to get around Belize, and is cheaper than hiring a taxi or renting a car. Most flights are aboard loud, twin-engine puddle hoppers (10 to 20 passengers) that feel like flying jalopies. The ride will either thrill or unnerve you, depending on your level of adventure, though you will no doubt find the scenery from above unsurpassed on the ground. Local flights leave from either the **Philip S. W. Goldson International Airport** in Ladyville, nine miles north of Belize City, or from the **Belize City Municipal Airport,** on the north end of town.

Tropic Air (2-45671 in Belize City; 800-422-3435 in the U.S.) operates an hourly shuttle from Belize City to San Pedro, Ambergris Caye, and also flies to Caye Caulker, Corozal in the north and points in the south. Tropic Air also has flights to Flores, Guatemala, the gateway to Tikal, that are more or less dependable. **Island Air** (26-62435 or 26-62484 in San Pedro, Ambergris Caye) flies to the cayes. For flights to southern Belize, **Maya Airways** (2-72312 in Belize City; 800-552-3419 in the U.S.) is the best choice.

For service to Belize's out islands, such as Lighthouse Reef, and to remote inland areas of Belize and Guatemala, call **Javier's Flying Service** (2-45332). In the late 1980s, Captain Javier Bosch flew *National Geographic* writers and photographers working on the *La Ruta Maya* issue around Central America and the Yucatán. Javier's low-flying planes offer enthralling views of the mountains and jungle, as well as the barrier reef running through iridescent blue waters.

BOATS

Shuttle boats cruise from Belize City to Ambergris Caye and Caye Caulker, with usually a morning and an afternoon departure. Launches leave from two Belize City locations: (1) across from the Bellevue Hotel, at 5 Southern Foreshore, and (2) at the Shell Station near the Swing Bridge, on the north side of Haulover Creek. At both places, you'll meet a number of sweet-talking skiff owners ("Hey nice lady, let me take you in my fast boat") anxious for your patronage. If there's not much business that day, you might negotiate a lower-than-normal fee. Otherwise, it's US$10 for the one-hour trip to Ambergris Caye; US$7.50 for the 30-minute ride to Caye Caulker. Trips to St. George's Caye and other out islands can be arranged.

DRIVING IN BELIZE

Nothing makes you feel more Belizean than bounding down a rocky, washed-out jungle road in a rented four-wheel-drive, Maya beads swinging from the rear view mirror and punta rock music pounding from a radio that's ready to pop out of the dash. The scenery is priceless—barefoot village kids racing through banana groves, iguanas darting across the road, Maya women toting fresh-cut corn for their tortillas—but the pace is painfully slow. Except for three paved "highways," inland Belize is a tangle of dirt and rock roads. After a few days, you will learn that every dirt road is not created equal, but fall into three general categories:

- Type 1: a wide, clay washboard surface that allows you to travel at a nice 35 mph clip.
- Type 2: narrow marl limestone road with scattered rocks the size of golf balls. Maximum speed: 25 mph.
- Type 3: a narrow, roller-coaster trail that looks like the scene of a bomb explosion. Rubble everywhere; rocks the size of base-balls. Maximum speed: 10 mph, with the windows clattering.

Inevitably, it is the Type 3 roads that lead to the best lodges, Maya ruins and nature reserves, and so have to be reckoned with. After awhile, your body becomes used to the jarring, and you learn to accept how long it takes to go a short distance. And perhaps for the first time in your life, you become over-joyed at the sight of asphalt.

Belize's three paved "highways" (actually two-lane roads) are in fairly good shape. The **Northern Highway** runs from Belize City north to the Mexico Border; the **Old Northern Highway** parallels the Northern Highway for about 40 miles; and the **Western Highway**, which starts near Belize City, heads west to the Guatemala border. On the Western Highway, distances are meas-ured in "mile posts," little white cement markers planted beside the road.

The badly worn **Southern Highway** extends 202 miles from Belize City to Guatemala, which locals call "painful driving." I recommend flying to sights in southern Belize, but driving a four-wheel-drive everywhere else. If you visit dur-ing the rainy season, check local road conditions before setting off through the jungle. Many roads flood and are impassable from June through September.

Belize is so undeveloped that it's virtually impossible to get lost while driving. Most towns have only a handful of roads (many without names), and getting around is as easy as driving around the block. When asking directions, don't be surprised if you get a reply like, "Head toward the ocean and take a right at the third palm tree." Only Belize City requires any real navigation, and even there the streets are laid out in an easy-to-get-around fashion. Pick up a free city and country map from the **Belize Tourist Board** (89 North Front Street, Belize City; 2-77213). Car rental companies also provide good maps.

CAR RENTALS

Renting a car gives you the freedom to explore at leisure (and avoid the hot, tiny public buses). Reputable companies recommend four-wheel-drives—a ne-cessity for Belize's rocky roads. Be prepared to pay dearly; four-wheel-drives run about US$80 per day, including unlimited miles and mandatory insurance.

Beware of companies that offer lower rates for old, gas-guzzling American cars. After paying for gas (and possibly breaking down), you will have spent more than if you had rented a new four-wheel-drive.

All the car rental companies are in Belize City. The one with the best reputation is **Budget Rent A Car** (Bella Vista Road, two-and-a-half miles north of Belize City; 2-32435, fax: 2-30237), which offers four-wheel-drives in top condition. Budget owner Alan Auil will brief you on the area, and provide essential driving tips.

Elsewhere, try **Avis Car Rental** (at the international airport and the Radisson Fort George Hotel, Belize City; 2-31987, fax: 2-30225); **Hertz Rent A Car** (Bella Vista Road, two-and-a-half miles north of Belize City; 2-32710, fax: 2-32053); **World Auto Rentals** (at the international airport; 25-2586, fax: 2-32940); or **National Car Rental** (126 Freetown Road, Belize City; 2-31586).

In towns such as Corozal and San Ignacio, travel agencies can sometimes arrange a rental car for you. It may take several hours' advance notice or several days, depending on what local resident's car is available!

If you reserve a car through a company's toll-free U.S. office, be sure to reconfirm with the office in Belize City. The easiest, least expensive way is to send a fax. Anyone 25 years or older, with a passport, a driver's license and a major credit card, can rent a car in Belize. Take the optional extra insurance that lowers your deductible for damage to the vehicle. Rental cars in Belize lead hazardous existences, subjected as they are to the rocky, mountainous terrain and pothole-laced roads.

It is not currently possible to drive a Belizean rental car into Guatemala or Mexico or vice versa. It's best to take a bus or a taxi when crossing the border.

GAS

Belize gas is leaded. Sold by the gallon, it costs slightly more than gas sold in the U.S. Most major towns have gas stations that are open during the day. If you plan a long excursion into the countryside, fill up beforehand. Otherwise, if you stick to the paved Western and Northern highways, you're never far from a gas station.

BUSINESS HOURS

Professional and government offices are open from 8 a.m. to noon and 1 to 4 p.m. Monday through Friday. Retail businesses open from 8 a.m. to 5 p.m. weekdays, except for Wednesday afternoons, when they are closed. On Fridays, some stores reopen from 7 p.m. to 9 p.m.

TIME ZONES

Belize is on Central Standard Time year-round. Daylight Savings Time is not observed here.

COMMUNICATIONS

TELEPHONES

Belize has an excellent phone system. Calling into Belize is usually as easy as calling long-distance in the United States. The country code for Belize is 501, and local codes differ depending on where you're calling *from*. If you're calling from abroad, use the one-digit abbreviated local code (available from an international operator). If you're calling within Belize, use the full local code, which has a zero prefix. For instance, to call Belize City from the United States, you would dial 2. To call Belize City from elsewhere in Belize, you would dial 02. If this system sounds confusing, that's because it is!

Many establishments in Belize have no phones because of the expense and, in many communities, because it literally takes years on a waiting list to get one installed. For local or long-distance calls, your best bet is usually to ask your hotel manager for assistance in placing the call. You will pay any long-distance charges plus a small fee for the service.

AT&T and some other U.S.-based long-distance companies have special numbers you can dial in Belize that will connect you with an operator and let you charge international calls to your calling card, often at a lower cost than you would pay through the local phone company. Ask your long-distance carrier for a directory of international numbers.

To phone home without a calling card, go to any office of **BTL** (Belize Telecommunications Limited). You'll find offices in all major towns. Give your calling information to the person behind the desk, leave a deposit of US$15, and wait until the call goes through, which can take a few minutes or several hours depending on how busy international phone lines are. Then you can take the call in a private booth and talk as long as your US$15 lasts (calls to the U.S. are about US$1.60 per minute). At the end of the call, you will be reimbursed for any unused minutes.

For placing calls unassisted, here are some key numbers to remember: long-distance operator: 91; international operator: 98; prefixes for dialing direct to the United States, Canada and Europe: 95 (station to station) and 96 (person to person).

MAIL

A yellow-and-red-winged *Catonephele numilia*, a star-eyed hermit crab, a common lettuce slug—you never know what you'll find on Belize stamps. The beautiful butterflies and birds, beasts and blooms, sea life and even Maya ruins that adorn these little squares of paper are a celebration of the country's flora, fauna and history. Belize stamps are said to be some of most colorful and attractive in the world. Take a look and you'll surely agree. Stop by the **Belize City Post Office** (Queen Street, on the north side of the Swing Bridge; 2-72201) or at one of the many town offices across the country (some are

run out of local homes). Besides decorating your postcards, stamps make unusual, inexpensive gifts. Postcard stamps to the United States are US 15 cents;
stamps for letters are US 30 cents.

Unlike mail in other parts of Central America and in Mexico, Belize mail
is highly reliable. From Belize to the U.S., mail takes one to two weeks; from
the U.S. to Belize, about a week.

LAUNDRY

After watching the local women scrub laundry every day in the rivers, the
idea of having your clothes dry-cleaned seems extravagant. However, there
is the **Belize City Dry Cleaners & Coin Laundry** (3 Dolphin Street; 2-
75153), which even offers delivery service that's more or less dependable.
Outside the city, you can usually have your wash taken care of overnight at
your lodge, though it's costly. I take a small bottle of laundry detergent, hand
wash everything in the lodge sink, and hang it to dry in the trade winds.

PUBLICATIONS

U.S. magazines, newspapers and paperback books can be found in Belize City
and at some lodges throughout the country. All major Belize publications are
in English. The country's newspaper is the *Reporter*, a quirky, homestyle tabloid
that reports on issues from screwworm eradication to the number of Guatemalan "aliens" who sneaked across the border that week. Pick up a copy—it's
local color at its best. More glossy but still offering gossipy tidbits is the bi-
monthly *Belize Currents* magazine.

PICTURE TAKING

While on the cayes and in larger towns, you can take pictures freely in almost
any public place. Outlying villages are a different story. Many villagers, particularly the older Maya and Garifunas, don't want their picture taken—a ta-
boo that we, as visitors, should respect. If you want to photograph village
people, ask first. You will no doubt be charmed by their colorful, elaborately
handcrafted clothing and their exotic features with faces expressing everything
from stoic nobility and ancient, mysterious wisdom to embarrassed amuse-
ment at the strange-looking tourist confronting them. With the coming of television to many villages, attitudes toward cameras are changing. Some people
are more willing than in the past to pose for photographs. And if you converse
with them for a while and let them get to know you, many people who would
deeply resent having their likeness captured by a stranger are more than willing to offer it as a gift to a new friend. You may want to reciprocate with
a small gift, either a monetary tip or a souvenir. Village children love pens,
hair barrettes, sunglasses—most anything a tourist has to offer.

Have your film developed back home. Belize's developing labs are not only expensive but few and far between. If you just can't wait to see your snapshots, take your film to **Spooner's One-Hour Minilab** (89 North Front Street, Belize City; 2-31043), which offers fair prices and dependable service.

HEALTH PRECAUTIONS

HEALTH CARE

Medical clinics and doctor's offices are available in towns and villages across Belize, but the level of care does not measure up to U.S. standards. The country's hospitals are typically sad-looking, overcrowded places that are not equipped to administer advanced health care. Belizeans who can afford it go to Miami or Houston for major surgery. For routine procedures and minor emergencies, **Belize Medical Associates Ltd.** (5791 St. Thomas Street, Belize City; 2-30303 or 2-30098, fax: 2-33837) is a private clinic recommended by some American expatriates. The facility employs seven physicians, including surgeons and specialists in internal medicine, pediatrics and obstetrics.

Outside Belize City, lodges can usually recommend the best local physicians. Contact your health insurance carrier before you leave to find out the extent of your coverage while abroad.

For true medical emergencies, a San Diego-based service called **Critical Air Medicine** (call collect to 619-571-8944) provides air ambulance service to anywhere in Central America or Mexico—24 hours a day, every day of the year.

TURISTA

The illness some people may encounter is diarrhea, euphemized as *turista*. Caused by food and drink carrying unfamiliar strains of bacteria, a bout can range from a 24-hour case of mild cramps to an all-out attack with several days of fever, chills and vomiting, followed by a lousy feeling that lingers on for weeks.

However, *turista* is much less common in Belize than in Mexico. This author, who consistently gets ill in Mexico (despite drastic precautions), has had no problems in Belize. No doubt it is because Belize, despite its Third-World status, adheres closely to British standards of cleanliness and health. In Belize City, the British government has installed a modern purification system that seems to work just fine. In remote areas, motels and lodges usually provide bottled water in the rooms or will direct you to a grocery store that sells it. Always drink bottled liquids—mineral water, sodas, fruit drinks, soft drinks or beer—whenever possible.

Take it easy the first few days. If you sock your system with unfamiliar food and heavy liquor right away, your stomach may seek revenge. In other words, eating spicy stewed chicken followed by fried gibnut chased by Caribbean rum is asking for trouble.

Remember, those who stay healthy use the best defense: prevention. Eat with discretion. If you're in a jungle or island lodge frequented by tourists, the food is usually high quality and delicious. If you find yourself in a remote outpost, where the pickings are limited to a suspect Chinese hole-in-the-wall or a grocery store, opt for the grocer. Consume only thick-skinned fruits that you peel yourself, such as oranges and bananas, and vegetables that are cooked through. Nuts with shells, such as peanuts and coconuts, are pretty safe bets, too. Steer clear of raw seafood—*ceviche* is renowned for causing *turista*—as well as garden salads.

Be careful about street food, especially in small villages. Meat, seafood, peeled fruit used in drinks and candies on which flies have taken their naps are more risky. However, a lot of the food from stalls is delicious and very well prepared. I especially enjoy the street food in Belize City and in San Pedro, on Ambergris Caye. If the facilities look clean and the food is hot off the grill, it's probably okay. Be the judge and take your chances.

Many people believe in preventive medicine. Some take a slug of Pepto-Bismol before every meal; others, a shot of tequila, believing it will extinguish any threatening organisms. The antibiotic Doxycyclin is commonly prescribed as a preventive, although it causes sensitivity to the sun—a major inconvenience in the subtropics. Belize bush doctors prescribe jackass bitters, an awful-tasting potion brewed with jungle plants, as both a preventive and remedy. One traveler from Texas, who contracted severe diarrhea, said jackass bitters cured him in several hours—though he could barely endure the taste. I also met several people, including former residents of Mexico, who swear by garlic pills as the best prevention. Lime juice is also a traditional preventive for stomach problems.

If you take all the necessary precautions and still get hit with *turista*, try these remedies: Lomotil, the stopper-upper. Use sparingly. Not a cure, it's a morphine derivative that induces a kind of intestinal paralysis. Stop the dosage as soon as symptoms disappear. Paragoric, Kaopectate, Kaomycin, Imodium AD and Pepto-Bismol help keep the cramps down. For diarrhea with a fever, you can take Septra or Bactrium if you are not allergic to sulfa drugs. But remember that prolonged use of any antibiotic is not good for your immune system and can make you more susceptible to other tropical diseases.

Hot chamomile tea and peppermint tea sooth the stomach and often work wonders. Papaya restores the digestive tract. Light, easy-to-digest foods like toast and soup keep your strength up. Lots of nonalcoholic liquids—any kind—prevent dehydration. Carbonated water with juice of a lime is another popular stomach soother.

Rest and relaxation will help your body heal faster than if you run around sick and wear yourself down further. The symptoms should pass within 24 hours or so, and a case of *turista* seems to have an immunizing effect—any subsequent bouts you may have will be less severe, and eventually your body will adjust to the foreign water's bacteria.

In rare cases, diarrhea may be a symptom of a more serious illness like amoebic dysentery or cholera. See a doctor if the diarrhea persists beyond three days, if your stool is bloody or foamy, or if you have a high fever.

MOSQUITOES AND OTHER PESTS IN PARADISE

Ask anyone who's spent a night in the jungle and they will tell you: The most ferocious animal is not a jaguar but a mosquito. **Mosquitoes** fiercely protect their territory in this region of the world, known aptly as "The Mosquito Coast." The little buzzers are thickest in rainforests, swamp areas and along coastal bush. The best defenses are long sleeves and pants, and plenty of good insect repellent.

What works for you may not work for someone else. People who wish to avoid DEET, the active chemical in most commercial mosquito repellents, may want to investigate some other methods. Herb shops and health food stores in the U.S. sell good-smelling potions that are more or less protective lotions made from oils and herbal essences. Some people swear by daily doses of Vitamin B-6 or garlic, others by tobacco smoke. The new electronic mosquito repellent devices, which emit a sound pitched at the high edge of human hearing, got high marks from a visitor to Guatemala's dense Petén jungle. Many Belizeans, following an ancient Maya custom, burn abandoned termite nests to chase away mosquitoes. After trying dozens of different brands, pills and treatments, I found that only the strongest repellent (such as Deep Woods OFF!) keeps me bugless. For areas of moderate infestation, the pleasant-smelling lotion Skintastic (also made by OFF!) does the trick.

Campers will find that mosquito netting is more important that a tent or a sleeping bag. Many jungle lodges drape mosquito nets over the beds, and provide mosquito coils that will burn all night.

Sandflies, also called flying teeth or no-see-ums, are mite-sized bugs with a giant bite. Like mosquitoes, sandflies steal the best part of the day, emerging in droves at dawn and dusk. Unlike mosquitoes, they will prey on the tiny grooves and crevices of the human body—ears, nose, eyelids. Besides a powerful repellent, wear a hat and a pair of sunglasses.

Booby

Less well-known but no less of a pest, **bottlass,** or "bottle-ass," flies are minuscule rainforest dwellers that inflict angry, itching blisters. As the flies fill with blood, their stomachs puff up and give the appearance of tiny flying bottles—hence the nickname.

Bottlass flies should not be confused with **botflies,** which don't bite in the traditional sense, but whose larvae burrow under the flesh after being deposited by a mosquito or bottlass fly. It causes only minor itching the first few days, but as the larva grows and feeds, its prickly body burns and pinches its victim. Botfly larvae breathe through a tiny hole in the victim's skin, so the way to kill them is to smother them by masking the hole (Belizeans use everything from Scotch tape and moistened tobacco leaves to petroleum jelly), then squeeze them out. If this sounds truly horrible, it isn't. Kids living and playing in the jungle get them all the time, and so do the animals. And chances are, unless you spend many days in the jungle during rainy season, you will probably never experience a botfly.

Before you head out to Belize's beautiful seas, you should become acquainted with **sea thimbles, sea lice** and **stingrays.** The first is a tiny brown, thimble-shaped jellyfish that scoots along the surface of the water. If you swim along the surface, it will scoot with you and inflict little bites that later turn into big red welts. Sea lice, the larvae of sea thimbles, also lurk on the surface and bestow measles-looking bite marks that itch for a week. Unfortunately, sea lice are invisible.

You can usually avoid sea thimbles by not swimming where you see them. Occasionally, they are so small and pervasive, they look like underwater particles. Sea lice are impossible to avoid, but you can minimize the bites by rinsing your body in fresh water. Don't rinse until you've removed your swimsuit; fresh water trapped under your suit could cause the larvae to swell and sting you even worse.

Like sea lice, stingrays are tough to see. The flat slippery creatures camouflage themselves in the sand along shallow areas and can deliver a wicked puncture with their stingers. To avoid being stung, shuffle away. If you're stung, see a doctor at once.

For various bug bites, Benadryl ointment and pills take the itch out and reduce swelling. Caladryl (a blend of Benadryl and calamine lotion) also works well, as does lime juice. For sea thimble and sea lice bites, Belizeans splash on vinegar to reduce swelling and take the heat out. If you do get zapped with a rash of bites, avoid the sun for a few days. Direct sun causes even more swelling and inflammation, and slows healing.

DRUGS

Marijuana farms abound in Belize. If you have any doubts, check a local map; the bigger fields are often clearly marked. Out in the bush, when locals want some "Belize breeze," they visit the village pot farmer. They *do not* help themselves to a local field; doing so could result in physical harm. If you should happen upon a marijuana field, resist any urges to go exploring. Many growers protect their crop as though it were their lives.

Smoking marijuana out in the jungle will probably bring few consequences, but back in "civilization," partaking could land you in jail, where getting out can take a lot of time and money. In certain locales, such as Belize City, Caye Caulker and Orange Walk Town, you will receive offers from whispering salesmen to purchase marijuana, cocaine, crack and other illegal substances, and may even see locals using drugs publicly. But what the police may accept from locals, they rarely tolerate with tourists. The United States government pays Belize a lot of money to enforce drug laws, and the substances are highly illegal. All things considered, when traveling in Belize, it's better to stay out of the war on drugs.

SAFETY AND THEFT

Belize is sparsely populated and has little big-city crime. Plus, Belizeans are extremely proud, family-oriented and peace-loving (the police carry no guns). Traveling here is like traveling through a jungle version of the American midwest—lots of country roads and friendly people. I spent several weeks crisscrossing Belize in a four-wheel-drive by myself and had not one problem. Even in Belize City, where everyone seems to have an "I-got-robbed" story, I felt quite at ease.

But Belize City *is* famous for petty thieves, just as certain U.S. cities have a well-deserved reputation for crime. When choosing a hotel, make sure it's in a safe part of town, preferably one that's frequented by travelers. All lodges recommended in this book are located in safe neighborhoods. After the stroke of dusk, stay away from the Swing Bridge, the infamous hangout of petty thieves. Even if you are with a group, the Swing Bridge is not safe at night. During the day, however, feel free to cross as often as you like!

The safest place to be in Belize City at night is at your hotel; the second safest is the Fort George neighborhood. Areas of downtown where there is a lot of activity after dark are safer than outlying neighborhoods. Don't tempt fate by wandering around dark back streets late at night. Stay away from drug deals. In short, exercise the same caution you would use at home. Observe these common-sense precautions, and feel fortunate that you are not in New York City, where—unlike in Belize City—the petty criminals carry guns.

Be aware that whenever you are in public, any thief who happens to be around will be checking you out. Foreign tourists are natural targets for theft because they stand out in a crowd and seem wealthy in a country where the average income amounts to US$10 a day. Use common sense. Watch out for pickpockets, purse-snatchers and backpack-slashers, especially in public markets and other crowded places. Carry your trip funds, passport and other important documents in a money pouch or hidden pocket inside your clothing. Keep cash in your side pocket, never a back pocket. Carry day-packs under one arm rather than on your back. Don't leave wallets or cameras lying on the beach while you go for a swim or sitting on a café table while you go to the restroom. Always lock your hotel room and car. Park in a secured lot at night. Don't leave radios, gifts, cassettes or other temptations visible inside the car. Dress with humility; a thief will focus on the best-dressed, richest-looking tourist around, so make sure it's not you.

Once you leave Belize City, relax. Except for the town of Orange Walk, which has its share of thieves and drug dealers, the rest of the country is rural and crime is rare. You should, of course, always exercise common sense. Never carry large amounts of cash or leave valuables unattended in public places. But don't be alarmed to find there aren't any locks on your lodge door—there are few thieves in the jungle!

EMBASSIES AND CONSULATES

Following is a list of foreign embassies and consulates in Belize:

Belgium Consular Representative: Queen Street, Belize City; 2-45769

British High Commission: 34/36 Halfmoon Avenue, Belmopan; 8-22146

Canadian Consulate: 120-A New Road, Belize City; 2-31060

Commission of European Communities: 1 Eyre Street, Belize City; 2-72785

Costa Rican Consulate: 8 18th Street, Belize City; 2-44796

El Salvador Consular General: 120 New Road, Belize City; 2-44318

German Honorary Consul: 2 Cork Street, Belize City; 2-77316

Honduran Honorary Consul: 91 North Front Street, Belize City; 2-45889

Israel Honorary Consul: 4 Albert Street, Belize City; 2-73991

Italian Consular Representative: 18 Albert Street, Belize City; 2-73284

Jamaican Consulate General: corner of Hyde's Lane and New Road, Belize City; 2-45446

Mexican Embassy: 20 Park Street, Belize City; 2-30193

Netherlands Honorary Consul: 14 Central American Boulevard, Belize City; 2-73612

Panamanian Consulate: 5481 Princess Margaret Drive, Belize City; 2-44940

Panamanian Embassy: 79 Unity Boulevard, Belmopan; 8-22714

Royal Danish Consulate: 13 Southern Foreshore, Belize City; 2-72172

Swedish Consular Representative: 13 Queen Street, Belize City; 2-77234

United States Embassy, Consular Section: 29 Gabourel Lane, Belize City; 2-77161

Venezuelan Consul General: 18/20 United Boulevard, Belmopan; 8-22384

NATIVE FOOD AND DRINK

FRUITS AND VEGETABLES

The Belizean landscape, so pristine and prolific, yields an extraordinary array of tropical fruits and vegetables. Many Belizean backyards are like "mini" produce markets, with selections ranging from papayas, mangoes and passion fruit to cacao beans, custard apples and habañero peppers. Banana plants and coconut palms abound, as do cohune palms, whose tiny white nuts taste like coconut and whose innermost cores, called hearts of palm, are considered a delicacy. You'll also find tamarinds, guavas, plantains and carambola, or star fruit, throughout Belize, and breadfruit on the cayes. Maize, or corn, is grown in *milpa* fields, and has been a diet staple of the Maya for thousands of years. In the tuber family, there are shaggy, white-fleshed malangas; the waxy, fibrous cassava, whose toxins are dispelled during cooking; and the knobby, rose-colored *boniatos*, the sweet potatoes of Central America.

For an introduction to Belize fruits and vegetables, visit the Belize City **Market** (Regent Street, at the southeast corner of the Swing Bridge), where bamboo bins display dozens of colorful varieties. Opened in early 1993, it's a gleaming, indoor place where Belize women are more than happy to tell you about each produce item.

Another excellent source of information are the Belize bush guides, who are infinitely versed in local fruits and vegetables. They'll tell you how the ancient Maya used the produce, and how you can prepare it today.

Even if you don't forage the countryside for fresh produce, you'll find yourself enjoying it at virtually every meal. Belize lodges take advantage of the earth's bounty to supply their tables, and many have organic gardens. For breakfast, wedges of papaya and mango might be tucked around the eggs, and slushy watermelon juice served alongside steaming tea or coffee. At lunchtime, when the sun is hottest and humidity highest, locals cool off with fresh squeezed lime juice, swirled with water and unrefined sugar. Dinner could bring malanga mashed with garlic or corn tortillas baked that very day. For the finale, it might be banana cake, mango fool (a custardy dessert, made with brown sugar, cream and sweetened condensed milk) or perhaps papaya slices flambéed with Belizean rum over ice cream.

Here are a few tips on identifying and using Belize's best produce:

Breadfruit: Breadfruit trees are massive, towering above houses and other trees, while the fruit, which is really a vegetable, is the size of a cannonball. Plucked when still green, it ripens quickly, developing soft, brown patches much like a ripening avocado. It is typically sliced in rounds and fried, though sometimes the flesh is scooped out and baked in a variety of ways, including into breadfruit bread.

Cashew: The cashew tree is a dull tree, with plain round green leaves covering a plain round canopy that disappears amongst the more beautiful Belize trees. Its only distinguishing characteristic is its fruit, the cashew apple, which appears in the spring. The apple is pale red and fleshy, and its sweet meat is turned into mild jellies and strong wines. At the apple's crown is the curly cashew nut, whose kernel is roasted and then coveted by people around the world. The best time to experience Belize cashews is in May, at the Crooked Tree Cashew Festival, held in the village of Crooked Tree in northern Belize. In case you're tempted to pick your own, be aware that the oily liquid inside the cashew shell is poisonous, and not only burns the skin but can kill you if ingested.

Cassava: A ruddy white tuber, and perhaps the humblest of Belize vegetables, it is a symbol of the Garifuna (African Carib) culture. In southern Belize villages, Garifuna women rise before the sun to dig hundreds of cassava roots from the hard clay ground. Then the roots are peeled, pressed through a grinder, and the juice wrung from it. The resulting mush is baked into a white waferlike bread. Other Belizeans use cassava widely, either mashing it like potatoes or slicing it into soups, stews and "boil ups," where it is boiled with whole fish, chicken or cow's feet.

Custard Apple: Like nature's own pudding cup, the custard apple has a creamy, rose-scented flesh designed to go straight from fruit to mouth with a spoon. About the size of an orange, with bumpy green skin that turns blackish-brown when ripe, the custard apple tastes best chilled. To eat, simply slice it in half and scoop out the black seeds.

Habañero Pepper: This is the hottest pepper on earth, registering 200,000 to 300,000 on the Scoville Chart, the Richter scale of chile peppers (jalapeños measure 5000), which sounds like enough to cause stomach meltdown. But the habañero can be eaten, indeed enjoyed, when tamed with shredded carrots and other vegetables and bottled as Marie Sharp's Hot Sauce. Marie Sharp's is consumed in mass quantities around Belize; the bottles sit on tables throughout the land. Many families have their own habañero bush. If you want to see fields of the lantern-shaped chilies, visit Melinda Farm in southern Belize, where Marie Sharp's is made (see Chapter Ten).

Hearts of Palm: It takes a great deal of strength and skill to hack into a palm tree and extract its heart. But once you have tasted the satiny core, encased in folds of delicate white flesh, you will understand why someone would go to all the trouble. After being wrenched from its tree, the heart is boiled until tender, then fanned across salads or served as a side dish, usually with a light sauce or a squeeze of lime juice.

Maize: Together with beans and rice, maize has been the foundation of the Maya diet for thousands of years. Maya villagers today still rely on corn as a primary staple; the men harvest it and the women soak it overnight in lime juice. The next day, the women grind the corn into a powdery meal, mix it with water, and knead it on a cornmeal stone called a *metate*. Then they shape it into wafer-thin disks called tortillas, and grill the disks over an open fire on a *comal*, or griddle stone. The tortillas are kept warm until the meal, at which time a typical Maya man may consume up to 20. If you are lucky enough to visit a rural Maya village, you can watch the women squatting over the fires, making their daily tortillas.

Mango: There are more than 100 varieties of mango, which can weigh anywhere from a few ounces to a few pounds, with flesh that can be fragrant, lush and golden or stringy and tasteless. The best way to tell a good mango from a bad one is to sniff it. It if doesn't smell sweet, it's probably no good. A choice mango smells and tastes like a cross between a peach, pineapple and banana. To eat a mango "on the half shell," slice the fruit right next to its flat pit to get two fleshy "cheeks." With the skin-side down, score each cheek into small chunks, then slice the chunks away from the skin.

A word of caution: Mangoes are in the poison ivy family; the juice and peel may swell and blister the skin of some people. But even those who are allergic to it can usually eat the ripe fruit without any side effects.

Papaya: American food writer Elizabeth Schneider likens the papaya tree to "an Indian fertility goddess." No doubt it is because the branchless trunk dangles its lobes of luscious fruit beneath a sprawling, lacy canopy. Yellowish-green to pinkish-purple, papayas have slippery peach-colored flesh and glassy black seeds that are edible. Simply cut it in half lengthwise and scoop out the meat.

Passion Fruit: One would hope this fruit was named for the sensations it arouses when eaten. Alas, it was named by a most dispassionate group, European missionaries, who upon landing in South America thought its flower looked like a crown of thorns and other Crucifixion symbols. The fruit, for its part, bears a sweet-tart, gelatinous pulp that is indeed sensory-heightening. To eat, slice the purplish-yellow globe in half and scoop out the pulp and edible seeds.

Soursop: There is nothing like the taste of soursop, so spicy and perfumed and tropically addictive. There is nothing quite like the looks of it either— pimply, plump and evergreen. Inside, the fruit's pale custardlike flesh is the color of pale pink abalone. The flesh is rarely cooked, but rather strained, and the soursop juice used in ice creams and rum drinks.

THE BEANS AND RICE SYNDROME

Except for Marie Sharp's Hot Sauce, nothing appears on more Belize tables than beans and rice. Since the time of the Maya, this fiber-starch duo has sustained generations of people on a short but endless cycle: They'd eat beans and rice to get energy to work in the fields planting, growing and harvesting beans and rice, which they'd eat for energy to work in the fields, starting the cycle all over again. Today, some villagers carry on the cycle, but most people who eat the dish do not grow it.

As humble as the dish sounds, beans and rice come in a variety of preparations, from a fiery mélange of vegetables and ground meat or lobster stewed in coconut milk to a dry, bland combo cooked way too long. It's not hard to tell the difference. Good beans and rice look moist and colorful (the beans will be crimson red to bright purple and slightly cracked). Bad beans and rice look dry, and the beans will be cooked to little hard pieces. Most dishes are made with red kidney beans, though you will find concoctions prepared with black beans, turtle beans and even pink beans. Some of the tastiest beans and rice come from street vendors, who toss the brilliant mixture in drum-sized frying pans.

You may not become a beans and rice fan overnight, but you will quickly learn that the dish is remarkable human fuel. For climbing Maya ruins, hiking through the jungle or kayaking the seas, few foods keep you going like beans and rice.

Of course, beans aren't always paired with rice. One of the best dishes I had in Belize was the spicy refried bean dip served at Chan Chich Lodge. When the dip is brought out every evening at sunset, guests literally mob the bowl.

CHAN CHICH'S SPICY REFRIED BEAN DIP

½ pound dried red or black beans

1 medium green pepper, chopped

1 small onion, diced

2 pickled jalapeño peppers, chopped, plus 1 tsp. of their juice

2 cloves garlic

¼ cup vegetable oil

salt and pepper to taste

tortilla chips, preferably blue corn chips

Rinse beans and place in a 2-quart pan. Cover beans with 2 inches of water, then cover with lid. Bring to a slow boil, reduce heat to medium-low, and simmer beans, partially covered, for 1½ hours. Add more water during cooking if necessary.

Remove beans from heat and cool. In a blender, combine beans and their water, green pepper, jalapeños and their juice, and garlic. Blend until smooth. In a large skillet, heat the oil over medium heat. Add the onion and sauté until pale brown. Stir in the blended bean mixture and cook over medium-low heat until thick, about one hour, stirring occasionally.

Cool slightly and spoon dip into serving dish. Serve with tortilla chips. Recipe makes about 2 cups of dip.

GIBNUT, BAMBOO CHICKEN AND COW'S FOOT SOUP

One reason people come to Belize is for adventure. That's why you might want to try gibnut, bamboo chicken and cow's foot soup. When cooked right, it's Belizean soul food at its best, food that's crisp-fried tender or simmered all day until the meat falls off the bone.

Gibnut, or paca, is a large nocturnal rodent whose tender white flesh is considered tastier than steak. Sometimes it's breaded and fried; more often it's stewed in a big, dilapidated pot over a gas stove or open fire. In the late 1980s, Queen Elizabeth elevated the dish to "royal gibnut" after she ordered it (and purportedly cleaned her plate) at a Belize City hole-in-the-wall called Macy's. But before the queen's discovery, it was plain old gibnut.

Bamboo chicken is the nickname for iguana, which, when fried or grilled, does look and taste a lot like chicken. Cow's foot soup is also just like it sounds: a broth made hearty by slow cooking with a cow's foot (or, if company's coming, two cow's feet). Carrots, onions, garlic, cassava and other vegetables are simmered with the foot, and sometimes a pig's tail, oxtail or chicken foot is thrown in. If you can get past the sight of feet in your soup, you will find the porridge is truly delicious.

Few hotel restaurants serve gibnut, bamboo chicken or cow's foot soup. Unless you're invited to a local home for dinner—an adventurer's dream—your best bet for soul food is a Belizean diner. These are typically tiny, meager establishments with fans teetering from the ceiling, a TV or transistor radio blaring, and a powerful-looking woman in the back hovering over numerous steaming pots.

The less adventurous will also find more familiar local cuisine. Fried chicken is ubiquitous, followed closely by "stew" chicken and "stew" fish, fried fish, fry jacks (sweet fried corn cakes) and johnnycakes (biscuits that are *not* fried). Street vendors sell spicy, flaky meat pies that are some of the best in the Caribbean. Tortillas and tamales are found in northern Belize, near the Mexican border, while lobster and conch prevail on the cayes. Order them only in season—July through October for lobster; October through June for conch. Chinese restaurants abound in certain small towns, with food of wildly varying quality. Some of the best Chinese food I ever had was in Belize, as was the worst. Ask around before you dine.

BEER AND RUM

Belize's national beer, Belikin, must have the best beer label in the world: a Maya temple. It's the Temple of the Sun God, found at Altun Ha. If you don't get to see the temple in person, you'll see its likeness all over Belize, since Belikin is wildly popular. The mild, medium-amber beer costs about US$1 a bottle in groceries and local restaurants, and double that in tourist areas.

There are several different rums made in Belize, but by far the best and most pervasive is Caribbean rum. It comes in light or dark, and both are surprisingly good, considering no one's ever heard of Caribbean rum. Buy some for your friends; a 750 ml bottle will only set you back about US$5.

Every Belizean has his or her own special recipe for rum punch, but I love the one served at Maruba Resort & Jungle Spa. It's a frosty swirl of just-picked tropical fruit, lime juice, unrefined sugar, rainwater and Belizean dark rum, served in a big hairy coconut shell. What gives it a distinctive sweet-tart taste is the soursop fruit. If you can't find the fresh fruit, substitute frozen fruit or canned juice.

MARUBA RESORT'S RUM PUNCH

3 cups chopped tropical fruit (such as papaya, mango, pineapple and soursop)

juice from half a lime

4 tablespoons unrefined sugar (or regular sugar)

2 cups water

¾ cup dark rum

Fill a blender almost to the top with crushed ice and add the above ingredients. Blend until well mixed and frosty.

Makes 4-6 drinks.

RESTAURANTS

Belize is not known for its culinary achievements. In fact, its restaurants suffer a dismal reputation among travelers, a reputation that's not deserved. No matter where you travel in the country, you will have access to tasty, well-prepared food. The problem is, many eateries are inconsistent. The place that served a memorable meal one night may serve a forgettable one the next. Cooks hopscotch between restaurants, and high-quality ingredients are not always available. But if you ask around town, locals will point you to the best spot.

In populated areas, such as Belize City and Ambergris Caye, you can choose from fresh seafood, Italian, Chinese and the ubiquitous Belizean soul food. In remote areas, you will rely on your lodge for meals—not a bad option, considering Belize lodges offer some of the country's best fare. Jungle lodges often grow their food organically and employ Maya or Creole cooks who know their way around a kitchen. And don't be surprised to learn that your delicious, filling entrée was prepared with low salt and low fat and without meat. Many innkeepers believe healthy, no-meat diets are in keeping with the principles of ecotourism.

In this book, restaurants are separated into the following price categories: *budget* restaurants cost $5 or less for dinner entrées; *moderate*-priced restaurants range between $5 and $12 at dinner and offer pleasant surroundings and a more varied menu; and *expensive* establishments tab their entrées at $12 and over, featuring cuisine that's more sophisticated, plus decor and more personalized service. A few hotel restaurants add a 15-percent service charge.

National Parks, Reserves, Refuges and Biotopes

MEXICO

0   50 kilometers

50 miles

Belmopan

Belize City

Northern Hwy.

Old Northern Hwy.

Western Hwy.

Hummingbird Hwy.

Ambergris Caye

CARIBBEAN SEA

A

B

C

D

E

F

G

H

I

J

K

L

M

LAKE PETÉN ITZÁ

Melchor de Mencos

13

Santa Elena   Flores

N

O

BELIZE

13

Dangriga

GUATEMALA

Southern Hwy.

GULF OF HONDURAS

Punta Gorda

N

LAKE IZABAL

Q

P

Puerto Barrios

9

HONDURAS

9

EL SALVADOR

A	Hol Chan Marine Reserve
B	Half Moon Caye Natural Monument
C	Community Baboon Sanctuary
D	Crooked Tree Wildlife Sanctuary
E	Shipstern Nature Reserve and Butterfly Breeding Centre
F	Monkey Bay Wildlife Sanctuary
G	Guanacaste National Park
H	Blue Hole and St. Herman's Cave National Park
I	Five Blues Lake National Park
J	Mountain Pine Ridge Forest Reserve
K	Melinda Forest Reserve
L	Bird Caye Bird Sanctuary
M	Cockscomb Basin Wildlife Sanctuary
N	Tikal National Park
O	Biotopo Cerro Cahui
P	Río Dulce National Park
Q	Biotopo Chacón Machaca

FIVE

The Outdoors

Belize *is* the outdoors. Here life revolves around the endless cycles of the rainforest and the sea. The complexities of the outdoors, the mysterious web of birth, death and dependency, overshadow everything else. Those who seek outdoor experiences and true adventures will find them everywhere—in the mangrove flats churning with fishing possibilities, in the primal forests riddled with hiking passages, and in the deliriously beautiful reefs offering incomparable scuba diving. You can explore 3000-year-old cities on horseback, canoe down rivers edged in jungle, bicycle to secret coves on hidden islands. You can even join a week-long climb up the treacherous, stony face of 3675-foot Victoria Peak—the ultimate Belize outdoor high.

NATIONAL PARKS AND RESERVES, WILDLIFE REFUGES AND ARCHAEOLOGICAL PRESERVES

More of Belize lies inside the boundaries of a reserve than outside of one. Some 80 percent of the country's original rainforests have been preserved (a sharp contrast to its neighbor El Salvador, which has saved only 2 percent), and most are protected by the government. More than 25 parks, wildlife refuges and archaeological preserves exist today. Some are so wild and impenetrable, they are impossible to visit. But most can been seen, indeed extensively explored, by outsiders.

Access to parks, reserves and refuges varies widely. By far the easiest to reach are Guanacaste National Park and Blue Hole and St. Herman's Cave National Park (not to be confused with the Blue Hole in the sea), located a short stroll off main roads. At the other extreme is the lost Maya city of Caracol, which requires an arduous, hours-long journey on rocky, oft-flooded jungle roads. Trips to Caracol require not only a special guide but a permit from the Belize Department of Archaeology.

The majority of reserves, however, fall somewhere in between. Prepare to spend at least an hour or two on rough roads (and don't lose your cool if the truck breaks down; Belize has a way of murdering vehicles!). And plan to do some serious walking and/or hiking—five miles in one reserve is not uncommon. Neither are 12-hour days.

No matter where you visit, go with a guide. Unless you've had guerrilla training, you won't know your way around the jungle. There is no substitute for having someone along who knows the land, and who can point out all the life hiding in the forest. Many Belize guides are Maya bushmen, earnest pioneers whose expertise range from baboon and jaguar calls to wild fern species and bizarre rituals performed by their ancient Maya ancestors. Some do not wear shoes, preferring to feel the jungle while they see and smell it. Their everyday conversations take on mystical proportions, with talk of Maya planet worship, universal energy and the healing secrets contained within the plants. When the day is done, they often retreat to the most comfortable home they know—the jungle.

For recommendations on bush guides, check with your lodge. For general information on reserves and wildlife refuges in Belize, contact the **Belize Audubon Society** (Box 282, Belize City; 2-77369) or the **Programme for Belize** (1 King Street, Belize City; 2-75616). For information on archaeological preserves, call the **Department of Archaeology** (Belmopan; 8-22106). Information on national forests is available from the **Department of Forestry** (Belmopan; 8-22166).

CAMPING

There is little organized camping in Belize. You will find makeshift shelters scattered throughout the reserves, but you have to bring your own equipment, food and water. Sometimes that means toting it through the jungle, *after* driving down a long bumpy dirt road. If you do camp in the forest, make sure it's the dry season. Summer rains can not only wash away your camp (and hatch zillions of mosquitoes), they can flood surrounding roads and strand you for days.

The best bet for camping is on the cayes, where palmy, open seashores make way for tents, and trade winds cool you down at night. In fact, the only real campground in all of Belize is on Caye Caulker. It's called Vega Inn and Gardens and it's a far-out place, with pooka-shelled hippies smoking weed and young bright-eyed backpackers grilling fish on the beach under the stars. This and other camping possibilities are mentioned throughout the book.

FISHING

Belize has many secrets, not the least of which is this: There are fish in Belize. Fish so big and so plentiful that even the most amateur angler can catch his limit in a few hours. Fish so anxious to impale themselves on a hook that they will rush toward a skiff, or toward a pair of human legs wading in the flats.

Belize owes its fishing phenomenon to a remarkably diverse underwater world—it boasts one of the hemisphere's most healthy reef systems—and a lack of people. Whether you fish in one of the many inland rivers or on the mangrove flats, along the barrier reef or out in deep blue water, it is likely you will not see another angler *all day*. Of course, as more people "discover" these wonders, the solitude and diversity will diminish. In the meantime, if you love to fish, don't miss the chance to cast your line in Belize.

FLY-FISHING   If you're into angling's hottest trend, saltwater fly-fishing, you'll find it in Belize, where bonefish, tarpon and permit churn up the flats everywhere. Belize's most renowned flats are those around the Turneffe Islands, where the bottom is a mix of hard-packed sand and sea grass, and the water is virtually always wadeable. Turneffe's popularity means it is more crowded than other spots around Belize, though for those used to fishing in Florida or other "discovered" areas, it will no doubt seem secluded.

Also popular are the flats off Ambergris Caye, famed as one of the world's most lucrative tarpon spots. Year-round, you can count on at least a small tarpon (20 to 50 pounds), though 100-pounders also abound. Schools of scrappy ladyfish, jack crevalle, permit, bonefish and barracuda are plentiful here.

The waters off Placencia are famous for permit, who thrive on the crystalline coral and mangrove "ocean flats" that emerge from deep water. The best time to try is at the end of an incoming tide, when tailing permit swarm the flats looking for food. Then even this most elusive of fish is inclined to strike your fly.

Other superb places to cast your fly: the flats at St. George's Caye, Hickes Caye, Tobacco Reef, South Water Caye and Glover's Reef. If you're just learning to fly fish, most lodges offer instruction.

Peak fly-fishing seasons vary from place to place, but generally you'll find that tarpon are most plentiful from October through mid-December and in June and July; bonefishing is best from September through January; and permit fishing peaks from August through October and March through June. Be aware that March can be windy with scattered storm bursts, and July and August are usually rainy and buggy.

RIVER FISHING   If it's too windy to fly fish, or if you feel more comfortable with a spinning rod, Belize's rivers offer snook, snapper, jack and tarpon fishing in an incomparable jungle setting. One of the most scenic and prolific inland waterways is the Belize River, which climbs down northern Belize and empties into the Caribbean Sea near Ladyville. Here along placid waters, walls of bamboo and troops of monkeys decorate the shore, and tarpon roll across the surface like a pack of piranhas thrashing at a hapless victim. Cast your lure into a pack of these tarpon, and you can't help but catch one, though don't be surprised when he rears up out of the water—several times.

South of Placencia, the deep Monkey River is similarly striking, framed with massive vines and sugar cane and teeming with tarpon and snook. Southern

Belize's inland backwater lagoons, pockets of shallow, muddy water between the Caribbean Sea and the Maya Mountains, are ideal for permit fishing since they are sheltered from wind.

Remember that during the rainy season, from June through October, rivers often flood and drive the fish (and fishermen) out to sea. The best time to river fish is from February through May, when the water is low and clear and the fish most plentiful.

REEF FISHING   The ribbon of coral reef paralleling the Belize coast glints with healthy schools of big fish. Whether you're trolling or fishing the bottom, you're apt to catch big grouper, cobia, kingfish, wahoo, king mackerel, jack crevalles and prize snapper, including the ubiquitous yellowtail and the brawling cubera. The barrier reef is so warm year-round, and the food so abundant, that reef fish do not migrate. Hence, expect good fishing here year-round.

Belize is not known for its blue water fishing. In fact, few charter boats are available for deeper waters. However, during the spring and fall, sailfish and marlin are occasionally caught along the seaward side of the reef.

FISHING LODGES   Belize has several first-rate fishing lodges offering week-long packages that include daily outings (usually 10- to 12-hour days) with an accomplished guide. Accommodations are usually rustic, but you can fish to your heart's content, assured that if you *don't* catch something, you are in the minute minority. Most locations feature every kind of fishing and include all meals. Tackle is not included, so bring your own. Fishing permits are not required in Belize. Descriptions of the best fishing lodges can be found throughout this book.

In the United States, **Angler Adventures** (P.O. Box 872, Old Lyme, CT 06371; 800-628-1447) will arrange stays at Belize fishing lodges. The tour company offers a wealth of Belize fishing programs, and has a fine reputation in angling circles. With your reservation, you'll be informed about everything from weather conditions and the best tackle to what fish are running where.

If you'd rather schedule a day of fishing after you're in Belize, check with one of the following Belize City tour companies: **Native Guide Systems** (1 Water Lane; 2-75819); **Belize Tours, Ltd.** (115 Albert Street; 2-75443); **Belize Land and Sea Tours** (58 King Street; 2-73897); **Mayan Tours Travel & Rental** (5536 Leslie Street; 2-31531); **Zippy Zappy Boating Services** (36 St. Thomas Street; 2-32844); or **Blackline Marine Service and Dive Shop** (Northern Highway, two-and-a-half miles north of Belize City; 2-44155).

Fishing guides are abundant in Belize. In fact, some are former poachers who are now strict proponents of catch and release. On Ambergris Caye, check for a guide along the waterfront in San Pedro. On Caye Caulker, **Chocolate** (Belize City; 22-2151), **Rally Badillo** (22-2190) and **Ricardo's Adventure Tours** (22-2138) offer customized fishing trips around the cayes. In Placencia, check with **Joel Westby** (6-23138), **Whiprey Caye Guiding** (6-23130), **Blue Runner Guiding** (6-23153) or **Kingfisher Sports** (6-23125).

DIVING

Ancient Maya treasures may lie deep in the Belize jungle, but offshore, glorious treasures await in the mysterious underwater world of the sea. Here, on the world's second-longest barrier reef, dive spots come in endless varieties, from bright shallow waters marbled with dazzling reefs to deep, dark holes dripping with underwater stalactites. In most places, visibility averages 100 feet, though on a clear spring day 150 feet is not uncommon. The scenery often resembles a silent, blossoming dream or dazzling hallucination. To dive here is to enter another planet.

The coral reefs, though they look like inanimate rock, are actually living colonies of polyps that absorb food from the nutrient-rich Gulf Stream and have slowly grown into a coral jungle as complex as the Amazon. Finger coral, elkhorn, mountainous star, brain coral, purple leaf and orange tube, precious black coral with sepia age rings, plus green stinging coral and red fire sponges, which burn when touched, are a few of the species that bloom to towering heights on the sea floor. Hewn into breathtaking landscapes, this coral world is dappled with vivid sea fans, treelike gorgonia, prickly sea urchins, sea whips and lush anemones.

Throughout this subterranean garden are brilliant schools of fish and myriad other sea creatures: candy bass, shortnose batfish, spiny puffers all bloated and prickly, polka-dotted rays, stoplight parrotfish whose scales look tie-dyed, tiny blond razorfish diving into the mottled sand, coral crabs skittering sideways like moving shards of reef, turquoise angelfish, flamefish and sea cucumbers, colossal sea turtles and guitar-shaped guitarfish—an astonishing visual symphony rippling by, beautiful beyond belief.

But Belize's most famous place to dive is not on the barrier reef. The Blue Hole, a monstrous sinkhole in the sea, lies within an atoll—a ring of coral isles surrounding a lagoon. The hole does not glint with blinding color or fantastic fish. It is dim and eerie, a pit of inky water streaked with tiny tremors of light and looking like a scene from the Ice Age. Deep in its jowls, great shafts of rock imitate giant icicles and shelves of deep sand resemble snow banks. Prehistoric-looking sharks peer out from narrow ledges, and caves tunnel back into the walls. Caverns drip with stalactites formed by eons of percolating rain.

Back near the surface, the mouth of the hole is encased in exquisite coral, and the water is ten feet deep, swimming-pool-clear and wriggling with fish, sponges and sea fans.

Despite its fame, the Blue Hole does not attract crowds of divers, primarily because it is about three hours by boat from the mainland. There is one nearby resort, **Lighthouse Reef Resort** (located on Northern Caye; 800-423-3114 in the United States), accessible by plane from Belize City, which includes a trip to the hole in its extensive daily dive program. My favorite dive lodge in Belize, it offers a variety of dives around the gorgeous Lighthouse Reef atoll with views of walls and wrecks and basket sponges blossoming over a 15-foot span.

Several dive outfits offer excursions to the Blue Hole. From Ambergris Caye, **Out Island Divers** (26-2151) has one-day trips to the Blue Hole aboard its fast *Reef Roamer I*. Also on Ambergris, **Fantasea Watersports** (at the Victoria House, San Pedro; phone or fax: 26-2576) also offers day trips to the Blue Hole.

Like the Lighthouse Reef atoll, Belize's other two atolls—Glover's Reef and Turneffe Islands—are actually coral rock top hats of the Maya Mountains. The underwater ridges, valleys and ravines around the atolls make for sensational diving, and the varying terrain will please all levels of divers. And, because the atolls are circular in design, they always offer a leeward side where you can escape the wind and seas. Anyone who has dived in four- to six-foot swells—quite common on the barrier reef—knows the advantages of a leeward dive spot.

One of the most popular and challenging atoll dives is The Elbow, located in the Turneffe Islands, where the fish are big and the currents erratic. Turneffe is also famous for its miles of mangrove forests teeming with fish seeking shelter in the underwater roots. Manatees love the warm waters created by mangroves, and can sometimes be seen lumbering through the water.

Glover's Reef atoll boasts different forests—ones comprised of luscious elkhorn coral that stretch up from depths of 100 feet. Dolphin, turtles and mantas are abundant in this remote southernmost atoll, and the waters are gin-clear and warm year-round. It's no surprise, then, that Glover's Reef is reputed to have some of the most extravagant underwater scenery in the Caribbean. Best of all, much of it lies inside the reef, where calm waters make for unparalleled diving.

Note: The fate of this resplendent scenery, and the rest of the Belize reef, lies with divers and others who visit it. Protecting the reef is as easy as not touching it. Even a slight brush from a fin is enough to damage a coral forever. No matter how tempted you may be, never take a piece of coral. That small souvenir will destroy in one second what it took nature thousands of years to build.

Always anchor your craft in the sand or grass flats, away from the reef. If you can't see where you're anchoring, send a diver down to check the sea bottom. Unfortunately, some Belize dive boats still anchor on the reef, lopping off huge pieces of coral and spreading disease. Perhaps if enough divers frown on the practice, dive operators will be more careful to preserve the future of their livelihood.

For your own protection, avoid touching sea creatures. Inside crevices, where you should never poke a prying hand, live moray eels, whose saw-toothed fangs hold decayed food particles that can fatally poison an unsuspecting victim. Some anemones and sea urchins are poisonous, and their spines inflict painful, lasting wounds. An encounter with fire coral, a brownish, innocent-looking coral found everywhere, can leave you peppered with flaming welts that outlast your vacation.

Be a safe diver. Always dive with a buddy, preferably a Belizean buddy familiar with local waters and conditions. Stay well within the boundaries of the dive tables, and limit your dives at the beginning and end of your vacation. If you overdid the rum punches the night before, take the day off. A hangover can affect your judgment and even contribute to decompression sickness.

In case of decompression sickness, there is a recompression chamber (26-2851 or 26-2073) next to the airstrip in San Pedro, Ambergris Caye. However, some Belize dive operators prefer to send their guests to U.S. medical facilities. For a $25 annual fee, **Divers Alert Network** (Duke University Medical Center, Box 3823, Durham, NC 27710; for emergencies, call 919-684-8111, for non-emergencies, call 919-684-2948) provides air rescue from anywhere in the Americas, for dive accidents or other medical emergencies. The international, nonprofit organization also offers dive accident insurance for an additional $25 a year that covers up to $30,000 in medical expenses, including visits to a hyperbaric chamber.

DIVE LODGES   Whether you're a four-tank-a-day diver or one who enjoys the feel of a hammock as much as a BC, you will find your place in Belize. Half a dozen lodges specialize in diving, and another dozen offer some type of dive program. Most specialty lodges are located on secluded out islands and require minimum stays of four to seven nights. But they vary considerably when it comes to amenities (or lack of) and approach to diving. Some stress rigorous diving with little time for relaxation, while others strike a balance between diving and doing nothing. I stayed at one lodge that was so regimented, guests were either diving, eating or attending meetings about diving. This is dive dreamland for some people, but not for others. When making reservations at a lodge, ask about the facility's dive philosophy, the number of dives offered each day, and the experience of the divemasters. For critiques of individual dive lodges, see Chapter Six of this book.

DIVE INSTRUCTION   If you've been thinking about getting certified, why not do it in Belize? The pace is slow and the weather dependably warm, and there's not much to distract you from studying! More importantly, there are many experienced, first-rate dive instructors. Most dive lodges offer PADI or NAUI instruction, and most classes are so small (one to four people) you'll get special treatment. Allow at least four days for the course, which includes four open water dives divided between two days. Prices range from US$250 to US$400 per person, depending on the lodge and size of the class.

Many dive lodges also offer one-day resort courses for those who'd like a taste of diving, as well as advanced certification, refresher courses and specialty diving, such as rescue diving or night diving.

DIVE SHOPS   On Ambergris Caye, **Indigo Divers** (San Pedro; 26-21301) will take you to nearby reefs or farther out to the atolls. Also here is **The Dive Shop Ltd.** (at the San Pedro Holiday Hotel pier; 26-2437) and **Bottom Time Dive Shop** (at the SunBreeze Hotel; 26-2348). On Caye Caulker, **Belize Diving Services** (22-2143) has scuba excursions. To rent snorkeling equipment on Caye Caulker, check toward the middle of town, across from the park, in a little building that says "Snorkel Rental-Pastries."

In Belize City, **Blackline Dive Shop** (Mile 2, Northern Highway; 2-33187) offers certification and numerous dive packages to the cayes. In Placencia, stop by **Placencia Dive Shop** (at Kitty's Place, one-and-a-half miles north of Placencia Village; 6-22027). The Belizean guides here specialize in scuba and snorkeling tours to remote areas such as Laughing Bird National Park. At **Pisces Dive Service** (Placencia Village; 6-23183), Mike and Beverly McCarty provide a wide range of services, including certification courses.

If you'd like to record your dive experience, consider renting a camera. Underwater cameras are available on Ambergris Caye from **Joe Miller Photography** (in Fido's Courtyard, seafront in San Pedro; 26-2577). For classes in underwater photography, check with **Pisces Dive Service** (6-23183), located in the village of Placencia.

LIVE-ABOARD DIVE BOATS   The way to get in the most diving around Belize's fantastic reefs is to stay on a boat. Several live-aboard dive boats ply the waters around the cayes, dropping anchor at the Blue Hole, Half Moon Caye, the walls of Turneffe and other famous dive spots. Boats range from 16-passenger skiffs with dorm-style camping to 40-passenger yachts with staterooms. Trips typically last from one to seven nights.

The 54-foot **Manta IV** (800-468-0123 in Florida) has one-night "camp-aboard" trips, while the 50-foot **Offshore Express** (26-2013) offers birdwatching expeditions as well as dives. The 50-foot **Reef Roamer II** (800-258-3465) anchors near Half Moon Caye and provides tents for those who want to camp on the island. The fancier, 110-foot **Aggressor** (800-348-2628) has air-conditioned cabins that accommodate up to 18 people. By far the most luxurious is the 120-foot **Wave Dancer** (800-932-6237 or 305-669-9391 in Florida), whose air-conditioned staterooms are more than 90 square feet, twice the size of most live-aboard cabins. *Wave Dancer* offers a seven-night itinerary from Belize City, with a visit to the Turneffe Islands and Lighthouse Reef. The final night, guests stay at the plush Radisson St. George in Belize City.

SWIMMING AND SNORKELING

Washed by stunning seas and crisscrossed with smooth-flowing rivers and jungle waterfalls, Belize offers many ways to get your body wet. Virtually anywhere inside the barrier reef, you'll find calm, shallow waters as clear as air, perfect for swimming and snorkeling. Unlike the Caribbean waters off neighboring Yucatán, which are plagued by strong currents, the seas here are sheltered by the barrier reef. Rip currents are rare, and the water is warm year-round—75 to 80 degrees in winter, and up to 85 degrees in summer.

But while the barrier reef provides protection, it prevents the formation of beaches. Like the Florida Keys, which have their own barrier reef, Belize's cayes are ringed with mangroves and pebbly dirt, not sugar-white sand. Except at the atolls and a few resorts with imported sand, swimming beaches are scarce. Better to swim and snorkel from a boat.

Take your mask, snorkel and fins to Belize. Rentals are expensive, and sometimes unavailable on remote islands.

Inland, freshwater rivers are framed in lush jungle, where you can watch monkeys play while you swim. Incidentally, when monkeys swim across a river, they thrash about like they're drowning. If you see one, don't offer your assistance or you will have one angry monkey on your hands!

Here are some of the top swimming spots in Belize:

❖ Hol Chan Marine Reserve, off Ambergris Caye, is the place to snorkel

❖ The Cut, at Caye Caulker

❖ The shallow, protected lagoons within the Turneffe, Lighthouse Reef and Glover's Reef atolls.

❖ The Sibun River beaches within Monkey Bay Wildlife Sanctuary

❖ The Belize River, especially at Guanacaste National Park

❖ Rio On Pools in western Belize, where clear water tumbles down rock terraces

❖ Along the Curassow Trail at Cockscomb Basin Wildlife Preserve

❖ Blue Creek, outside Punta Gorda

BIRDWATCHING

Birders love Belize. They love rising at 5 a.m., sneaking into the darkened web of jungle, and listening for the *hoot-hoot* call of a blue-crowned motmot. To see one of these exquisite birds in the sun-dappled dawn is a great event, especially since they are somewhat rare. Daybreak brings out other species of extraordinary beauty, including oropendolas, red-legged honeycreepers, slaty-tailed trogons, great curassows and white hawks. Toucans and macaws are fairly common in Belize, and so are unexciting to birders, although the layman rarely grows accustomed to seeing these ravishing creatures color the sky.

Birdwatching in Belize has only come into vogue in the past two years. As new trails are carved through dense jungle and bird sanctuaries made more accessible, birders are discovering the thrills of this little country. Several areas offer wonderful birding. At Chan Chich Lodge in northwestern Belize, exotic birds actually nest near your jungle hut. When was the last time you walked out your front door to see a toucan feeding her young? Or an ocellated turkey preening for a mate?

Other prime birdwatching spots include Half Moon Caye Natural Monument, Crooked Tree Wildlife Sanctuary, the jungles around the Caracol ruins, and Cockscomb Basin Wildlife Preserve.

Lineated woodpecker

In the United States, top organizers of birdwatching tours are scheduling more treks to Belize. For dates and details of various birding tours, contact **Field Guides** (P.O. Box 160723, Austin, TX 78716; 512-327-4953), **The Massachusetts Audubon Society** (South Great Road, Lincoln, MA 01773; 800-289-9504) or **Victor Emanuel Nature Tours** (P.O. Box 33008, Austin, TX 78764; 800-328-8368).

In Belize, the **Belize Audubon Society** (Box 282, Belize City; 2-77369) is an excellent source of information on birdwatching.

OTHER OUTDOOR SPORTS AND ACTIVITIES

KAYAKING

If you like the idea of navigating your own vessel, fishing for your own dinner, and sleeping under the stars on faraway islands, consider sea kayaking. **Slickrock Adventures** (P.O. Box 1400, Moab, UT 84532; 801-259-6996) offers week-long expeditions around the 82 square miles of Glover's Reef atoll. Most of the cayes are uninhabited poster islands ringed with palms and sugar-fine sand, and the waters are brilliantly clear and filled with sea life.

During the day, kayakers snorkel, fish and paddle between islands. At night, they cook around a campfire and sleep in hammocks.

Elsewhere around the cayes, you can rent kayaks by the hour or day. Check with your lodge. On Ambergris Caye, contact **Travel & Tour Belize** (Barrier Reef Drive, at the San Pedro airstrip; 26-2031).

Inland, the calm, twisting Macal River in western Belize is terrific for kayaking. To rent kayaks, check with Yoli Mendez at **Mayan Coast Tours** (Belmopan; 8-22556), **Red Rooster Inn** (2 Far West Street, San Ignacio; 92-2506) or at **Eva's** restaurant (22 Burns Avenue, San Ignacio; 92-2267). From Belize City, **Native Guide Systems** (1 Water Lane; 2-75819) will arrange kayaking trips.

CANOEING

Few experiences are so truly Belizean as canoeing down a silent, shimmering river draped in lavish jungle, fat iguanas sunning on tree limbs, monkeys skittering along the shore, parrots squawking in the air. Just 50 years ago, the rivers were the highways of Belize. Now that there are roads, the rivers are used by tourists as much as villagers, though they are hardly crowded.

The best place for canoeing is in the Cayo District, where the Macal and Mopan rivers offer splendorous scenery and splendid sightseeing stops. Several outfits offer canoe rentals, including **Float Belize** (San Ignacio; 92-2188), **Toni Canoes** (22 Burns Avenue, San Ignacio; 92-2267), **Windy Hill Cottage Tours** (Western Highway, just west of San Ignacio; 92-2017), **Chaa Creek Inland and Jungle Expeditions** (on the Macal River, about eight miles outside San Ignacio; 92-2037) and **duPlooy's** (nine miles outside San Ignacio; 92-2057).

Just east of San Ignacio, **Caesar's Place** (Mile 62, Northern Highway; 92-2341) will also arrange various canoe outings. Near Belmopan, you can canoe along the scenic Belize River from **Warrie Head Ranch** (Western Highway, six miles west of Belmopan; 2-77185).

Birdwatchers will find the ultimate canoe trip at Crooked Tree Wildlife Sanctuary in northern Belize. Rentals are available at the visitors' center or at nearby **Bird's Eye View Lodge** (2-75145) or **Paradise Inn** (25-2535).

HOUSEBOATING

One of the most unusual and enjoyable ways to experience outdoor Belize is to drift down a jungle-cloaked river in a houseboat. **River Haven** (at Freetown Sibun, off the Western Highway, south of Hattieville; 2-30063; fax: 2-32742) offers houseboat rentals ranging from a day to a week, giving you the freedom to pilot and sleep on your own craft. The journey takes you down the curling Sibun River to Northern Lagoon, site of two bird sanctuaries, and to Southern Lagoon, home to numerous manatees and to the charming Creole fishing village of Gales Point. Along the way you're likely to see monkeys looping through treetops, tarpon churning along the water's surface, soft white beaches trimmed with river palms and sweeping views toward the Maya Mountains.

BICYCLING

The most relaxing bicycling is on the hard-packed sand streets of Ambergris Caye and Caye Caulker. On Ambergris Caye, you can rent bikes at **Travel & Tour Belize** (Barrier Reef Drive, at the airstrip, San Pedro; 26-2031).

On Caye Caulker, bike rentals are available at **Island Sun** (near the middle of town; 22-2215).

Belize City's narrow, bustling streets don't make for great cycling, but you might try riding around the Fort George neighborhood and nearby Barracks Road. Bike rentals are available from **Bike Belize** (104 New Road, Belize City; 2-33855), which also offers trail bikes, minibikes and scooters for striking out on the Western and Northern highways. You can also rent bicycles just outside Belize City at **E & L Bicycle Rental** (4 Eighth Street, Kings Park; 2-31157).

HORSEBACK RIDING

What could be more enjoyable that a scenic ride through the countryside? Out in western Belize, **Mountain Equestrian Trails** (Mile 8, Mountain Pine Ridge Road; 8-23180 or 8-22149) is a popular, well-run facility offering rides across 60 miles of trails, including former logging trails. The ranch also features river cave float trips.

HIKING

You could hike forever in the Belize jungles. Some of the best trails are in the archaeological zones, where ancient Maya cities harbor a labyrinth of trails through cool, exhilarating forest with views of temples and pyramids and the green countryside. My favorite place to hike is at Chan Chich, a lodge built on a Maya plaza and enveloped by 275,000 acres of interminable jungle. Nine trails, offering a variety of lengths, difficulty and scenery, cover eight miles through the forest. The lodge publishes an excellent book, *Exploring the Rainforest*, that details 130 marked sites along the trails, including tombs, creeks and "nest condominiums" often inhabited by toucans, woodpeckers and red-lored Amazon parrots. If you're feeling unusually adventurous, take one of the lodge's night hikes through the jungle. There's nothing like shining a flashlight into a pitch-black thicket, only to discover a pair of jaguar eyes glowering back.

Elsewhere, the Community Baboon Sanctuary and Cockscomb Basin Wildlife Sanctuary offer splendid hiking through dense broadleaf rainforest. Both facilities sell inexpensive trail maps (about US$1), and the wardens can point you to the best spots. For hiking through cool, mountainous slash pine forest, head for the Mountain Pine Ridge. The terrain harbors vast caves, thundering waterfalls, scenic lookouts, racing rivers studded with black boulders, and marvelous views of wild animals. Maps of various trails are available from most lodges in the pine ridge. One resort, the 18,000-acre Hidden Valley Inn, offers a trail system so vast it takes days to hike.

Around Belize, numerous companies offer hiking guides and/or excursions. They include: **Native Guide Systems** (1 Water Lane, Belize City; 2-75819); **Belize Tours Ltd.** (115 Albert Street, Belize City; 2-75443); **Melmish Mayan Tours Travel and Rental** (5536 Leslie Street, Belize City; 2-45221);

Island and Inland Travel Services (San Ignacio; 92-2421); **Chaa Creek Inland Expeditions** (near San Ignacio; 92-2037); **Maruba Resort** (Old Northern Highway, about 40 miles north of Belize City; 3-22199); **Jungle River Tours** (20 Lovers Lane, Orange Walk Town; 3-22293); **Jal's Travel and Tours** (49 Fourth Avenue, Corozal; 4-22163); **Pelican Beach Resort** (north end of Dangriga; 5-22044); and **Placencia Tours** (Placencia Village; 6-23186).

The Cayes

MEXICO

0   20 kilometers

20 miles

Ambergris Caye

✈ ■ San Pedro

N

Hol Chan Marine Reserve

Caye Caulker

Caye Chapel

St. George's Caye

✈ Belize City ■

Gallow's Point Caye

Spanish Lookout Caye

Sergeants Caye

Water Caye

Goff's Caye

English Caye

Bluefield Range

Northern Caye

TURNEFFE ISLANDS

Blackbird Caye

Blue Hole ●

LIGHTHOUSE REEF

Half Moon Caye

Big Caye Bokel

✈ ■ Dangriga

Tobacco Caye

GLOVER'S REEF

South Water Caye

Southwest Caye

Carrie Bow Caye

C A R I B B E A N   S E A

SIX

The Cayes

The Belize Cayes stretch eastward from the mainland, a sprinkling of coral rock and mangrove isles basking in the fabulous blues and greens of the Caribbean Sea. They range in size from tiny mangrove specks inhabited only by sea birds to substantial islands with thriving fishing villages. Their first inhabitants were the Maya, who established intricate island trading routes during the Classic Period, from 250 to 900 A.D. Seven hundred years later, British pirates used the isolated, scrubby isles to stash the treasure they had plundered from Spanish galleons. Today, little evidence exists of either the Spanish or the Maya, but the islands remain pristine and isolated.

The cayes (pronounced "keys") are why most visitors come to Belize, for here can be found some of the best diving and fishing in the world. Along this 200-mile-long barrier reef—the longest in the Western Hemisphere—is an underwater Eden of dazzling sea creatures, wildly colorful coral and see-through waters ribboned with sunlight. The marine life here, biologists say, is perhaps the most complex and diverse in all the Caribbean. Indeed, some claim Belize's reef sustains a greater variety of sea creatures per square foot than any other barrier reef in the world.

Beyond the barrier reef are secluded patch reefs with travel-poster islands, sandy flats superb for fly-fishing, and warm slurpy waters that beckon swimmers year-round. Then there are the atolls, pronounced a-TOLS, ringlike bands of coral isles surrounding lagoons. Belize's three atolls offer the ultimate in fishing and diving, for their circular shape ensures there is always a leeward side where you can escape wind and waves.

The pace of life is slow in the Cayes. There are no paved roads—only sand streets—and electricity is often provided by a generator, solar panels or even windmills. Getting to a caye usually means taking a small plane or boat, though hopefully the boat is not too small, as most voyages are from two to four hours. In fact, travel around the Cayes holds promise of adventure, considering the shaky dependability of boat motors and captains, the even less predictable weather, and the fact that Cayes' time is even slower than regular Belize time!

Though Belizeans don't particularly frown on nudity, there are no official nude beaches in Belize. However, there are dozens of deserted out islands with beaches perfect for sunbathing in the buff. Around Ambergris Caye and Caye Caulker, I've noticed birthday-suited tourists buzzing around in boats. Maybe the latest fad?

Surprisingly, beaches are scarce in the Belize Cayes, since, like the Florida Keys, they are formed of mangroves and coral rock. The choicest beaches are on the out islands, and so not within easy reach of the average visitor. On Ambergris Caye, the largest island, there is no official public beach, but good beaches can be found behind hotels on the north and south end of the island.

Lodging on the Cayes ranges from charming seaside motels and thatched bungalows on the beach to fishing cabins on a secluded island. Most of the upscale accommodations are on Ambergris Caye, Belize's largest caye, and those are not ultra-luxurious. In fact, most cayes' hostelries are what you'll soon come to know as funky-Belizean: full of charm and personality, but lacking in creature comforts. Only the expensive and very expensive few lodges offer air conditioning, but sea breezes are adequate on all but the muggiest of summer days. To make sure you catch the breezes, ask for a room (preferably with lots of windows) on the windward side of the island. You'd be surprised what a difference a breeze will make—usually between a restful or a restless night.

Many cayes have only one or two lodges, offering that rare opportunity to stay at a castaway island. These out-island lodges are most popular with anglers and scuba divers who prefer nature over civilization. Some lodge owners take ecotourism quite seriously, even limiting the number of anglers allowed per week.

Lodge owners themselves can determine whether or not you love a place. When you're staying on a near-deserted island out in the middle of nowhere, the personalities running the show become quite crucial. (You should know that most lodge owners, like the guests, are Americans.) I have had experiences where lodge owners were so intrusive, it was difficult for guests to relax and have a good time. Lodging reviews in this chapter reflect my impressions of each place. Before you book an out-island lodge, however, it's helpful to talk to someone who's stayed there recently.

Depending on how "out" the island is, you may be required to stay at least a week. Any less would be impractical, since getting there requires a lengthy boat trip (four hours, in some cases) or chartering a small plane. All lodges will arrange your transportation. Most people find the journey not only an adventure but a marvelous window to the unspoiled Caribbean of Belize.

Like the lodges, Cayes' eateries possess those typical Belizean elements: eclectic decor, sand floors and fascinating characters hailing from all corners of the earth. Few restaurants keep "official" hours, but you'll always find something open to suit your needs. Besides the Belizean staple of rice and beans (which can be quite tasty), expect plenty of fresh seafood when dining on the islands. Here is a good place to try your first Belikin beer, Belize's ubiquitous national brew, which, by the way, happens to be very good beer.

On the out islands, you'll be dining at the lodge restaurant—the only one on the island—but most times you'll find the food quite good. A few resorts take advantage of their captive audience and charge ridiculously high prices for food. To avoid price gauging, buy a lodging package that includes meals. Most out island bars are run on the honor system—no problem if there are only 20 people on the whole island.

AMBERGRIS CAYE

Twenty-eight miles long and the country's biggest island, Ambergris Caye boasts the most and best resorts and the finest array of restaurants, shops and bars in all of Belize. Yet Ambergris is where people still go to get away, whether it be hippies escaping to a secluded campground or the rich and famous retreating to Journey's End, a posh resort literally at land's end. Ambergris also is still home to much wildlife, including many shore birds, nesting sea turtles and even ocelots, who find refuge in the swamps and mangrove forests unspoiled yet by people.

Situated northeast of Belize City, about a one-hour boat ride away, Ambergris is actually closer to Mexico than Belize. Only the skinny Boca Bacalar Chico Channel, dug by the ancient Maya, separates the north tip of the island from the Yucatán Peninsula. The caye gets its name from "ambergrease," the waxy secretions of sperm whales that was found on the beaches by 18th-century British explorers. Once a pricey substance used in making perfume, ambergrease can sometimes be seen today clouding sea waters in the area.

Most of Ambergris' activity is concentrated near the island's south end, in the seaside village of **San Pedro**. Named for Saint Peter, patron saint of fishermen, the fishing village was founded in 1848 and was a refuge for *Mestizos* (persons of mixed Spanish and Indian blood) fleeing Yucatán's War of the Castes. Eleven years later, Englishman James Hume Blake bought San Pedro and the rest of Ambergris Caye for just $625 during a bankruptcy auction by the British government. Soon coconut plantations abounded on Blake's island, and San Pedro residents made their living husking and shredding the nuts. By the mid-1900s, the coconut business had gone bust and most plantations abandoned, and San Pedroans returned to fishing for a living.

Today, a boat is just as likely to be hauling tourists as fish. Tourism is the biggest business on Ambergris. During high season, visitors to San Pedro outnumber its 2000 residents. No matter when you visit, the village will seem a busy little place, with golf carts buzzing up and down the sand streets and punta rock music drifting from outdoor bars. Wobbly docks loaded with boats are strung along the seafront, and old clapboard buildings huddle against new concrete condominiums.

Unlike anywhere else in Belize, San Pedro has a definite feel of American influence, from the stark new buildings financed by American companies to the American-owned hotels, restaurants and bars. Yet, for now at least, Ambergris Caye is still a place where visitors aren't subjected to the rigors of mass tourism. Locals frequent the same restaurants and shops as tourists, and everyone is treated with the usual brand of Belizean hospitality. And though most residents are of Mexican descent, they are bilingual, and are just as happy to converse with you in English as Spanish.

Only about seven blocks long and three blocks wide, San Pedro is easy to navigate. It will take you all of about one hour to stroll every sand street, not including tiki bar stops! You'll soon learn that most everything happens on Barrier Reef Drive, also called Front Street, San Pedro's main drag and the street closest to the sea. Hotels and businesses are here, and so is the **San Pedro Town Hall and Police Station** (26-2788), a humble seaside building with peeling paint and a hand-painted sign imploring readers to protect the Belize reefs. There's also **Travel & Tour Belize** (26-2031), an excellent source for island information and excursions.

Walking west from Barrier Reef Drive, you'll find Middle Street and Back Street. North and south are various unmarked and unnamed streets, and a couple of lanes called different local names just to keep things interesting. The 2600-foot **San Pedro Airstrip** is at the south end of town, where visitors fly in and out every 20 minutes or so.

If you're lucky enough to be in San Pedro on a Saturday night, you'll see local families gather in the town square for their weekly get-together. It's a festive occasion, with folks cooking dinner on makeshift grills and kids playing basketball. Small children come all dressed up, then promptly get dirty playing in the sand streets.

About four miles southeast of town, the **Hol Chan Marine Reserve** is a five-square-mile underwater park accessible only by boat. Hol Chan is Maya for "little channel," and it was the Maya who first discovered the plethora of sea life in the narrow passage through the barrier reef here. Overfishing in the early 1980s nearly destroyed the area's fragile reef system and drove most of the life away. In 1987, the Belizean government made it a national reserve, and installed buoys for boats to tie to, thereby avoiding anchoring on the reef. Today, the reef is thriving again, and snorkelers can admire its brilliant brain and star coral, ethereal sea fans and resplendent sponges.

Most fascinating, though, are the green moray eels that inhabit the walls of the reserve's channel, which is only 15 to 30 feet deep. You will likely see divemasters feeding the eels (which they shouldn't), but don't try it yourself. Morays become aggressive when fed, and can nip off a finger in an instant. At a minimum, they can inflict a nasty poisonous sting.

Many dive boats also stop at **Mexico Rocks**, just outside the barrier reef and the reserve. Slightly shallower, with depths of 8 to 15 feet, the water is clear and etched with constellations of elkhorn and staghorn coral, and churning with exotic fish.

Snorkeling excursions to Mexico Rocks or Hol Chan can be arranged with one of the many boats at the San Pedro docks, or through most hotels.

LODGING   Budget and moderate accommodations can be found in the town of San Pedro, while expensive and very expensive resorts tend to be on the north and south ends of the island. Staying in town means you can walk to restaurants, stores and tiki bars, but town is also noisier, and there are no real beaches. Outside of town, you'll pay more for solitude and for having a generous beach out your back door. However, lodging on the north end is accessible only by boat—something to consider if you plan to spend a lot of time in San Pedro. Hotels there do provide ferry service to and from town, though schedules are infrequent. If you stay on the south end of Ambergris, you'll need a bicycle or golf cart (available from most hotels) to get to town.

One of the southernmost hostelries is also one of the most engaging. Nestled on a sublime stretch of beach, the ✪ **Victoria House** (about two miles south of San Pedro; very expensive; 26-2067 or 800-247-5159 in the United States) boasts 29 rooms spread among a pretty Victorian plantation house, several row houses and Mexican-style *casitas*. Most desirable are the *casitas*, wrapped by spacious porches and warmly adorned with Mexican tile floors, hardwood furnishings, high-beamed ceilings and Belizean paintings. Rooms in the houses, though slightly smaller, are attractively appointed with white wicker. All rooms have small refrigerators. Complimentary bicycles, as well as van service to town throughout the day, are included in the rate.

For contemporary, condominium-style accommodations, check into ✪ **Caribbean Villas** (about one-and-a-half miles south of San Pedro; air conditioning; expensive; 26-2715, fax: 26-2885). The white-stucco buildings, resting right on the beach, feature fashionable rooms and apartments with plenty of privacy and space. There's no restaurant, but most rooms have kitchenettes with plenty of cooking gadgets, and all come with complimentary bicycles for getting back and forth to town.

Situated along a curving, palmy beach, **Ramon's Village** (just south of San Pedro; ceiling fans; very expensive; 26-2071, or 800-624-4215 in the United States) enjoys the liveliest atmosphere of any island hotel. The sands are alive with volleyball games, the saltwater pool is always filled with people, and the outdoor bar stays busy from morning till late night. Accommodations are in 60 *palapa*-style cabanas, squeezed together along the sand, with louvered windows, wood or tile floors and comfortable furnishings. The very expensive price buys atmosphere, not cushy rooms.

With its white-stucco arches, spindle rails and Mexican tile floors, the **Sun-Breeze Beach Resort** (seafront, south end of San Pedro; air conditioning;

very expensive; 26-2191, fax: 26-2346) recalls the architecture of San Pedro's native Yucatecans. The low-slung hotel also enjoys a swimming pool and a splendid location: a generous beach, right at the end of town. Everyone eventually shows up here and stays for a while, and that's why the place is always abuzz. Decor in most of the 39 guest rooms is brown and drab, though the air conditioning, cable television and telephones more than make up for it. Best here are the five spacious rooms that feature modern decor as well as jacuzzi tubs.

Popular with divers, the seaside **Coral Beach Hotel** (Barrier Reef Drive, near the middle of San Pedro; air conditioning; moderate; 26-2001) is better known for its topnotch scuba program than its accommodations. Though unspectacular, the 20 rooms are clean and decorated with new wallpaper. Many offer views of the sea. There's no beach, but there is the uproarious Tackle Box Bar, which sits at the end of a pier.

Sea-weathered white clapboard, faded gingerbread and dormer windows make the **Barrier Reef Hotel** (Barrier Reef Drive, San Pedro; some air conditioning; moderate; 26-2075, fax: 26-2719) look perfectly Belizean. This friendly seaside guesthouse, opened in 1907 and one of San Pedro's oldest, is also a good buy. The ten rooms, with white plaster walls and Belizean tile floors, are basic but comfortable. Seven rooms have air conditioning. There's also a good restaurant and popular lounge.

Lily's (Barrier Reef Drive, San Pedro; ceiling fans; budget; 26-2059) is a congenial, tumbledown sort of place, with a myriad of levels and cluttered rooftops. Wood-paneled walls and vinyl floors are standard decor in the ten bare but clean rooms. By far the best rooms are the three that face the sea. The owners, long-time residents of San Pedro, also offer delicious home cooking in a tiny restaurant.

If you prefer comfort to character, check into the new, American-style **Mayan Princess Resort Hotel** (seafront, near the north end of San Pedro; air conditioning; very expensive; 26-2778, fax: 26-2784). Opened in late 1992, the coral-coated building boasts 23 stylish suites with white ceramic floors, whitewashed wicker furnishings, and french doors that open onto a private veranda. The well-stocked kitchens are especially helpful for families. Every room faces the sea.

Luscious landscaping on a generous expanse of sugary white beach makes the **Paradise Resort Hotel** (on the north end of San Pedro; four rooms have air conditioning, the rest ceiling fans; expensive; 26-2083, fax: 26-2232) instantly appealing. To match the surroundings, 15 palm-thatched cabanas are outfitted with straw mat floors, bamboo closets and wood shutters. For those who crave less indigenous quarters, there are four contemporary villas and two condominiums—all right on the sea.

For those who yearn for the luxuries of home, **Rock's Inn** (just north of San Pedro; air conditioning; expensive; 26-2326, fax: 26-2358) offers some of the most modern, spacious rooms in all of Belize. Facing the sea, with a tiny beach, the white Mediterranean building houses 14 apartments with comfortable beds, sofas, dinettes, kitchens and big windows wrapped in pretty drapes.

Serious anglers will point you to ✪ **El Pescador** (north end of Ambergris Caye; ceiling fans; very expensive; phone or fax: 26-2398), whose nearby flats are world-renowned for tarpon and whose remote seaside setting feels worlds away from the daily grind. The two-story, wood-frame lodge is set among coconut palms on a lovely stretch of sand, and harbors 22 tidy but plain rooms typical of a homey fishing camp. There is a seven-night minimum stay, and packages include flats and/or reef fishing, daily guide, all meals, and the flight from Belize City.

Like some sanctuary for shipwrecked souls, **Captain Morgan's Retreat** (north end of Ambergris Caye; ceiling fans; very expensive; 26-2567 or 800-447-2931 in the United States) is stashed on a deserted ribbon of beach, accessible only by boat. The 21 simple, thatched-roof *casitas* virtually disappear into the palm trees, and the bamboo restaurant and sand-floored bar look like they were built by Captain Morgan himself. Furnishings in the *casitas* are simple but tasteful, with louvered wood windows, plank floors, vaulted ceilings and roomy porches facing the sea. A favorite of honeymooners, and others who really want to escape.

Robin Leach, on his "Lifestyles of the Rich and Famous" television program, has extolled the virtues of **Journey's End** (north end of Ambergris Caye; air conditioning; very expensive; 26-2173 or 800-447-0474 in the United States), a dream getaway resort that ranks among Belize's finest. Indeed, this sprawling, secluded retreat would seem to have it all: a fantasy palm-speckled beach, stylized swimming pool with nude sunbathing deck, small casino, lovely beach cabanas and modern hotel rooms with televisions (rare in Belize!), along with a staff that sees to your every need. The restaurant's accomplished chef turns out daily gourmet delights, as well as twice-weekly beach barbecues that are culinary shows. Besides all this, there's complimentary boat service to and from San Pedro (the resort is reached only by boat) several times daily.

RESTAURANTS   In a lovely South Seas-style building that looks across the beach, **Jade Garden** (a half-mile south of the airstrip, San Pedro; moderate to expensive; 26-2506) invites with its polished wood floors, soaring wood ceilings and pink and white linens. The Chinese fare does not shine as much as the decor, but it is a welcome change of pace. Chop suey, chow mein, sweet and sour and foo yong dishes are available, as well as American specials such as ribeye steak and seafood kebabs.

Elvi's Kitchen (Pescador Drive, San Pedro; budget to moderate; 26-2176) has sand floors, long picnic tables and a tree growing up through the middle—the perfect venue for trading tall tales. The food plays second string to the atmosphere, but it's filling fare nonetheless. Choose from burgers, fish sandwiches, fish platters, steaks and rice. Popular for breakfast, too.

The Hut (south end of San Pedro, near the airstrip; moderate) looks just like it sounds: a hunching old clapboard building, buried along a side street. But inside is a cozy little dining room, adorned with colorful tablecloths, wood beams and plenty of potted plants. The blackboard menu features fresh seafood and produce, with specials such as shrimp curry, roast pork with creole gravy, stone crab claws and fish in wine with dill sauce.

Mary Ellen's Little Italy (Barrier Reef Drive, San Pedro; moderate; 26-2866) is an immensely romantic seaside venue with a touch of Southern charm. The latter comes from Mary Ellen, a former attorney from Tennessee. Classical music and sea breezes stream through the dining room, decorated with red-and-white checked tablecloths, flickering red candles and tropical flowers. Here also is some of the island's best Italian cuisine, from bubbling deep-dish pasta to chicken and pork dishes smothered in garlic and wine sauce.

If you arrive at San Pedro by boat, you'll immediately spot **Fido's** (Barrier Reef Drive; budget; 26-2409). The big and breezy marketplace, crowned with a giant thatched roof, is the place for burritos, burgers, buffalo chicken wings, pizza by the slice and other quick bites.

Lily's (Barrier Reef Drive, San Pedro; budget; 26-2059) is widely known among locals for its hefty home-cooked portions. For breakfast, there's huevos rancheros and shrimp omelettes; for lunch or dinner, try the fried shrimp or fish simmered in Mexican barbecue sauce. The surroundings—battered rattan chairs, laminated wood clocks and turtle shells parked on the walls—are perfectly Belizean.

SHOPPING   For a terrific selection of Belizean art, stop by **Iguana Jack's** (on the main street, San Pedro; 26-2767). The cozy seaside gallery displays original paintings and color prints, painted clay vessels and exotic jewelry.

Belizean Arts (in Fido's marketplace, San Pedro; 26-2638) also carries original paintings of Maya and island scenes, as well as artsy T-shirts.

Next door to Belizean Arts, the **Salty Dog** has Guatemalan woven satchels and wallets.

NIGHTLIFE   San Pedro has the best nightlife in Belize, with possibilities ranging from intimate seaside bars to over-the-water pubs and sand-floored discos. Knowing these possibilities, the British sailors and pilots stationed in Belize flock to San Pedro, adding an uproarious nighttime dimension.

Big Daddy's (seafront, toward the south end of San Pedro; 26-2052) is the last word on disco around these parts. Nothing fancy, the bamboo shanty on the beach rocks until the wee hours of the morning. Bands play on Saturday nights. Cover.

The obvious choice for a pub is the ever-popular, sand-floored **Tackle Box Bar** (at the Coral Beach Hotel, seafront, San Pedro; 26-2001), perched over the water at the end of a pier. Sadly, the owners have corralled numerous sea turtles outside the bar and called it a tourist attraction. Perhaps as more travelers become ecotourists, they will complain, and the poor creatures will be set free.

For a before- or after-dinner drink, nestle up to the long padded bar at **The Pier Lounge** (seafront, near the center of San Pedro; 26-2002). On weekends, there's live blues and folk music.

The tiny **Purple Parrot Bar** (seafront at Fido's marketplace, San Pedro) draws big crowds with occasional reggae and punta rock bands. On off nights, it's a quiet spot for a drink.

Sandals (on the main street, near the north end of San Pedro; 26-2281) is the local pool joint, with sand floors, recorded reggae and dusty sandals parked on the walls.

GETTING THERE: If you're staying on Ambergris Caye, your lodge will arrange transportation from Belize City. If you're arriving on your own, Tropic Air and Island Air have regular flights to the San Pedro airstrip from Belize City. Or, shuttle boats make the one-hour cruise to Ambergris Caye from two Belize City locations: (1) across from the Bellevue Hotel, at 5 Southern Foreshore and (2) at the Shell Station near the Swing Bridge, on the north side of Haulover Creek. The one-way cost is about US$10 per person.

CAYE CAULKER

Just 20 scenic minutes by boat from Ambergris Caye, but decades away in spirit, is **Caye Caulker**. Despite its designation as the second-most populous caye in Belize, Caye Caulker hasn't changed much since the 1960s. Electricity did arrive in the mid-1980s, but there are still only a handful of old cars that cruise the sand streets. Life here feels like a slow-motion film, with dogs lazing everywhere, rickety picket fences running in all directions, and rows of battered clapboard homes tilting ever so slightly to the wind. Barefoot children tote tubs of bananas on their heads, and fishermen wrestle conch meat from their shells along crooked docks. The post office doubles as a store, and the pastry shop also rents snorkel equipment.

Spanning a five-square-mile area, Caye Caulker is mostly swamp and mangroves. The village itself is only four streets wide and ten streets long, all sand, of course. On the main drag, sometimes referred to as Front Street, there is a speed bump of knotted rope and a sign that cautions to "Go Slow," though no one is quite sure who they're meant for—maybe the island's four cars?

Perhaps it is the swamplands, or the island's thin ties with reality, that give Caulker its mysterious edge. Listen to the perpetual breezes that blow across the island and you will hear small-town whispers of strange people and places. There is a woman storyteller, locals will say, who spins yarns late at night, but only when storms are brewing. And somewhere is a lagoon filled with crocodiles, a disco that is haunted, and a mangrove forest where Maya cults worship. Who knows, they shrug, maybe it's the same place where the ancient Maya worshipped long ago.

Some 2000 years ago, the Maya were Caye Caulker's original islanders. Then followed the buccaneers, who never stayed very long but whose English accents gave the island its current nickname—Caye *Corker*. But most of Caulker's present-day residents are descendants of the *Mestizos*, who fled here after Yucatán's War of the Castes. In 1870, a *Mestizo* named Luciano Reyes bought the island for US$150 when he lost the bid for Ambergris Caye. Reyes' descendants still live on the island and are some of its most prominent residents.

Through the years, Caulker has always existed in the shadow of Ambergris, which is larger and more sophisticated than its tiny neighbor. But Belizeans today speak of Caulker with fondness, recalling the days when Ambergris was as laid back and not yet tainted by foreign development.

The boats on Ambergris transport many tourists, but those on Caye Caulker arrive burdened with fruits of the sea. Indeed, Caye Caulker is still very much a fishing village; every afternoon along the seafront, crayon-colored sloops arrive laden with snapper, grouper and, in season, pearly conch and bright pink lobsters. Some sloops suggest they may be loaded with something else; notice the boats named "Suspect," "Miss Conduct" and "Bong" tied to the village docks. Right next to the docks is the tiny island cemetery, overgrown with weeds.

Caye Caulker's 800 residents are ever protective of their little paradise. When local officials announced plans to open an airstrip, residents rallied against it, saying it would bring too much tourism. In 1991, the airstrip did open, but so far the visitors are only trickling in. If you do arrive in one of the infrequent commuter planes, you'll be deposited in a place that looks like the mangrove boonies, with only one house in sight. Not to worry. Just pick up your bags and start walking north (toward that house), and you'll soon find yourself in town.

Lodging on Caye Caulker ranges from modest accommodations to bare-bones; the best hotel is the Tropical Paradise, though whose idea of paradise could well be a point of debate. But the traveler looking for a slice of yesterday and an unhurried pace will find the island a paradise. Flowers and trees of raging color decorate the scenery—flaming red flamboyants and purply bougainvillea, canary mandavilla and ruby hibiscus. Coconut palms are so plentiful their fruit litters every sandy street. Breadfruit trees grow so big they camouflage stilt houses, and their fleshy fruits dangle like green bowling balls. In the morning, village women pluck the fruit and turn it into breadfruit bread; you can smell it baking through their open windows.

Visitors can learn about the island, and Belize's fragile reef system, in a slide show offered most weeknights at **Sea-ing is Belizing** (near the soccer field, toward the north end of town; 22-2189; admission), a photo gallery and book exchange. The slides are taken by gallery owner James Beveridge, an underwater photographer and Belize conservationist. Other than the slide show, nighttime activities are pretty much limited to dining on catch-of-the-day, drinking rum at a tiki bar, or gazing at the stars.

For island information and tours to other cayes or the mainland, stop by **Dolphin Bay Travel** (Front Street, near the middle of town; 22-2214). Here is also the village message board with formal notices and odd bits of advertising ("Reflexology! Go to Little Blue House next door to Frenchies.").

During the day, snorkeling, scuba diving and fishing are top pursuits. Several boats offer excursions, but by far the most popular trips are with **Chocolate** (22-2151), the island's most famous boat captain. Chocolate lives in a thatched-roof house along the seashore with his partner, aptly named Annie Seashore.

At the northernmost tip of town, **The Cut** was created in 1961, compliments of Hurricane Hattie. It's now the place to hang with locals, who cool off in the air-clear aquamarine channel and warm up on little sun docks. The "public beach" is really a small patch of dirt with palm trees. There's a couple of marooned boats, and a popular tiki bar that looks like it may topple over any day now.

LODGING   If modest, back-to-nature accommodations are your style (and budget), you've come to the right place. Most lodging on Caye Caulker is a notch above camping, with clean, nondescript rooms that have ceiling fans

Trumpetfish and Smooth trunkfish

and hot water that is more or less dependable. The water on Caye Caulker is not purified, so use *only* bottled water for drinking and brushing your teeth.

Oddly, the best place to sleep is next door to the cemetery, at the **Tropical Paradise Hotel** (seafront on the south end of town; some with air conditioning; budget to moderate; 22-2124). Owned by the Reyes family, descendants of Luciano Reyes, the hotel offers rooms in a main concrete building or along two rows of tiny, tin-roofed, plywood cabanas parked next to the beach. The cabanas, by far the best choice, feature vinyl floors, wood-paneled walls and newly remodeled bathrooms. Four cabanas have wall-unit air conditioners—offering the only air-conditioned lodging on the island.

Next door, the **Seabeezzz** (seafront on the south end of town; budget; 22-2176) really is a breeeezzy place to stay. Constant trade winds cool three small clapboard buildings, where six tidy rooms provide clean, comfortable lodging. Best of all, the rooms open onto an immaculate courtyard brimming with tropical plants and exotic fruit trees. Open from November through April.

The road stops at Seabeezzz, so you'll have to walk along the beach to get to **Shirley's Guest House** (seafront, south end of town; ceiling fans; budget to moderate; 22-2145). In a secluded, peaceful spot swept by sea breezes are six rooms in a low-slung building and three whitewashed cabins, all with Mennonite mahogany furnishings. The rooms share baths (including three outdoor facilities), while the cabins have private baths. Budget for rooms with shared bath; moderate for those with private baths.

Deisy's Hotel (south end of town; some with ceiling fans; budget; 22-2150) resembles a spiffy boarding house. All 12 rooms are newly painted and neat as a pin. Unfortunately, the community bathrooms are not as pleasant. Ask for a room with ceiling fan.

The ✪ **Vega Inn and Gardens** (seafront near the middle of town; budget; 22-2142) has a handful of tidy rooms for rent, as well as a lovely camping area right on the sea. The hot showers are the indoor-outdoor kind, but things seem private enough. The local family who owns the place treats the guests like family, and cookouts are quite common.

For rock-bottom rooms at rock-bottom rates, check into **Riva's Guest House** (north end of town; budget; 22-2127). You'll sleep above a Chinese restaurant, but you'll have clean sheets and generally clean surroundings. The bathroom's down the hall.

The prettiest pastel buildings on the waterfront can be found at the **Rainbow Hotel** (north end of town; budget; 22-2123). Inside the 16 rooms are attractive green tile floors, battered dressers and mattresses that range from firm to slightly lumpy. For television lovers, the cable televisions in each room are a real find.

RESTAURANTS   Caye Caulker's eateries are offbeat, super casual (don't mind the cats or dogs) and full of weird possibilities. A hippie will serve you tonight, but tomorrow night's waiter may be a moonlighting preacher or even a kid from down the street. Chairs and tables never match—that would be boring—and hours are apt to change with boating conditions.

Considering the norm, then, the restaurant at the **Tropical Paradise Hotel** (south end of town; budget; 22-2124) seems almost formal. Red and blue starched linens cover every table, and the service is dependably good. The breakfast, lunch and dinner fare isn't spectacular, but most meals are under $5. Fresh fish and shellfish, fried chicken, burgers and creole dishes are available.

To really get into the Caye Caulker mood, walk up into the **I & I Upstairs Café** (south end of town, a block from the Tropical Paradise; budget). The outdoor terrace is as funky as can be, with haphazard tables, plants potted in plastic buckets, and the owners' pet rabbits hopping around the floor. The menu, scrawled on notebook paper, features three or four fresh tasty seafoods of the day, usually grilled or baked, plus a hearty fish soup. For romantic dining, ask for one of the two tables on the rooftop—the best view in Caye Caulker.

Pinx Restaurant & Bar (seafront, near the middle of town; budget) is the spot for cheap, creole-style chicken and seafood, and the island's best pies (try the key lime, coconut or banana cream). Dine inside a little pink clapboard building, or outside on picnic tables overlooking the sea.

The place for lunch is **Syd's** (down a side lane, mid-island; budget; 22-2108), a battered little house with mesh screens and Christmas lights strung across the ceiling. Syd is not in sight, but his wife will gladly throw a cheeseburger or grilled cheese on the griddle, or whip up some burritos.

Paper lanterns, Mennonite mahogany tables and sea views lure diners to the **Sand Box** (facing the sea on the north end of town; budget). Once you're there, the talented chef and owner, a woman from southern Florida, treats you to fresh, inventive pasta and seafood dishes. Top choices are shrimp lasagna, conch fritters, and snapper stuffed with spinach, shrimp and mushrooms. Easily the island's best food.

Expatriates gather at **Aberdeen** (north end of town; budget; 22-2127) for fried rice, curries, chop suey, chow mein and other Oriental fare. Or, if you crave plain old American-style food, go for the T-bone steak or baked lobster.

SHOPPING   Shopping is a loose term here; it's more like whatever you happen to find that's open *and* has merchandise that day. A few possibilities: **Galeria Hicaco** (south end of town), owned by a California marine biologist, who carries a fine array of Belizean arts and crafts; **Regine's Gift Shop** (near the middle of town; 22-2167), which has pricey Guatemalan shorts and wristbands and good books on Belize; **Island Sun** (near the middle of town; 22-2215), the place for sundresses, straw hats and ship's models; or **Chocolate's** (near north end of town; 22-2151), where Chocolate's partner, Annie Seashore, sells good quality T-shirts and tropical wear.

NIGHTLIFE   The one and only true watering hole on Caye Caulker is **The Reef Bar** (seafront, on the north end of town; 22-2196), a bamboo hut with sand floors and dart boards. Recorded blues and reggae entertains nightly crowds, many of whom are British sailors, who gladly heed the bar's sign that says "No Shoes, No Shirts, No Problem."

GETTING THERE: Tropic Air and Island Air offer regular flights from Belize City to Caye Caulker. Shuttle boats make the trip to Caye Caulker from two Belize City locations: (1) across from the Bellevue Hotel, at 5 Southern Foreshore and (2) at the Shell Station near the Swing Bridge, on the north side of Haulover Creek. The 30-minute trip is about US$7.50, one-way.

CAYE CHAPEL

If you started at the southern tip of Caye Caulker, you could swim to Caye Chapel in about ten minutes. Most people take a boat or a plane (there's a good landing strip), and arrive to find the most diminutive, picture-perfect island, with throngs of coconut palms waving from sugary beaches that run along its two-mile length. The palms are Chapel's historic signature; they were planted by 19th-century settlers who made the island a thriving plantation that bore more than 50,000 coconuts a month.

Besides the trees and beaches, the main thing here is the Pyramid Island Resort, which owns Caye Chapel. Unfortunately, the resort is not as perfect as the island, and in recent years has had its share of management problems, even closing briefly when staff members deserted. It was once an exclusive facility (for Belize) offering everything from tennis and windsurfing to a golf driving range and extensive marina. Perhaps the latest management team, which took over in early 1993, will return the resort to its lively old self. At this writing, though, I cannot recommend staying there. However, the resort welcomes visitors from Caye Caulker and other islands who will patronize its facilities (restaurant, bar, water sports center) and spend a day on its beautiful beaches—an experience I do recommend.

GETTING THERE: Tropic Air and Maya Airways have fairly regular flights from Belize City to Caye Chapel. Or, you can easily catch a boat from the docks at Caye Caulker.

ST. GEORGE'S CAYE

The idyllic caye called St. George's is nearly two miles long and 800 feet wide at its broadest point, and is shaped like a wriggly crescent. From Belize City, it's just 20 minutes by boat across the clear sand flats, making it Belize's most accessible isle of escape. Little wonder that St. George's is a weekend haunt for wealthy Belizeans, whose charming stilt homes of painted clapboard are propped along the beach.

Given the island's eye-blink size, it is difficult to imagine that for two centuries it was hotly fought over by the Spanish and British. In fact, the Spanish called the island Cayo Casino even after the British made it the capital of the Belizean colony in 1650. By then, the island's residents were mainly English logwood and mahogany traders who grew numerous crops on the caye, despite the ban on crop growing, which kept the colonies dependent on the Crown. The Spanish regularly raided the crops. As one islander tells it: "Every couple of years the Spanish Navy would sail in, burn all the crops, hoist up the Spanish flag, and sail away. By the time the crops were good and growing again, the Spanish were back. It was a frustrating cycle."

The tug-of-war continued until 1798, when the Spanish lost the Battle of St. George's Caye. Belizeans commemorate the battle with a national holiday and much revelry. Some, however, claim it was not a battle at all, but simply some Spanish galleons retreating after being confronted by a ragtag band of Belizeans in boats. Official history, however, records the presence of a British schooner and the volleying of many cannon balls before the victory.

Appropriately, a single cannon on the beach remembers the battle today. Near the cannon are several graves, some occupied by early settlers and others by the recently deceased. A footpath wends past the graves to St. George's other inhabitants: two lodges, a few lobster fishers whose rickety traps are stacked higher than the palm trees, an aquarium builder (you can peek your head in, but there's not much to see), and the British Joint Forces "Adventurous Training Centre." The training, judging from the troops' activities, involves playing volleyball in the sand and drinking Belikin beer by the sea.

LODGING   **St. George's Lodge** (some rooms with ceiling fans; very expensive; for reservations, call 2-44190 in Belize City or 800-678-6871 in the United States) is ideal for hard-core divers who prefer a rigorous schedule. Each day's agenda, organized and directed by owner Fred Good of Texas, calls for diving interspersed with dive instruction and discussion, with time for three meals but little time for relaxation. Which is too bad, considering the lodge enjoys a picturesque location on the sea. Guests can choose from six rustic cabanas perched on stilts over the water or 12 bedrooms in a main house that are narrow and breezeless, quite monkish in design. Meals, dives and boat transfers from Belize City are included in the rates—among the highest lodging rates in all of Belize—and, in my opinion, not worth it.

At the opposite end of St. George's Caye is ✪ **Cottage Colony** (air conditioning; very expensive; for reservations, call 2-77051 in Belize City, fax: 2-73253), where 14 prim cottages are painted in sherbet colors, trimmed in gingerbread and framed by a white picket fence. Their interiors are airy and modern, with floors of linoleum and furniture of white wicker, and their porches face a shady courtyard next to the beach. All have air conditioners—lifesavers on hot days! The official gathering place is the second-floor bar and restaurant overlooking the sea. Main activities: diving, fishing and beach bumming. Rates include meals and boat transportation to the island.

GETTING THERE: Guests of Cottage Colony and St. George's Lodge will have prearranged boat transfers from Belize City to St. George's Caye. Independent sightseers can usually hire a boat from the docks across from the Bellevue Hotel, 5 Southern Foreshore; the docks at the Shell Station near the Swing Bridge; or from Blackline Marina, two miles north of Belize City on the Northern Highway.

THE ATOLLS

Farther out to sea lie three atolls, coral isles that form rings around lagoons. These dazzling island necklaces actually sit atop the Maya Mountains; over the eons, the coral blossomed on the mountains until it rose above the sea. The sea, in turn, pulverized their rocky shores into cushiony white sand that makes the atolls look like some exotic Pacific isles. Most of the world's atolls do in fact lie in the Pacific. Only four exist in the Western Hemisphere, and three of these are in Belize. The fourth atoll, Chinchorro, is in Mexico just across the Belize border.

From the air, the Belize atolls appear as stunning oddities, with the calm emerald waters of the lagoons seemingly corralled by the blustery blue waters of the sea. On land, the scenery is just as compelling. The faraway isles that make up **Turneffe Islands, Lighthouse Reef** and **Glover's Reef** atolls are the quintessence of tropical paradise: pearly beaches studded with swaying coconut palms and washed with warm, shallow waters. Bird life is prolific and bountiful, and giant sea turtles build their nests in virtual privacy. Northern promontories attract swarms of grouper and snapper, who spawn each year with little interruption from a hook and line.

Just offshore, the sea bottom plummets, then becomes wildly etched with spiked ridges and rolling canyons and lattice-like caverns. The ridges have brought down many a ship, laid them to rest in what is now a virtual nautical graveyard of the 18th and 19th centuries. These sunken ancients, together with the many sheer walls webbed with sea life, make the surrounding waters an extraordinary place to dive.

Only a few years ago, Belize's atolls were considered the outer limits of Caribbean diving. But as word spread, they have become the "in" place to dive; their virtues are whispered on the diving grapevine and exalted in glossy dive magazines. The place most divers hear about first is **Turneffe Islands**, the largest and westernmost of Belize's atolls, located about two-and-a-half hours from Belize City by boat. Here, one can dive the Black Beauty, where ebony coral blankets a reef, and The Elbow, where curtains of huge fish waft up and down a 150-foot wall of coral. There is an excellent dive lodge on Turneffe, as well as a fishing camp and an ecotourism retreat.

Besides its size and fantastic diving, what really sets Turneffe apart is its mangrove forests. Brilliant orchids drape from the mangrove limbs, and schools of fish seek protection in their roots. Mangrove lagoons provide safe haven for many manatees and dolphins, which are the main reason **Blackbird Caye Village** opened in 1991. The research center and ecotourist resort is the venture of Belizean Ray Lightburn and American Al Dugan, who have hired scientists to study marine life in the area. The 4000-acre island and its surrounding waters are still extremely pristine, and sea life is profuse. The village focal point is a dolphin research center, where scientists are studying the communication and other behaviors of the gregarious mammals. Lightburn and Dugan hope the village will make the Turneffe atoll a national park.

There are few mangroves on the **Lighthouse Reef** atoll, but there are ravishing beaches, whose promenades of luxuriant, crisp white sand are sprinkled with palms and washed by pleated seas dyed green and blue and, at sunset, blazing violet.

Within the atoll are numerous natural wonders, most notably the **Blue Hole,** explored in the 1970s by Jacques Cousteau. Actually an ocean sinkhole, it measures a spectacular 1000 feet across and plunges 480 feet down from the atoll's ten-foot-deep lagoon. Riddled with stalactites and stalagmites and pitch-black caves, the Blue Hole is difficult to reach (on a calm day, it's three hours by boat from Belize City), but that only adds to its mystique. Several dive operators offer one-day trips, but dedicated scuba divers should consider staying at **Lighthouse Reef Resort** (800-423-3114), which includes a trip to the Blue Hole in its one-week package.

The resort also offers excursions to **Half Moon Caye Natural Monument** (for information, contact the Belize Audubon Society; 2-77369 in Belize City)

Frigate bird

at the southeast corner of Lighthouse Reef. The 45-acre sanctuary, Belize's first national park, boasts sensational beaches and about 4000 red-footed booby birds, who nest on the southern end of the caye and are very rare. Among the other fascinating creatures living here are mangrove warblers and frigate birds, wish-willie lizards, and loggerhead and hawksbill turtles, who lay their eggs on the eastern beaches. A raised platform provides bird's-eye views of all the animal action. Arrive at dusk and you may catch one of nature's intense shows: aerial bird fights between the frigates and boobies.

Because of its extreme remoteness, Belize's southernmost atoll is also its least visited. **Glover's Reef** is five hours by boat from Belize City—not a pleasant trip on rough seas. But on calm days, it is a fantastic voyage, with mesmerizing vistas of sapphire waters that meet blue skies and the tiniest, most serene little islands.

The atoll is named for English buccaneer John Glover, who set up camp here during the 1700s, not knowing he was living on the hemisphere's most shapely atoll. Glover's coral outcroppings form a nearly unbroken oval whose vertical sides fall away to inky depths. If drained of their seas, they would look like a Pacific volcano.

Inside the coral lies an 80-square-mile lagoon of the most intensely beautiful water, riddled with hundreds of patch reefs and sea creatures of flamboyant colors and shapes. Outside its borders are the wrecks of five 18th century English merchant ships, which met their doom on jagged coral. Glover's has but six cayes, all fringed with fabulous white sand and palm trees, and all located on the southeastern corner of the atoll. Here also is the atoll's one and only lodge, Manta Resort—a true dream getaway.

LODGING   The most popular atoll resort is ✪ **Turneffe Island Lodge** (Caye Bokel, Turneffe Islands atoll; ceiling fans; very expensive; for reservations, call 800-338-8149), situated on a private 12-acre caye. A cluster of charming frame bungalows, swallowed in palm trees, line the sandy shore and offer comfortable rooms with private baths and views of the sea. Guests spend most of their time in the sea, either diving the fabulous reef or fishing the flats. The waters around Turneffe are renowned for bonefish. To help keep them that way, the lodge limits the number of anglers to six per week. Minimum stay is one week; included are all meals and boat transportation from Belize City—about a two-and-a-half-hour trip.

If you've ever had the urge to be a marine scientist, check into **Blackbird Caye Resort** (Blackbird Caye, Turneffe Islands atoll; ceiling fans; moderate; for reservations, call 713-658-1142 in the United States, fax: 713-658-0739). Here, on a 4000-acre, jungle-covered island, you can help researchers collect marine samples, monitor the activities of local manatees, and videotape dolphins as they play and speak with each other in a sheltered lagoon. It's not a resort in the traditional sense, but an "ecotourist resort," with woodsy accommodations in four thatched beach bungalows, meandering nature trails and several laboratories, including a dolphin research center. Meals and transfers from Belize City are included in the rate.

For thousands of years, the site of **Turneffe Flats** (on Northern Bogue, on the northeast side of the Turneffe Islands atoll; ceiling fans; very expensive; for reservations call 605-578-1304 in the United States) has been a fishing camp, first for the Maya and now for visiting anglers who come armed with fly rods. Flats fishing is naturally the big draw, but guides are also available for reef and deep-sea fishing. The lodge can also arrange dive trips. Guests stay in one of six comfortable wood-frame bungalows with porches on the beach. A 24-hour generator turns the ceiling fans in each room and provides the hot water for showers. There's a bar and family-style dining room, where tasty meals of fresh fish are the highlight. Minimum fishing or diving package is one week, which includes one night in Belize City at the Radisson Fort George, all meals and guides.

Lighthouse Reef Resort (Northern Caye, in the Lighthouse Reef atoll; air conditioning; very expensive; for reservations, call 800-423-3114) resembles a tropical illusion: a castaway island, ringed in coconut palms and powdery white sand, with lovely cabanas strung along the beach. Offshore, the underwater panorama is no less spectacular, which explains why so many scuba divers stay here. Dives are offered several times a day and at night, including trips to the famous Blue Hole. Accommodations are in casual, roomy concrete cabanas or in gleaming new apartments or suites. Every room has modern decor and a porch with rocking chairs. The restaurant serves unusually good food, and there's a real feeling of camaraderie among guests. But perhaps the best part of staying here is arriving. After your plane bumps to a halt on the rocky airstrip, you'll be greeted by the friendly, always-barefoot manager named Dennis, wearing a parrot on his shoulder. Weekly packages only; all meals and air transportation from Belize City included.

Five hours by boat from the mainland and offering only six cabanas, ✪ **Manta Resort** (Glover's Reef; some air conditioning; very expensive; for reservations, call 2-31895 in Belize City or 800-342-0053 in the United States) is a seclusionist's paradise. It's nestled on its own 12-acre fantasy island, with nothing but fluffy white sand, palm trees and sapphire waters that plunge to inky black depths. The lodge attention-getter is a vast thatched cantina, stuck way out in the sea at the end of a pier. Here, guests meet for eating, drinking and partaking of the gorgeous sea views. Nothing fancy, the thatched-roof cabanas are made of mahogany and feature solar-heated showers and tiny porches over the sand. For those who want more creature comforts, there's a modern two-bedroom family house with air conditioning, kitchen, and even television and VCR (unheard of in the out islands!). Rates include all meals and boat transfers from Belize City.

GETTING THERE: Boat or air (in the case of Lighthouse Reef) transportation to the atolls is arranged through your resort.

OTHER CAYES

Hundreds of other beautiful cayes are scattered off the Belize coast, including many that are uninhabited but can be visited by boat. Such is the case with **Spanish Lookout Caye, Sergeants Caye, Water Caye** and **Goff's Caye.** About 45 minutes by boat from Belize City, the teeny sandy cayes are popular day destinations for Belizeans who love to picnic and snorkel here. Also popular is nearby **English Caye,** which marks the entrance to the shipping channel and has a lighthouse, a lighthouse keeper and a few private houses.

If you'd rather spend the night on one of these out islands, head a few minutes north to **Gallow's Point Caye.** At **Gallow's Point Resort** (moderate; for reservations, call 2-73054 in Belize City) you'll find four primitive bedrooms on the second floor of a big white wooden house. Other than fishing, snorkeling or lying prone on the powdery patch of beach, there's absolutely nothing to do! Rates include meals and boat transfers from Belize City.

Farther south, you can experience the life of a lobster fisher on the string of mangrove isles called the **Bluefield Range.** Belizean Ricardo Castillo runs a commercial lobster camp on one of the islands, and also runs **Ricardo's Beach Huts** (expensive; for reservations, call 2-77593 in Belize City). He invites guests who stay in his four super-rustic stilt huts (no showers—the sea is your bathtub) to accompany him as he fishes for lobster. Or, guests can do their own fishing and snorkeling in the surrounding crystalline waters. Meals (including much lobster, of course!), a day trip to surrounding cayes, and boat transfers from Belize City are included in the rate. For the true adventurer who doesn't mind really roughing it, this is a memorable experience—even for Belize, where *everything's* an adventure.

Looking like a wedge of sand and palm trees set adrift, **South Water Caye** is encircled by the clearest, shallowest water, and beyond that, the resplendent coral reef, beckoning for exploration. Unlike most of the "other cayes," South Water has a little more going on, thanks to the **Blue Marlin Lodge** (air conditioning; very expensive; for reservations, call 800-798-1558), which has lately become popular with anglers and divers. Here, numerous buildings are sprinkled atop the sand, including several clapboard ones with casual, beachy rooms and several concrete cabanas that offer air conditioning but smell musty—a hazard of island existence. The most coveted room is a spacious wooden bungalow the juts right out over the water and catches constant sea breezes. There's a glorious sand beach here and congenial thatched-roof restaurant and bar. Minimum stay four nights. Rates include all meals and transportation from Dangriga.

Next door, you'll notice a sandy jewel called **Carrie Bow Caye,** spanning all of one acre, and acting as a field station for the Smithsonian Institute during the spring and summer. Smithsonian researchers, searching for a good field station site, accidentally landed on the island in 1972 during a bad storm. They fell instantly in love, and struck a deal with the Bowman family of Dangriga, who own the island, to use it for half the year. If you swim or motor over to Carrie Bow, the scientists will be happy to show you around. Research changes every season, of course, but in 1993 they were studying the mating habits of worms and jellyfish.

GETTING THERE: Day trips to these outer cayes can be arranged through **S & L Travel** (91 North Front Street, Belize City; 2-77593, fax: 2-77594).

Belize City

0   0.25 kilometer

0.25 mile

HAULOVER CREEK

N. Front St.

Barracks Rd.

Eve St.

Queen St.

Handyside St.

Hutson St.

Vernon St.

Water Ln.

Front St.

Orange St.

Church St.

Bishop St.

King St.

Prince St.

Dean St.

South St.

Collet Canal St.

Euphrates Ave.

West St.

George St.

W. Canal St.

E. Canal St.

Albert St.

Regent St.

S. Foreshore Dr.

Kut Ave.

Mex Ave.

Queen Charlotte St.

Birds Isle

Cork St.

Fort St.

Marine Parade

CARIBBEAN SEA

N

POINTS OF INTEREST

A Fort George and
Embassy Row
B Baron Bliss Memorial and
Fort George Lighthouse
C Memorial Park
D Belize Tourist Bureau
E Swing Bridge
F St. John's Cathedral
G Supreme Court
H Bliss Institute

SEVEN

Belize City

Although the Cayes are the most popular destination in Belize, Belize City is the place most travelers see first, after arriving at the international airport. Unfortunately, it is not the best introduction. Sweltering hot all the time, it is crowded with crumbling streets, tin-roofed shanties and British colonial buildings that have seen better days. Murky Haulover Creek slices through the center of the city, bubbling with sailboats and makeshift skiffs and fed by open sewage canals that line the streets. The 60,000 people who live and work here create a continuous grind of activity—quite unlike the rest of the country, where life is slow and the land virtually empty.

In the early 1700s, the city was conceived by a band of British Baymen, logwood cutters who were former pirates but who still clung to their buccaneer ways. From their stilt-shack settlement at the swampy mouth of the Belize River, they would occasionally cut logwood and load it onto ships headed for England. Most of the time, however, "their chief Delight" was "in drinking," rum punch being their favorite, according to Captain Nathaniel Uring in 1720, who adds he "had a very unpleasant time living among these people." Little wonder that 18th-century mapmakers obelized, or marked the settlement with a symbol warning of a corrupt place, which, over time, was itself corrupted into the word "Belize."

More than a hundred years later, when Maya explorer John Lloyd Stephens sailed into the port city, conditions had changed considerably. Gleaming white colonial houses paraded up and down the waterfront and nearby streets, culminating in the elegant Government House, designed by famous 19th-century architect Christopher Wren. There was also an ornate Gothic church with a soaring spire and groves of coconut palms that, from the sea, reminded Stephens of the palm trees of Egypt and "gave the appearance of actual beauty."

Despite its new-found sophistication, vestiges of the unsavory Baymen remained deep in the city's foundation. As late as 1917, workers who dug down 60 feet found "mahogany chips mixed with rum bottles, with surprising regularity," according to one account in *The Baymen's Legacy, A Portrait of Belize City.*

103

It is a city that should not have been built, for its land is swampy and low-lying, confronted by water on three sides and forever vulnerable to rains and tides and hurricanes. The no-name hurricane of 1931 extinguished ten percent of the capital city's 15,000 residents, most of whom tragically believed the barrier reef would prove a natural force field. Thirty years later, Hurricane Hattie virtually picked up Belize City and flung it out to sea in a day of hell described by many as "an earthquake in a storm." It was Hattie that finally drove the country to move its capital inland, to a place called Belmopan.

Today, Belmopan is the official capital, but Belize City is the life pulse of Belize, the country's only genuine city. Despite its teetering existence, "it continues to swell and expand against all odds and without any plan," or so said the *Amandala*, Belize's biggest newspaper, in a 1986 editorial that became an infamous essay on Belize City. The editorial denounced the city as having a culture that "copies America too slavishly, and which has no stomach for sacrifice. But it is the culture that gives Belize City identity and makes it flashy and attractive, like a Saturday night hooker."

It is also that culture, that spicy slice of post-Colonial life by the sea, which eventually tends to win visitors over. Of course, Belize (as locals call the city) does have its high points, not the least of which is its people. Like all Belizeans, city residents are gregarious, laid-back and ever helpful to newcomers. Some are too helpful, though, as they hustle visitors to lend pocket change, buy drugs or join them in finding "some action." But visitors who stick to the better neighborhoods, and avoid venturing out alone at night, will find Belize City safer than big cities back home. At night, the infamous scene of petty crime is the Swing Bridge; avoid walking it from dusk to dawn, no matter how many people you're with.

The very best neighborhood is the **Fort George neighborhood,** named for the fort built here in 1803 but since destroyed. At the time, the area was a swampy island, but today it is draped across the tip of a peninsula on the northern side of Haulover Creek. The neighborhood's beauty lies in its big old whitewashed homes trimmed in filigree and framed by white picket fences and well-groomed lawns, and in the lavish traveler's palms and poinciana trees that decorate the yards and street corners. Here, along the waterfront Fort Street and Marine Parade, is **embassy row,** where several countries are represented by picturesque architecture (and, hopefully, competent staffs). One of the most appealing buildings in all of Belize, the **United States Embassy** (29 Gabourel Lane; 2-77161) is a distinguished, whitewashed building that was actually constructed in New England and brought to Belize in the 1800s.

At the tip of the peninsula stands the stately **Radisson Fort George Hotel.** Built in 1953 as a hotel, it once boasted the only swimming pool in Belize. (Times have changed, and now there are more than two dozen.) A block from the hotel is the **Baron Bliss Memorial** (Marine Parade), an unspectacular slab of stone commemorating a spectacular act of generosity. In 1926, Englishman Henry Edward Ernest Victor Bliss, known as Baron Bliss, sailed into the harbor at Belize City. Sick with food poisoning he'd contracted in Trinidad, he was unable to leave his boat. For the next few months Bliss lived onboard, fishing and trying to recover from his illness. He never recovered, but he did befriend many Belizeans, who brought him food and took care of him. When he died, he left his $2 million fortune to the people of Belize.

The baron's generosity made him a national hero and paid for numerous public buildings, including health clinics and schools and the Bliss Institute museum. And though he never walked on Belize in life, he is buried here in a tomb, where land meets the sea. The **Fort George Lighthouse** stands sentinel nearby.

North on Marine Parade and facing the sea, **Memorial Park** is a rambling grassy area with queues of concrete benches, a tin-roofed gazebo, amphitheater and obelisk honoring the 40 Belizean men who died in World War I. Around the bend is the headquarters for information on Belize. The **Belize Tourist Board** (83 North Front Street; 2-77213) has helpful employees, maps and guides.

Continue west a few paces and you'll notice the white clapboard **Paslow Building** (corner of Front and Queen streets), looking tired but dignified, and housing numerous government offices, including the **Belize Post Office** (2-72201). On the west side of the building, hiding out in a teeny room, is the **Belize Philatelic Bureau,** showcasing the country's marvelous stamps. You can purchase souvenir sheets of various editions; my favorites: the dazzling Coral Reef series and the poignant, infinitely detailed Maya Monuments.

From here, you can spot the **Swing Bridge** and its constant hum of activity. The city's geographic frame of reference, the bridge crosses Haulover Creek and swings open at about 5:30 a.m. and 5:30 p.m. daily, causing instant gridlock. Built in Liverpool, England, and brought to Belize in 1923, it is thought to be the only manually operated swing bridge still being used in the world. If you watch the four skinny men straining with their long poles to open the bridge every morning and night, you will know why it is the only one.

South of the bridge lies the heart of the city, centered around Albert and Regent streets and the Southern Foreshore. Here, buildings crowd shoulder-to-shoulder and street vendors hawk baskets of bread and tropical ices. Bicyclists, pedestrians with parasols, rickety old school buses and kamikaze taxis compete for the same narrow stretch of pavement. At high noon, the roadside park benches get so hot they burn right through your jeans.

At the southeastern foot of the Swing Bridge, you'll be met by the sparkling, modern, yellow-with-black-trim **Belize Commercial Center.** Opened in 1993, it feels like a mini-convention center, with a first floor crowded with Creole and Latin American foods and second and third floors lined with vendor-style shops, businesses and eateries. The first-floor **market** features wobbly tables and baskets overflowing with produce, from glassy red scotch bonnet peppers and shaggy boniato (a tuber) to silky red beans and juicy passion fruit. You'll also find catches of the day—anything from grouper and snapper to live iguana and sea turtles. The latter are endangered, so don't support the industry. If you have questions about produce, the friendly Belizean women (anxious to make a sale) will happily answer them. *Remember:* Buy only what you can peel yourself, and wash everything in purified water.

Away from the bridge, and where everyone seems to be heading, is **Brodies Department Store** (255 Albert Street; 2-77070). It's Belize's official department store, but don't expect Macy's; it's more like a crowded K-Mart with iffy air conditioning.

Near here, Belize's own **Central Park** (bounded by Albert, Regent and Church streets) is bustling, small and strange, a sort of outdoor way station for street vendors, street people and salesmen of questionable character. Banks and other businesses line the park, and so does the white clapboard **Supreme Court** (Regent Street across from Central Park). The third Supreme Court to be built on the site (fires destroyed the first two), it's an attractive two-story building with neoclassic columns, a four-sided clock tower (pay no attention to the time—it's usually wrong) and a filigreed iron balcony, the prettiest in town.

A couple of blocks over along the sea, you'll find the **Bliss Institute** (1 Bliss Promenade; 2-77267), a weathered white concrete edifice and center of Belize culture. Inside, there's the extensive National Library and a few permanent exhibits, including limestone altars uncovered from the ancient Maya city of Caracol. Traveling exhibits, sponsored by the resident Belize Arts Council, feature bamboo crafts and paintings by Belizean and international artists.

Belize City's most flamboyant personality can usually be found at his **Admiral Burnaby's Art Gallery and Coffee House** (9 Regent Street; 2-77453). But his name isn't Burnaby; it's Emory King. The cigar-smoking, panama-hatted man-about-town is a writer, lecturer, real estate salesman, tour guide and self-proclaimed expert on antique bottles. The American expatriate ended up in Belize in 1953 after his boat, the *Vagabond*, got snagged on some coral offshore. By the time his boat was fixed, King had already fallen for Belize. He never went home. If you don't catch him at his coffeehouse, you can see him in the 1986 movie *Mosquito Coast*, where he played a bit part with Harrison Ford.

Near the southern end of Regent Street, visiting dignitaries are often entertained at the graceful **Government House,** built around 1812 and designed by famed architect Christopher Wren. Across the street, you'll instantly recognize **St. John's Cathedral** (corner of Regent and Albert streets; 2-72137) by its manicured lawns and dignified red-brick facade. The oldest Anglican church in Central America, it was built by slaves from 1812 to 1826, who were conveniently emancipated by the church in a formal ceremony in 1838. Despite many fires and hurricanes, St. John's still boasts its original sapodilla roof, mahogany beams and 1826 organ.

For a real slice of Belize City life, wander the side streets between Regent Street and Southern Foreshore. Under the canopies of shady poinciana trees, brilliant parrots squawk from cages and women scrub their wash in big tubs. Children tote heavy strings of fish, fresh from the painted wooden sloops bobbing in the nearby harbor.

West of the city center are neighborhoods not worth visiting but whose street names are worth mentioning: Armadillo, Iguana, Antelope, Gibnut, Raccoon and Pelican.

On the north end of Belize City, a half-mile offshore from the airstrip, you can look over to **Moho Caye**. Earlier this century, the mite-size island yielded more historical mementos than all of Belize City. Pottery shards, pottery rings used as fishing sinkers, spear heads and two burial grounds testify to its days as a Maya fishing outpost. Even more remarkable were the thou-

Yellow-headed parrot

sands of manatee bones washed on the northern shore. Today, manatees still seek the warmth of nearby waters, and the tiny island is owned by **Maya Landings** (2-45798, fax: 2-30263), a marina and dive/sail boat operation offering week-long trips to the Blue Hole and to the Río Dulce in Guatemala.

LODGING   For the most part, accommodations in Belize City are extremely basic, with four walls, hot water and a bed, plus a ceiling fan if you're lucky. Considering the often suffocating heat and the nagging problem of street hustlers, I highly recommend you take a room in or near the Fort George neighborhood, where several pleasant hotels offer air-conditioned rooms.

The city's most distinguished establishment is the **Radisson Fort George Hotel** (Marine Parade; air conditioning; very expensive; 2-77400, fax: 2-73820), whose 76 rooms are among the plushest in Belize—and worth the price. Favored by business travelers, its lush, walled grounds with brick lanai and pool seem worlds away from the bustling street life. Rooms in the main building offer commanding views of the sea, and have that Belize rarity, cable TV. Near the gardens, rooms take on a tropical flavor. A fine restaurant and lounge round out the amenities.

Across the street, also owned by Radisson, is the pretty **Villa Belize** (13 Cork Street; air conditioning; expensive to very expensive; 2-77400, fax: 2-73820). Everything in the lobby is vivid and tropical, from the green wicker settees to the shiny ceramic floors. Of the 41 rooms, 30 offer splendid sea views. There is a little swimming pool, but it overlooks neighboring apartment balconies strung with laundry. Of the many pluses: a helpful staff, topnotch restaurant and terrific location in the Fort George neighborhood.

Located in the Fort George neighborhood and definitely one of the best bargains in town, the 1930s' colonial ✪ **Colton House** (9 Cork Street; ceiling fans; budget to moderate; 2-44666) invites with its front porch with double swings, polished pine floors, lacy draperies and shelves lined with good books. Alan and Ondina Colton are congenial innkeepers, making sure guests are comfortable in the four spacious bedrooms. Each room has pine floors, plush carpets and a private entrance. Two have private baths. Rates include complimentary coffee.

If the Colton House is booked, try the **Fort Street Guest House** (4 Fort Street; ceiling fans; budget; 2-30116, fax: 2-78808). It's not as classy, but the six bedrooms are quite cozy with their tongue-in-groove ceilings and floors, woven Guatemalan rugs and battered assortment of furniture. Unfortunately, the beds take up most of the room. There's a shared bath. It gets hot in the summer.

The stately white **Château Caribbean** (6 Marine Parade; air conditioning; expensive; 2-30800, fax: 2-30900) is showing some wear, but it still imparts an island charm. Overlooking the sea, with a large swimming pool encased in palmy grounds, the colonial mansion offers 23 pleasant rooms with private balconies and cable television.

Mom's Triangle Inn (11 Handyside Street; ceiling fans; budget; 2-45523, fax: 2-33966) is about what you'd expect from a Belizean mom: a comfy old parlor with yawning cats all over the place, clean but funky bedrooms with ancient ceiling fans and worn carpets or vinyl floors, and a place to wash your dirty laundry. The best part, as everyone knows, is the downstairs restaurant that offers inexpensive home cooking. Young backpackers and environmentalists love this place.

Though only opened in mid-1993, the 12-room **Bakadeer Inn** (74 Cleghorn Street; air conditioning; moderate; 2-31286, fax: 2-31963) is quickly gaining a reputation as one of the best values in Belize City. Indeed, for a moderate price, visitors not only get friendly service and assistance with sightseeing tours, they enjoy attractive rooms with virtually every modern amenity, from cable television to telephones and mini-refrigerators. Budget-priced breakfasts are extra special, and there's a secured lot for parking rental cars.

Just outside the Fort George neighborhood, but in the same class with the Radisson Fort George, is the **Ramada Royal Reef** (Newtown Barracks; air conditioning; very expensive; 2-32670, fax: 2-32660). The best choice for young couples and families, the attractive teal building is set along the Caribbean Sea and boasts a fantasy pool (the best in Belize) with swim-up bar. There are 113 rooms, each with a sea view and decor that's contemporary but tropical: textured concrete walls, cane headboards and striking tones of plum, teal and auburn. Besides cable television, amenities include a hair salon, marina and several good restaurants and bars.

If you have to stay downtown, the best choice is the **Bellevue Hotel** (5 Southern Foreshore; air conditioning; expensive; 2-77051, fax: 2-73253), whose two-story brick facade with arched windows curve along the seafront. It's a comfortable, timeworn place with a little garden, a wedge-shaped swimming pool and a bar called the Maya Tavern. All 37 rooms are carpeted and decorated with seashell-patterned bedspreads and rattan tables and chairs in unexciting shades of brown and olive. A few have a view to the sea, but, unfortunately, it's through chain link tacked over all the windows.

Reminiscent of a youth hostel, **Seaside Guest House** (3 Prince Street; budget; 2-78339) has dormitory accommodations plus two single and three double rooms, all with twin beds and shared baths. Sea breezes help cool things down, but it's still hot and noisy. Hot breakfasts are US$1. Clean but funky.

Even if you don't stay at the **Mopan Hotel** (55 Regent Street; some air conditioning; ceiling fans; moderate; 2-73356, fax: 2-77351), you should stop by and meet Jean and Tom Shaw. For decades, the two environmentalists have attracted a coterie of archaeologists, zoologists and other conservation devotees, who converge at the hotel bar for nights of impassioned discussion, and who don't seem to mind that the hotel is entirely run-down. The 12 bedrooms, scattered between an old frame house and an unfinished concrete block addition, are spartanly furnished but have clean sheets and private baths, and jalousie windows that let in the city noises. Several rooms have wall-unit air conditioners.

RESTAURANTS   Despite its reputation as a rice-and-beans country, Belize has much to offer in the way of skillfully prepared seafood dishes and gratifying home cooking. In Belize City, fine dining exists in hotel restaurants, while soulful fare can be found in seedy diners tucked here and there.

The fresh, inventive cuisine at **Radisson Fort George Hotel** (Marine Parade; moderate; 2-77400) is not only delicious, it's reasonable. Situated along the sea, with pink starched linens and vases brimming with tropical flowers, the handsome dining room turns out dishes such as grouper filet with shrimp and white wine sauce, shrimp amaretto, bouillabaisse, lobster thermidor (in season) and stuffed baked stone crab. For breakfast, there are thick slabs of french toast and saucy eggs ranchero; for lunch, try the cobb salad, bacon cheeseburger or American-style pizza.

Top of the Town (Holiday Inn Villa Belize, 13 Cork Street; expensive; 2-32800) holds the designation as the restaurant at the highest elevation in Belize. As you might expect, it also dispenses terrific city and harbor views. The cuisine, a medley of lobster, shrimp creole, conch ceviche and Oriental stir-fry is average to very good. Early American woods, draped with linens, create a warm, classy aura.

Glimmering oil lamps, brilliant tropical flowers and white eyelet tablecloths make **Fort Street Guest House and Restaurant** (4 Fort Street; moderate to expensive; 2-30116) an intimate place to dine. Set in a big whitewashed colonial house, the piped-in blues and Bogey and Bacall decor give a feeling of bygone days. The chalkboard menu is read tableside, listing five or six items the cook has prepared for the evening. Cajun shrimp, kingfish with sour cream and pineapple, and snapper baked in foil with onions and peppers are a few choices.

Visitors inevitably ask: "How do we get to **Mom's**?" (11 Handyside Street; budget; 2-45523). It's a little tough to find, tucked as it is along a crowded side street. But find it you should, since you won't want to miss the crisp-fried chicken and mashed potatoes oozing with thick, peppery gravy. Wash it down with sweet, pulpy limeade, then finish with creamy bread pudding or banana cake. For lighter appetites, there are BLTs and burgers; for breakfast, fat omelettes with refried beans and johnnycakes. Mom's will also fix you a box lunch. Mom's is dearly loved by American and English expatriates.

The Grill (164 Newtown Barracks; moderate to expensive; 2-45020) has a reputation as an on-again, off-again establishment, but when I tried it, I found it exceptionally good. Fresh seafood, beef and chicken, grilled or bathed in light sauces, are served in a seafront room framed by candlelight and white linens. Tables are well-spaced for privacy, and the service is above par.

One of the city's newest restaurants is also one of its best. Opened in 1993, **Kadel's** (second floor, Belize Commercial Center, southeastern foot of Swing Bridge; moderate; 2-70103) is the creation of Kadel Flowers, a Belize City native who was chef at Santa Monica College restaurant for 14 years. But Flowers' menu barely hints at California cuisine; instead, it focuses on original treatments of local fare such as Belizean spiced shrimp, warm chicken salad, blackened fish and peanut punch. His loft-style dining room, however, looks like a California counterculture scene: beaded doors, Gypsy-patterned chairs and throw rugs, and an overriding Black emancipation theme.

The dining room at the downtown **Bellevue Hotel** (5 Southern Foreshore; moderate to expensive; 2-77051) would be the last place you'd expect complex dishes. But here they are, served in a small but entirely cozy room of rattan chairs and carved wood sculptures by friendly, but slow-moving waitresses. For starters, try the smoked Belizean blue marlin, then move on to entrées such as grouper with cucumber cream sauce, chicken breasts filled with herbed cream cheese and served on a bed of pineapple and brandy sauce, or rock fish olé (stuffed with capers, olives and onions and topped with spicy tomato sauce).

Around the corner, on the first floor of a lovely whitewashed building decorated with arches and gingerbread, **GG's Café & Patio** (2B King Street; budget; 2-74378) serves down-home Belizean fare like stewed pork, beef or chicken, pork steaks and burgers slathered with hot sauce. Nothin' fancy, the inside is a mishmash of nautical and south-of-the-border decor, with plastic tablecloths, wood chairs and wood-paneled ceilings. Or, dine out on the shaded patio.

For pizza and nothing else, duck into the **Pizza House** (11 King Street; budget; 2-73966), which has four rickety tables and various meat and veggie pies. Don't expect Pizza Hut flavors here, but Belizean seasonings on a bed of chopped tomatoes with a little cheese.

Dit's (50 King Street; budget; 2-73330) is as Belizean as they come: friendly and uproarious, with plastic tables and local artwork, and Campbell's soup cans sold at the cash register. Choose from meat pies, "fry" chicken, *garnaches* (fried tortillas stuffed with tomatoes and onions), and rice and beans with stew chicken, beef or fish.

The funkiest diner in town, **Macy's** (18 Bishop Street; budget; 2-73419) became famous in the late 1980s when England's Queen Elizabeth dined here on gibnut (a large rodent). The rodent has been elevated to "royal gibnut" on the menu. Right beside it is oxtail soup, and more traditional offerings like stew rice and beans and grouper. Sweet local fruit juices, from pulpy papaya to slushy watermelon, come in tall cool glasses. It's all served in a little room with folding iron chairs, clanking screen doors and a TV playing American soap operas.

SHOPPING   Few people would think to go shopping at the **Belize Philatelic Bureau** (in the Paslow Building, corner of Front and Regent streets), but the country's exquisitely designed stamps really do make great gifts. Souvenir stamp sheets include dozens of historical and environmental themes.

You'll find vintage greeting cards at **The Book Center** (144 North Front Street; 2-77457), as well as Belizean literature, two-day-old copies of the *Miami Herald*, and references on local cuisine, history and art.

A little coffee with your art? **Admiral Burnaby's Art Gallery and Coffee House** (9 Regent Street; 2-77453) will serve you a cup, while you peruse Belizean watercolors, wood carvings and Guatemalan woven fabrics, right alongside jeans and baseball caps made in the United States. The pleasant, colorful **Go Tees** (23 Regent Street; 2-74082) purveys tropical clothing, wood jewelry, postcards by Belizean artists and books on Belize.

The **Belize Bookshop** (corner of Regent Street and Rectory Lane; 2-72054) stocks everything from coloring books and tattered, third-generation paperbacks to excellent books on Belize.

If you'd rather slum it for bargain prices, walk along King Street between Albert and Canal streets. The narrow stores here are jammed with electronics, sneakers, cosmetics, lingerie and T-shirts.

NIGHTLIFE   Most local bars are seedy joints and not places for tourists. Stick to the hotel bars, such as the Radisson Fort George's **Paddle Lounge** (Marine Parade; 2-77400), where a big-screen television shows the latest American sports.

With its rambling tiled terrace overlooking the sea, **The Lighthouse** (at the Holiday Inn Village Belize, 13 Cork Street; 2-32800) offers romance with its drinks.

Settle into a cane-back chair and watch the big-screen television or gaze at the pool at the **Blue Hole Lounge** (Ramada Royal Reef Hotel, Newtown Barracks; 2-32670).   A stereo plays Punta rock and American tunes.

The **Hard Rock Café** (35 Queen Street; 2-32041) is a pirate of the international chain, despite the ubiquitous T-shirts that claim otherwise. But the third-floor perch is wildly popular with young foreigners.

The Belize Arts Council sponsors concerts and theater and dance performances at the **Bliss Institute** (1 Bliss Promenade; 2-72458). The talent is both national and international.

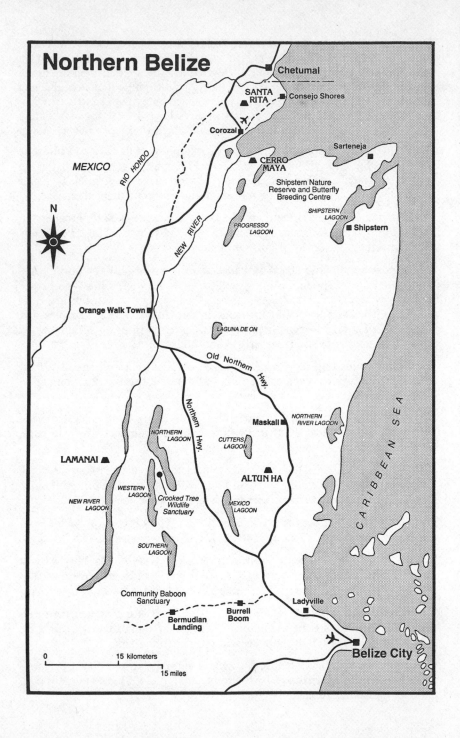

Northern Belize

Chetumal

SANTA RITA

Consejo Shores

Corozal

Sarteneja

MEXICO

RIO HONDO

NEW RIVER

CERRO MAYA

Shipstern Nature Reserve and Butterfly Breeding Centre

SHIPSTERN LAGOON

PROGRESSO LAGOON

Shipstern

N

Orange Walk Town

LAGUNA DE ON

Old Northern Hwy.

CARIBBEAN SEA

Northern Hwy.

NORTHERN LAGOON

Maskall

NORTHERN RIVER LAGOON

LAMANAI

CUTTERS LAGOON

WESTERN LAGOON

Crooked Tree Wildlife Sanctuary

ALTUN HA

NEW RIVER LAGOON

MEXICO LAGOON

SOUTHERN LAGOON

Community Baboon Sanctuary

Ladyville

Bermudian Landing

Burrell Boom

Belize City

0   15 kilometers

15 miles

EIGHT

Northern Belize

Just three decades ago, northern Belize was a forbidding land choked by dense jungle and mired in swamps, and the only road was a potholed trail that rarely got you from here to there without some calamity. Today, the Northern Highway is fairly smooth and lined with small villages, fields of shaggy sugar cane, and ponds populated by wood storks and egrets. Of course, the jungle retains its hold—thanks to conservation efforts by Belizeans—and "highway" traffic is just as likely to be a sprinting Jesus Christ lizard as a car.

From Belize City, the Northern Highway wends 100 miles to the Yucatán border, past several modern-day villages and two magnificent and mysterious ancient cities that are testaments to Maya greatness, Altun Ha and Lamanai, as well as endless remnants of stone houses and walls. Traveling this northern corridor, you are constantly reminded of the ancient Maya civilization, whether it's the house mounds at one's jungle lodge or the 1000-year-old well near a swimming hole.

LADYVILLE TO CROOKED TREE

The first town north of Belize City is neither ancient nor mysterious. Rather, **Ladyville** is best known as the site of Belize's **Phillip S.W. Goldson International Airport**. It's pintsized, as international airports go, but locals love to hang out on the receiving deck and watch the 747s come booming in. Just south of the airport on the Northern Highway, and one of the first sites visitors see in Belize, stands a steel monument depicting five Belizeans, each representing one of the country's five major ethnic groups—Creole, Garifuna, *Mestizo*, Mopan Maya and Kekchi Maya. North of the airport is "downtown" Ladyville: a gas station, tumble-down schoolhouse, several no-name bars and usually dozens of children playing along the street.

LODGING   If you need a room near the international airport, the place to stay is the **Belize Biltmore Plaza** (Mile 3, Northern Highway; air conditioning; very expensive; 2-32302, fax: 2-32301). Opened in 1991, the low-slung, coral-washed buildings encase a lush courtyard of traveler's palms and oleanders, a swimming pool and pond. The lobby is done in British colonial style, with white-paned glass, white wicker and attendants in pith helmets. Each of the 90 rooms opens onto the courtyard and gives the feeling of a spacious motel with contemporary comforts such as bathtubs (unusual in Belize), cable television and telephones. Popular with business travelers, who enjoy the hotel's clubby bar and semi-formal restaurant.

Just around the corner from the airport but worlds away in ambience, the **Belize River Lodge** (Northern Highway, Ladyville; very expensive; 25-2002, fax: 2-2298) offers total escapism. Here, tucked along a flourishing riverbank, with stands of coconut palms and banana plants and carpets of green lawn running down to the river, are several clapboard cottages whose mahogany walls harbor decades of fish tales. The lodge is indeed reputed among anglers, who return each year to stalk the giant tarpon that seethe, piranha-like, in the river. For those who prefer flats or reef fishing, Belizean owners Marguerite Miles and Mike Heusner have an ample fleet of skiffs and topnotch guides to take you just about anywhere. They also offer six- and seven-night fishing "cruises" aboard their larger cruisers. Those who stay at the lodge will find cozy, all-wood cottages with eclectic touches such as driftwood lamps, brown patchwork quilts and comfortingly worn books lining the shelves. Minimum stay is six nights, and includes family-style meals and guide for five days, with only two anglers per guide—the best way to fish.

RESTAURANTS   Rich maroon carpets, sheer lacy drapes and mahogany tables and chairs give the **Victorian Room** (in the Belize Biltmore Plaza, Mile 3, Northern Highway; expensive; 2-32302) a slightly formal air. For many travelers, it's a welcome change from the wear-your-flip-flops funkiness of most Belize eateries. Plus, the extensive menu satisfies both the domestic and international palate. For soups, there's onion gratinée, goulash or fisherman's soup; for salads, a tossed caesar or Belizean potato. Entrées include everything from spaghetti bolognaise and filet mignon to grouper with artichokes and stew chicken with beans and rice.

NIGHTLIFE   Your best bet is an after-dinner drink at the American-style **Squire's Lounge** (at the Belize Biltmore Plaza, Mile 3, Northern Highway; 2-32302). It's dark and cozy, with entertainment ranging from local balladeers and Caribbean artists to karaoke parties.

GETTING THERE: If you've just arrived at the International Airport, it's easy to rent a car inside the terminal. If you're coming from Belize City, you can take a Batty Brothers or Venus bus, which have frequent daily service. Taxis can also be chartered but are expensive, about US$15 one-way from Belize City.

CROOKED TREE

From Ladyville, the patchwork asphalt called the Northern Highway launches into wide open savannah and low-lying mangrove forests, with occasional pit stops like the cinderblock Chillville Lodge, announcing "cool A/C and

TV," but looking unlike like any place one would stop lest she were positively down on her luck, or had imbibed an unconscionable amount of Belizean rum.

After several miles comes the turnoff for the village of **Burrell Boom**, which will take you nine miles down a dusty, rocky trail into forests of pine-oak and cohune and swamp, until you arrive in **Bermudian Landing**. The Landing and surrounding villages were originally settled by Maya, who left their calling cards in the form of house mounds, which still pepper the wooded landscape, and in the Maya people—many direct descendants—who live and farm here. It was formerly called Butchers Landing because local cattle were brought here to be slaughtered before heading downriver to Belize City markets. Several decades ago, it was renamed for the band of Bermudian buccaneers who settled on this high bank in the 1600s.

It was the logging industry that shaped the area, starting in 1650 and continuing for some three hundred years. Villages testify to those logging days with their whimsical names of "boom," "landing," "bank," "walk" and "pen." Loggers first settling an area called it a landing or bank (for riverbank); once established, they would stretch a boom, or heavy iron chain, across the river to trap floating logs. They might also plant fields of crops where you could "walk," or raise cattle in pens. Today, you'll find villages such as Flowers Bank (formerly Flowers Walk), Lime Walk, May Pen and Isabella Bank. There's also Scotland Half-Moon, named for its Scottish settlers, and Ben Bow Creek, the namesake of one pirate Admiral Ben Bow, who supposedly spent several rum-crazed nights in these wilds.

Bermudian Landing may seem just as wild to visitors today. Few people own cars and fewer have telephones, but most any teenager can tell you the jungle cure for stomachache, and even small children know the difference between a good snake and a bad one. A sign here proclaims that the area has just received "24 Hours Electricity." No doubt it propels the fans that whir inside the little museum at the **Community Baboon Sanctuary** (admission), where there are absorbing exhibits on the endangered black howler monkeys, which in Belize are also known as baboons. Black howlers are found only in Belize, southern Mexico, the Yucatán and northern Guatemala, and are rarely spotted in great numbers.

Little was known about the howlers in 1980 when Dr. Robert Horwich, a Wisconsin primatologist, watched a documentary titled *Amate—The Fig Tree*. It was made by well-known filmmaker Richard Foster, who lives in Belize and who had captured footage of an endearing troop of howlers living in a fig tree near Bermudian Landing. Horwich immediately flew to Belize and began research on the howlers. What he found was not only a healthy population of the monkeys, but a group of villagers willing to protect them.

In 1985, at a small gathering in a tiny clapboard house, the villagers of Bermudian Landing and surrounding areas formally opened their Community Baboon Sanctuary. The event not only secured the future of the howlers, it began

Howler monkeys

what was perhaps the world's first grassroots sanctuary, where residents—not the government or some conservation organization—rallied to save the wildlife in their own jungle backyards.

Eleven villagers first signed a pledge to change their farming methods in a three-square-mile area. Their mission was to protect vegetation along the Belize River banks, various corridors of trees, and other areas where the howlers thrive. For the villagers—most of whom were surviving at poverty level—it meant using even less land to grow their crops; hence, less food for their families.

Over the years, the hardships have pulled the villagers together, and today 125 farmers and ranchers are members of the sanctuary, which, in turn, has blossomed to 20 square miles. Former howler and jaguar hunters now serve as sanctuary guides, and local families earn small fees by hosting visitors in their homes. Studies by sanctuary manager Camille Young show that about 90 percent of the villagers have kept their promise to protect the vegetation. Perhaps the most convincing evidence of success, however, is that while there were 500 howlers here in 1985, today there are more than 1400.

Which means that visitors to the Community Baboon Sanctuary will most certainly see a howler, even a whole family of howlers, who are instantly appealing with their cherub-like faces, beseeching eyes and tiny hands and feet. Their narrow throats magnify their thunderous roars—often mistaken for jaguar screams—so they can be heard more than a mile away.

To find the howlers, you will, of course, need a guide, and a museum attendant will be happy to fetch you one from "downtown" Bermudian Landing. Local guides are infinitely versed on the native flora, pointing out the spiny bamboo, red ginger, bromeliads and guanacaste trees that line the three-and-a-half miles of trails and the Belize River, which flows through the sanctuary.

Spiny bamboo, one learns, protects the riverbanks from erosion, and red ginger is called forest "Visine" because its juice takes the red out of irritated eyes. The petals of the bromeliads can store up to two gallons of water and provide a home for 12 species of insects, while the trunk of the guanacaste tree was used by the Maya to make dugout canoes. The acid-like sap of the poisonwood tree is so poisonous it burns its own trunk. The stately kapok tree—the rainforest's tallest—towers more than 200 feet, but alas, all its limbs cling to its crown. Here, also, are many mapola trees, whose canopies are loved by howler monkeys. On most days, you'll spot families of monkeys scurrying through the treetops. The babies are not much bigger than your hand.

The monkeys are just some of the thousands of jungle residents you're apt to see. Foot-wide butterflies dance in and out of forest shadows and red-eyed tree frogs emit flashes of color. Iguanas sun on splintered logs poking out across the river, and leafcutter ants parade across the jungle floor, hoisting freshly cut leaves in their own antish, Herculean style. My guide and I even encountered a boa constrictor, all seven feet of him, stretched across the footpath.

If you'd rather explore the sanctuary on horseback or by canoe, guided excursions are available. Fishing guides are also available for those who'd like to try for tarpon, snapper or catfish in the Belize River—though it's strictly catch and release. To make tour arrangements, call sanctuary manager Camille Young at 2-44405.

Back on the Northern Highway, about 19 paved miles north and four miles west down a white marl road, lies a sanctuary for birds. The centerpiece of the 3000-acre **Crooked Tree Wildlife Sanctuary** (admission) is the vast Northern Lagoon, whose shallow waters are perennially darkened by flocks of fantastic birds. Birdwatchers and birders (there *is* a difference, the former being a more casual observer) also flock to this place, setting up their telescopes and cameras along the shores, scouting out such unusual creatures as purple gallinules and ruddy crakes, social flycatchers and lesser yellowlegs, olive-throated parakeets and white-collared seedeaters. Most species have funny local names; the spot-breasted wren, for instance, has been creolized to "katy-yu-baby-di-cry," no doubt because a man claimed its song mimics the voice of a certain woman.

The unusual creature most people come to see is the jabiru stork. The Western Hemisphere's largest flying bird, it is formidable and fascinating, boasting a 12-foot wing span. Arrive during the dry season (October through February is the very best time), when the storks and thousands of other birds, including peregrine falcons and boat-billed herons, create a flurry of activity.

It is usually easy to get close-up views of the birds from the paths that wend along the Northern Lagoon, as well as from the Western Lagoon, located on the opposite side of Crooked Tree Village. Along the paths are many anhinghas, who dive underwater to snag fish, then emerge to dry their water-gorged wings on a tree branch. Locals rent boats and offer guided boat trips, but they're expensive (up to US$80), and the scenery is much the same. When the rainy season starts, the sanctuary floods and many birds leave. Before you visit, call the **Belize Audubon Society** (2-77369 in Belize City) to check current conditions.

Once at the sanctuary, stop by the **visitor's center** and pick up a map and list of birds. The warden there can also provide other information or arrange for a local guide, and can tell you about **Crooked Tree Village,** home to 700 people and seemingly just as many pigs, chickens and skinny dogs. Half a dozen dirt roads wind through the village, past Jones Bar, Alice Store, the town telephone, and the town generator that gets turned off at midnight (it used to shut down earlier, but local barflies complained).

If you have some time, take one of the horse and buggy rides (ask at the visitor's center) offered by several local farmers. Ask them to point out all the mango and cashew trees the village is known for. Every May, at the Crooked Tree Cashew Festival, locals go all out with nonstop parties, including Caribbean folktelling and outdoor theater. Attending visitors are invited on nature walks, river trips and tours of the nearby Maya ruins.

ALTUN HA   Just south of Crooked Tree Village and the sanctuary is a fork where the Northern Highway meets the **Old Northern Highway.** Formerly *the* highway in northern Belize, this sliver of lonesome, well-worn pavement bumps and turns for 40 miles past cohune palms, thick bush and a scattering of clapboard houses. It is so narrow, a taxi driver points out, that when he meets a car, "we play chicken."

The road is the reason **Altun Ha** (Old Northern Highway, 31 miles north of Belize City; admission) was discovered. In 1957, quarriers looking for stone to build the road selected some 2000-year-old specimens at this Maya site.

As they dug, they uncovered more than just rock mounds. There were 13 structures surrounding two plazas, including one 60-foot temple now called **Temple of the Sun God**. Several years later, as archaeologists did their own digging at the temple, they made a thrilling find: the head of Kinich Ahau, the sun god, carved around 600 A.D. from a single piece of jade. The largest carved jade artifact ever discovered on the Maya Route, it weighs nearly ten pounds and is masterfully sculpted. (Unfortunately, you won't be able to look upon its hideous countenance—fanged tongue, crossed eyes and cauliflower ears—as Kinich Ahau now resides in a Belize bank vault.)

What made the jade head even more spectacular was that it was located next to the remains of a priest. The holy man had been laid atop a wooden platform, adorned with jaguar and puma skins and necklaces of oyster and jade, and buried in a small pyramid. Rarely did the Maya bury their dead in temples, so what was the significance? The excavation team, led by Canadian archaeologist David Pendergast, never reached a conclusion. What they did find, however, were six more priests entombed in the temple—an exhilarating discovery in the first full-scale excavation in Belize. Several of the crypts had been defiled by fire, soil or broken roof slabs. The desecrators were not modern-day looters but early Maya, an indication, Pendergast wrote, that the society may have collapsed at the hands of revolting peasants.

A Classical city that reaches out for one-and-a-half miles, Altun Ha was a link in the Caribbean trade route that ran north through the Yucatán. It was a town and minor ceremonial center, lacking any stelae, yet Pendergast found remnants of jade and copal tree resin obviously used in rituals—a practice rare among the Maya. Many of the fragments were found on the round altar atop the Sun God temple, known as **building B-4** in **Plaza B**, including exquisitely carved pendants that had been shattered and cast into a blazing fire. Pendergast believes that this altar held some unique significance, noting that "the bits of jade, resin and charcoal were scattered over the floor around the altar, and left as some sort of fossilized ceremony, to be discovered some 1300 years later."

Like many Maya structures, the Temple of the Sun God was constantly being improved on; Pendergast noted eight separate construction periods. And while it was obviously the premier building, Altun Ha boasts five additional temples, surrounding **Plaza A**. Four are dedicated to the forces of nature—the sun, rain, wind and moon—while the fifth, the **Temple of the Green Tomb**, held human remains and hundreds of pieces of jade jewelry, some quite elaborate.

Away from the plazas, a quarter-mile trail through the jungle leads to a misty, lime-colored reservoir. Called **Rockstone Pond**, the clay-lined, spring-fed basin was enlarged by the Maya, as evidenced by the sharp stone blocks—probably digging tools—found around the shoreline. At the south end, they built a dam of stone and clay to keep the water from seeping into surrounding swamps. The reservoir is surrounded by house mounds, the remains of waterfront residences.

Standing at the lip of the pond, watching the parrots skip through the trees, listening to the *hoot-hoot* call of blue-crowned motmots, spying the tail of a fleeing opossum, it is impossible not to wonder if the occupants of those houses saw and heard these same creatures, felt the same steamy haze before an afternoon rain, inhaled the skunky smell of the forest floor. After all, more than 1000 years have passed, but the jungle has remained virtually unchanged.

And therein lies Altun Ha's added appeal. Though it is one of Belize's most popular Maya sites—it is close to Belize City and easy to find—Altun Ha still belongs to the rainforest. Except for the occasional mid-morning and mid-afternoon tour buses, there are no crowds—only mosquitoes, whose swarms will blacken your skin and attack your body in the most troublesome places. Coat yourself in repellent, then sightsee at leisure, exploring the ceremonial structures and house mounds sprinkled around the lush jungle clearing.

LODGING AND RESTAURANTS   Birders know **Chaux Hiix Lodge** (ceiling fans; very expensive; for reservations, call 800-765-2611 in the United States, fax: 2-77891 in Belize City) as one of the choicest spots for catching a glimpse of Belize's unusual winged creatures. Of course, it doesn't hurt that the lodge is wonderfully remote, located downriver from the Crooked Tree Wildlife Sanctuary and upriver from the Community Baboon Sanctuary. Just getting to Chaux Hiix usually involves animal encounters, as guests travel 45 minutes by boat down jungle-lined Spanish Creek from the outpost of Lemonal. Four

Red-eyed tree frogs

rooms in two duplex cabanas aren't fancy, but they are comfortable enough, offering hot showers and screened jalousie windows. The lodge is enveloped by 4000 acres of jungle and low pine ridge, but more importantly, it borders the ancient Maya town of Chaux Hiix, where archaeologists in late 1993 were still uncovering fascinating clues to its existence, including structures dating all the way from 1500 B.C. to 1500 A.D. There is so much yet uncovered that workers attempting to dig outhouse trenches kept finding layers of relics, including Maya satellites. Tours of the ruins, as well as guided nature tours and fishing excursions, canoeing and horseback riding, meals and snacks, and transportation from Belize City are included in the rate. Because getting there is so time consuming, a three-night stay is required.

In the village of Crooked Tree, three rustic lodges open their doors to visitors. All are extremely basic, so expect to rough it:

On the rim of Northern Lagoon, facing a dirt beach and a wobbly pier, **Crooked Tree Resort** (moderate; 2-77745, fax: 2-31734) features ten round bamboo cabanas peaked with thatch roofs and shaded by bullet trees. Furnishings are simple but clean, with well-swept mahogany floors, pine walls and private baths. There's a small restaurant serving home cooking, and the village bar is spitting distance—not a good situation if there's a party going on. Two birdwatchers I met stayed awake several nights, listening to the *boom-boom-boom* of a band that played till dawn. Translation: Before you book a room, ask if there are any special events scheduled at the bar.

The five cabanas at **Paradise Inn** (fans; moderate; 25-2535, fax: 25-2534) look remarkably like the ones at Crooked Tree Resort, located just south along Northern Lagoon. All face the water and catch a perpetual breeze, which is good considering the fans cut off at midnight when the town generator shuts down. Belizean specialties, including local fish plied with cashews from village trees, are served in the budget-priced restaurant here.

On the opposite side of the village, set along a picturesque shore of a lagoon, **Birds Eye View Lodge** (ceiling fans; moderate; for reservations, call S&L Travel in Belize City at 2-75145, fax: 2-77594) is a drab yellow cinderblock building whose two rooms are surprisingly attractive and comfortable. Belizean tile covers the floors and hot water emanates from the private bath. The dining room is the fanciest in Crooked Tree.

A soothing body massage, given in the warm, damp embrace of the jungle, is just one reason to stay at the secluded ☉ **Maruba Resort & Jungle Spa** (on the Old Northern Highway in Maskall Village, 40 miles north of Belize City; very expensive; 3-22199, or 713-799-2031 in Texas). There are many others, such as the peaceful, luscious grounds with pineapple orchard, coconut-lined paths and myriads of hummingbirds. Or the big jacuzzi, swirling under the cashew trees, and the swimming pool where water gushes from rocks. The 15 rooms are all different, from the chapel room with stave doors and bottle wall to the spacious jungle penthouse with sensuous wood art. But the resort specialties are massages, seaweed body wraps and other blissful body treatments, given by Chicagoan Franziska Nicholson, whose Trinidadian family owns the resort. There are no restaurants nearby, but delicious meals are provided by the resort. Don't be surprised if a monkey joins you for breakfast.

GETTING THERE: It's easy to drive to Crooked Tree Wildlife Sanctuary and Altun Ha. However, while Crooked Tree has plenty of available guides, Altun Ha has none. If you'd like a tour of Altun Ha, you'll have to hire a guide to take you there. Any area lodge, as well as the Crooked Tree visitors center, can recommend guides for Altun Ha.

ORANGE WALK TOWN AND LAMANAI

The modern-day hub of northern Belize lies 37 miles north of Altun Ha along the Old Northern Highway. You'll know you're getting close to **Orange Walk Town** when you see the old trucks stuffed with cut sugar cane, and notice a sweet molasses smell in the air. Sugar cane is the number-one business in this working town, one of Belize's biggest. Home to about 11,000 people, Orange Walk was originally a logging outpost that became a refuge for *Mestizos* fleeing the Caste War in nearby Yucatán. Mexican influence is evident everywhere, from the tortilla bakeries and Wild West-style storefronts to the weathered mission churches. Notice how at one house of worship, **La Immaculada** (3 Church Street; 3-2038), a strangler fig is attempting to conquer the bell tower.

Over the past few decades, Orange Walk has attracted a rich ethnic mix that includes Chinese, Hindu Indians, Maya and Mennonites. The latter, dressed in tattered straw hats and baggy overalls cinched with twine, ride into town in horse-drawn buggies to trade crops for sugar or supplies. There isn't much in downtown to attract a traveler, considering it's mainly tired cinderblock buildings, ice factories and a string of churches. In fact, the number-one reason most people come to Orange Walk is Lamanai.

The Maya would no doubt be pleased with the present-day way to arrive at **Lamanai**: a two-hour, backwater boat trip. After all, Lamanai means "submerged crocodile," a name befitting a city sprawled on the jowls of a gorged lagoon. The trip starts near Orange Walk, on the New River, which winds southward past an old rum factory, slash-and-burn farms, and Mennonite villages.

Along the way, women wash their clothes in the clear warmth of the water, and long-nose bats sleep in hollow tree trunks above the river. Long-legged jacana birds, flaunting fluorescent green wings and neon yellow beaks, trot across colossal lily pads, and fields of emerald sea grass wave beneath the water's surface. Shy boat-billed herons hide along the riverbanks, and snail kites whisk through the sky.

It would be enough just to witness the surreality of the river, but what awaits afterward is even more riveting. Here, where the river yawns into a wide lagoon, several thatched buildings gather at the water's edge. At their flanks is a once-grand city that still presides over this part of the jungle—an ancient Manhattan, some 720 buildings spread across 950 acres, obscured in a mantle of massive trees and greedy vines. Leaf and rubble paths curl between Lamanai's buildings, many of which tower above the jungle canopy and form a mystical maze. The rattling purrs of unseen cicada insects flood the forest, and the panicked squawk of a brown jay—the jungle siren—warns of impeding danger.

The waterfront thatched buildings are left over from the days of Canadian archaeologist David Pendergast, who excavated the area during the 1970s and 1980s. While Pendergast's teams resurrected buildings, they also sought clues to the lifestyles of Lamanai's former inhabitants. They took samples of lagoon sediment, for instance, which revealed good levels of pollen and suggested the Maya were growing corn as early as 1500 B.C. And they combed the primeval rot of Lamanai's garbage dumps, only to find that these ancient Manhattanites fancied deer and turtle.

Pendergast also brought some modern-day gentility to the jungle setting, for when *Equinox* writer Ronald Wright dined with him in the late 1980s, he recalls that their meal "was followed by cookies and tea, and it would have been hard to imagine oneself in the heart of Belize were it not for the tarantula that (one of the archaeology students) discovered in the teapot."

Today, Maya caretakers live in the thatched village, and excavations and restorations continue on several of the ancient buildings. Wandering around the hulking stone structures, it is difficult to believe that this great ceremonial center was begun around 1500 B.C. Even more astounding, it was still inhabited in the 19th century, making it one of the longest occupied Maya sites.

In 1860, the British Honduras Company Ltd. showed up on Lamanai's shores with dreams of building a sugar factory. It did indeed construct a mill and import laborers from Jamaica, Barbados and China, but the workers were not trained in making sugar and the mill was too primitive for the task. In 1875, sugar making became history at Lamanai, though the brief attempt is remembered today in the ruins of the old mill, including a flywheel and boiler, lo-cated south of the city center.

Two hundred years earlier, the Spanish had come to Lamanai and, eager to force their religion on the Maya, built a Christian church. The Maya were not so eager to convert and destroyed most of the building. Missionaries soon arrived and put up a second, more stylish church, but the Maya were not im-pressed. This, too, they tried to demolish, through more of it survived. Rem-nants of both missions can be seen today north of Lamanai's center.

Far greater than those houses of worship are the Maya ceremonial structures. The one known as **Lag**, or **structure N10-43**, rises to 112 feet and was the tallest in the Maya civilization when it was created in 100 B.C. Today, it is the largest Preclassic building on the Maya Route. A sturdy flight of stairs runs up the front, depositing visitors on a platform that looks across the pastoral Maya lowlands and slow, snaking New River. It is on this platform that the Maya likely performed complex religious ceremonies. Among the more bizarre, men pierced their penises with stingray spines and women dragged strings of thorns across their tongues. Prisoners of war were typically beheaded, though noble ones received special treatment: their hearts were torn out while still alive.

Lag faces a good-sized **ball court**, where Maya athletes played *pok-ta-pok*, a basketball-style sport using a small rubber ball. In the center of the court Pendergast found a massive stone disc; under the disc, he made one of his most thrilling discoveries: a pool of liquid mercury, the first ever uncovered at a Maya site. The mercury was among several pottery vessels containing jade and shell objects that were no doubt part of a special offering.

The offerings made at **structure N10-7**, south of the ball court, seem to have included children. Here, behind a remarkably detailed stone stelae of a Maya ruler, Pendergast found the bones of six children. Why the people of Lamanai would sacrifice their own children remains a mystery, since human sacrifice was not customary among the Maya. Across the plaza stands the **Jaguar Temple (structure N10-9)**, built in the 6th century and embellished with stairs in the 8th and 13th centuries. Among the finds here: a giant red and black bowl, a jade mask and a pair of Early Classic jade earrings.

North of here, the 60-foot-tall **Mask-Decorated Temple**, or **structure N9-56**, rises hauntingly along the New River Lagoon. It is wildly adorned with stone masks, though the eye is instantly drawn to one particular visage—the 12-foot-tall face of a man, his nose fat and flattened, his eyes heavily lidded and slitted like a jaguar's, his features markedly Oriental. The temple's ar-chitecture reveals four separate construction phases, beginning in 200 B.C. and ending, incredibly, some 1500 years later.

There are numerous other masks and stelae, and buildings containing flint and pottery, at Lamanai. In fact, it takes at least four hours to explore the two-square-mile city center—with a guide, of course. But don't count on find-ing any at Lamanai; it's best to hire a guide a day before you plan to visit.

LODGING   Few travelers have the need (or desire) to stay in Orange Walk Town, but if you find yourself stuck for the night, check into **Hotel Barons** (40 Belize-Corozal Road; some rooms with ceiling fans, some with air conditioning; budget to moderate; 3-22518). The downtown hostelry looks a little weary, but has basic rooms that are fairly clean and come with battered furniture, assorted tile designs and plenty of street noise. For a little more, you get cable television, telephone and air conditioning that not only keeps you cool but drowns out that pesky street noise.

RESTAURANTS   Of the many Chinese restaurants in Orange Walk, **Lee's** (11 San Antonio Road; budget to moderate; 3-22174) stands out. The interior is cool, clean and modern, if not utilitarian, and the portions generous and tasty. Besides the traditional sweet and sours, chop sueys and chow meins, there's baked fish and grilled pork chops.

GETTING THERE: Orange Walk is easily accessible by car or by taking a Batty Brothers or Venus bus from Belize City. Lamanai, however, is best reached with a guide.

Boats leave from various points around Orange Walk Town for the four-hour round-trip ride to the ruins. One of the more popular launch spots is **Jim's Cool Pool**, at the Northern Highway toll bridge south of Orange Walk. Brothers Joel and Anthony Armstrong, who live with their families and flea-bitten dogs in an old yellow school bus along the river, will usually take you to Lamanai in their motorboat. An excellent Lamanai tour is offered by the owners of **Maruba Resort** (Old Northern Highway; 3-22199), who provide a gourmet picnic lunch atop one of the pyramids. Or try **Maya World Safaris** (2-31063 in Belize City, fax: 2-30263), which offers excursions aboard the *Lamanai Lady* riverboat.

During the dry season (November through February), it is possible to drive to Lamanai from Orange Walk down a rocky, rutted path that looks a lot like a road. It's 36 miles one way, but the jarring trip takes about two hours. Before you strike out on your own, check road conditions and get directions from a local hotel or travel agency. **Caribbean Holiday and Travel Service** (51 Main Street, Orange Walk Town; 3-22803) is a good place to try.

COROZAL

If you've been awed by the brilliant butterflies weaving around the Belize forests, don't miss the **Shipstern Nature Reserve and Butterfly Breeding Centre** (about an hour's drive north from Orange Walk). Here, on a sunny day, butterflies are so thick they appear a constant whirlwind of color (they hide in the foliage on cloudy days). More than 200 species reside within a mesh enclosure that resembles a mini-forest. Visitors can wander through, learning about the butterflies' breeding cycles and extensive research being done here. Of course, many more creatures reside within this 22,000-acre reserve, which is unique in Belize because it takes in both hardwood and mangrove and swamp, or bajo, forests. Wading birds find the miles of salt lagoons and mangrove marshes safe places to raise their young, and white-tailed deer, brocket deer and tapir take shelter in the vast hardwood forests. Botanical trails offer peeks at these animals; guides are available at the reserve's visitors center. Tours to the reserve are offered by **Maruba Resort** (Old Northern Highway; 3-22199). Or check with **Tony's Inn** (south end of Corozal; 4-22055).

North of the reserve, the last real town before the Mexico border is **Corozal**. Curving along a pale blue, blustery sea, with a shore saturated in coconut palms, Corozal is scenic and peaceful. The expensive homes sprinkled along the water hint that this is a town with money, albeit mostly foreign money. Wealthy Belizeans do own vacation homes here, but it's the Americans and Europeans who fuel much of the real estate market. Local pride shines through in the picturesque **central park** (1st Street North, one block from the sea) with its pretty fountains and canopies of poinciana trees. Around town, you'll also notice the hand-written signs, tacked to electric poles, that read: "Don't Be Mean. Keep Corozal Clean."

On the outskirts of Corozal, two minor Maya sites offer interesting side trips. It's best to take a boat to **Cerro Maya**, located south of Corozal, near where the New River empties into Corozal Bay. Boats leave from downtown Corozal; or, check at **Tony's Inn** (south end of town; 4-22055). Cerro Maya, meaning "Maya Hill," is spread across more than 50 acres of forest, though the city center—resting on a gentle hill—is easily explored in an hour. Several plazas are surrounded by pyramids, including one that's 72 feet tall. Like these buildings, the ball courts and artifacts here date from 400 B.C. to 100 A.D.

Archaeologists believe **Santa Rita** (off the Northern Highway, just north of Corozal) was the Maya city of Chetumal, located about 35 miles south of today's Chetumal, Mexico. Situated on Corozal Bay, near the New River and Río Hondo river, Santa Rita likely controlled the trade arteries that funneled cacao, honey and vanilla from Belize to the northern Yucatán. The city was discovered around the turn of the century by Thomas Gann, amateur archaeologist and Corozal's town doctor. Gann uncovered fantastic Mixtec-style frescoes, jade jewelry and pottery, though the frescoes have since been destroyed. Today's site will not impress visitors as it did Gann. Only one structure survives: a Classic building, riddled with doorways and connecting rooms, including a main room where burnt offerings were made.

For the eight miles from Corozal to the Mexico border, the Northern Highway yields rural vistas of wide open pastures, scrub forest, and fields swelled with corn, bananas and sugar cane. There are a few eye-blink towns, including the pueblo-like Santa Clara and Santa Elena Concepción, that look more like Mexico than Belize. Mexico officially starts at the bridge spanning the Río Hondo river. The **border crossing** is quick and simple on the Belize side, long and often complicated on the Mexican side, especially if a public bus has just disgorged its riders. American citizens, who need a passport, will be issued a Mexican tourist card. The card will be reclaimed by the border officials upon reentering Belize. Most people crossing into Mexico are taking a day trip to **Chetumal,** mainly to shop the crowded, inexpensive markets. Buses are the cheapest way to go, costing about US$1.25 each way. Taxis are extremely expensive; the one-way trip is about $20. One exception is taxi driver **Anibal Orellana** (4-23456 in Corozal), who will take you to Chetumal for about $6.

LODGING   By far the best choice for Corozal lodging is **Tony's Inn** (south end of town; ceiling fans, some rooms with air conditioning; moderate to expensive; 4-22055), which feels like an upscale motor court. The crisp white, two-story buildings enjoy a breezy seaside locale, complete with outdoor palapa bar and precious patch of white beach. The rooms are big and modern, with tile floors. Some even come with satellite television.

If you're short on cash, check out the **Hotel Maya** (south end of Corozal; budget; 4-22082), situated across from the sea. The 17 rooms are very clean, but the dressers are beat up and the draperies look like sheets. The owners are a friendly local family.

Tucked on a finger of sandy, windy beach that juts out to sea, ✪ **Adventure Inn** (seven miles north of Corozal, Consejo Shores; ceiling fans, some air conditioning; moderate; 4-22187) looks like a castaway's hideout. The 21 stilt cabanas are basic island digs, with hardwood floors, white-stucco walls and waves splashing near the front doors. Several have outdoor showers. At the price, this is a splendid lodging choice.

RESTAURANTS   The fare is not spectacular, but **Tony's Inn** (south end of town; moderate to expensive; 4-22055) easily wins as Corozal's top restaurant. Choose from a variety of seafood dishes, baked, broiled or fried, as well as pork chops, fried chicken, and rice and beans. Linens cover the tables, and jalousie windows funnel in sea breezes. Breakfast and lunch are also available.

With only four tables, the **Hotel Maya** (south end of Corozal; moderate; 4-22082) feels like someone's private dining room. In a way it is, since it belongs to a family who prepares homestyle meals for a loyal local following. The menu changes depending on what's fresh each day, but entrées might include fried chicken or T-bone steaks. Breakfast features omelettes and eggs with refried beans.

It's out in the middle of nowhere, but worth a drive to **Adventure Inn** (seven miles north of Corozal, Consejo Shores; moderate; 4-22187) to soak up the time-forgotten island atmosphere. The floor is concrete and the bar U-shaped, while the patrons look like they sat down several years ago and never left. Grilled fish with garlic butter, seafood kebabs, beef tenderloin and liver pâté are a few specialties of the creative chef. Breakfasts are extra special.

NIGHTLIFE   The potential for next-morning stories is considerable at the seafront bar at **Adventure Inn** (seven miles north of Corozal, Consejo Shores; 4-22187), a local watering hole full of character and characters.

GETTING THERE: Batty Brothers and Venus buses service this northern area regularly from Belize City, although Corozal and most other points are easy to reach if you have a car.

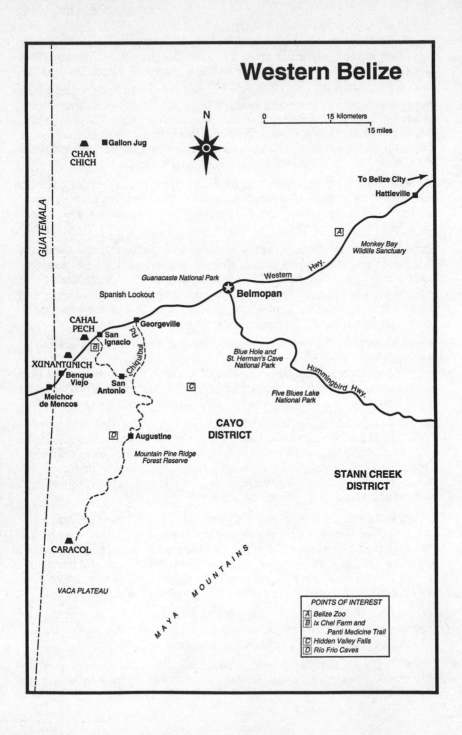

NINE

Western Belize

While the Belize cayes offer visitors a window to the world at sea, barely an hour away, western Belize opens onto a world of luscious jungle, forest-clad mountains and mighty temples shrouded in mystery. The gateway to this world is the Western Highway, which runs 82 paved miles from Belize City to the Guatemala border. Heading west from the city, the landscape is at once lonely and rugged, with scrub palmetto, mangrove swamps, and a few clapboard homes on stilts. Then mountains are slowly etched on the horizon, jagged summits with intense green forest cascading down their slopes.

This western route is measured in mile posts; you'll begin noticing the concrete posts with white signs and black numbers as you leave Belize City. You'll also notice the weedy cemetery, whose sunbaked, bone-white, above-ground tombs bid goodbye as you head west.

Western Belize is a land of country cottages, ranches and jungle lodges that seem etched into the earth. Many lie more than an hour from the paved road, down winding, rocky trails that look down the sides of hills. Most have not progressed to electricity (kerosene lamps light up the night), but accommodations are usually quite comfortable. Best of all, the nature encounters and cultural experiences are unmatched.

BELIZE ZOO AND MONKEY BAY

The first village is not for 16 miles, and it wasn't even meant to be a village. After Hurricane Hattie nearly blew away Belize City in 1961, survivors fled inland and set up a temporary camp that was, naturally, called **Hattieville**. Belize City was eventually rebuilt, and the capital of Belmopan opened to the west, but many people preferred to stay in their new clapboard homes dotting the scrub palmetto. Today, the homes don't look so new, but the 1179 residents of Hattieville enjoy their status as suburbanites.

Around Mile Post 29, you'll see a small sign for the **Belize Zoo** (admission). A wonderful introduction to Belize's wildlife, the zoo is home to Rambo the toucan, Balboa the boa constrictor, Pete the jaguar, Sarge the crocodile, and many other rare and colorful creatures. It seems inaccurate to call it a zoo, since the more than 100 species of animals do not occupy cages. Instead, they dwell in patches of forest veiled in wire mesh. Their spaces are so big and private that, if an animal is so inclined, he or she can hide from visitors, reiterating that this is *their* world.

Gravel paths wend through thick stands of slash pine trees dripping with moss and bromeliads, past a preening curassow, a fanged crocodile snoozing in the mud, a statue-still jaguar hunching beneath a palm frond, locking his eyes onto yours. His are not the beaten-down eyes of a zoo animal, but of a retired king come to rest in a comfortable home. Signs sprinkled among the enclosures plead for the animals' autonomy: "I'm a great black hawk, but guys who take shots at me are Great Big Turkeys," says the sign where a black hawk lives. And at the spider monkey home: "Listen! We make bad pets! We would much rather spend time with other monkeys than with human primates!"

The clever signs are the work of Sharon Matola, an American biologist who founded the zoo in 1983 after several animals were abandoned by a wildlife filmmaker. Since then, the zoo has gone from a funky little place with a few pens to one of Belize's shining ecotourism stars. In 1991, when a bigger and better Belize Zoo opened next to the old one, *National Geographic* filmed the animals moving into their new homes for a television special on animal caretakers. Included in the documentary were accomplished zoo curator, Belizean Tony Garel, and a staff of more than 20 villagers, some of whom were former wildlife poachers.

Many animals are born at the zoo, but those who aren't come from other zoos or from people who donate wild pets. Poachers are told to take their quarry elsewhere. In fact, Matola preaches her no-poachers policy on Belize radio and television, and few come around. Who does come around, almost every day of the year, are Belizean schoolchildren. The children of Belize may not know about Mickey Mouse, but thanks to an active field trip program, they're well acquainted with April the tapir, which is Belize's national animal. Back in the early zoo days, Matola constantly pestered schools to offer field trips. She would hop on her Kawasaki 650, with a boa constrictor and slide show in tow, and visit classrooms in rural areas.

While Matola is known around Belize as an animal rights radical, she has also been elevated to folk hero, a Belizean version of Dian Fossey (portrayed in *Gorillas in the Mist*). The former Florida lion tamer, Mexican circus showgirl and Central American fungi specialist has received publicity from *Sports Illustrated*, *National Geographic* and numerous other magazines.

Today, Matola lives about a mile from the zoo in a thatched bungalow where, in the predawn hours of the jungle, she writes children's books. Her latest title, *I Live In An American Forest*, features an accompanying soundtrack of animal voices. During her early mornings, the former showgirl also pumps iron in a screened, thatched-roof gymnasium she built single-handedly. Working out keeps her in shape for the expeditions she leads across Belizean mountains and through the jungles. In summer of 1992, she led the first all-woman expedition to the top of Victoria Peak, Belize's highest at 3675 feet. A few months earlier, she was the only woman on a grueling ten-day hike across the Maya Mountains divide. The expedition included British military troops who acquired jungle training and researchers who learned about Maya history at numerous ruins along the way.

Some of Matola's hiking terrain lies just two miles west at the 1070-acre **Monkey Bay Wildlife Sanctuary** (Mile Post 31, Western Highway; 8-23180, fax: 8-23235). Here, in a privately owned reserve that welcomes visitors, slash pine, scrub palmetto and supine savanna stretch for miles against a hazy backdrop of jagged foothills. There are no monkeys (the park is named for its founders, Monkey Bay Wildlife Sanctuary Tokyo), but there are many species of birds to be found, as well as peccaries. A picturesque beach on the Sibun (pronounced Si-BOON) River is ideal for daytrippers who don't mind hiking 45 minutes from the sanctuary entrance. There are many other solitary trails waiting for hikers; ask for directions at the wood stilt house near the entrance. The house is a loosely run place that is more or less the sanctuary headquarters and home to various wayfarers getting to know Belize. It's also home to American Matt Miller, who runs Monkey Bay, organizing visits from numerous United States student groups each year.

Another mile west, looking like nothing much but being one of Belize's most famous stopovers, is **J.B.'s** (Mile Post 32, Western Highway). The open-air cabana bar and infamous watering hole has been the stomping grounds of many a British soldier, Belizean politician and imported movie star (Harrison Ford hung out here during the filming of *Mosquito Coast*), having begun its illustrious career in the late 1970s at the hands of an American expatriate who everyone knew simply as "J.B." Reputed around town as either a flamboyant, highly entertaining character or a hard-drinking scoundrel, depending on who you talk to, J.B. brought the bar to great fame with his sardonic stories, late-night rock 'n roll parties and endless supply of rum and ice cubes (the latter

Collared peccary

being a luxury around these parts). Alas, J.B. picked up and left one day—some say he got all the way to Canada—but only after selling out to two teen-age waifs. The girls are there today wiping tables and playing video games, looking like they're waiting on their parents, but actually running the place and doing a bang-up business.

LODGING   If you'd literally like to sleep under the stars, bunk down at **Monkey Bay Wildlife Sanctuary** (Mile Post 31, Western Highway; budget; 8-23180, fax: 8-23235). A dozen or so thatched camping platforms are scattered among the scrub savanna, including some with little thatched roofs (but no walls, so pray it doesn't rain) for those who don't bring a tent. Cold showers and meals are available at a main house run by sanctuary director Matt Miller, an American raising his family in Belize. Rates, as you might expect, are rock-bottom.

RESTAURANTS   Near the Belize Zoo and Monkey Bay Wildlife Sanctuary, and the only place to quench your hunger or thirst for miles, is **J.B.'s** (Mile Post 32, Western Highway; budget). A local legend created by a flamboyant American named J.B., it's now run by two expatriate teenagers who can rustle up the Belize basics—burgers, fried chicken and rice and beans—but are best at playing obscure old and new rock 'n roll tapes. British soldiers hang out here, so the scene can get raucous.

GETTING THERE: I highly recommend that you drive a rental car here, but Batty Brothers, Novelos and Z-Line buses also service the area regularly from Belize City.

BELMOPAN

Belmopan became the capital of Belize in 1961, when Hurricane Hattie devastated Belize City, the then-capital. Though the government was moved, residents were slow to follow, preferring to live in Belize City even though they worked in Belmopan. In fact, the town was so desolate at night it was called the "City of Sadness." But Belmopan is slowly attracting new residents, and today it is home to 5000.

It takes about five minutes to see the entire city, built in a contemporary Maya style but resembling an aseptic cluster of cinderblock buildings corralled by chainlink. One Maya gem within this complex is the **Archaeology Department** (8-22106), where a clammy underground vault houses an ever-changing collection of ancient relics uncovered in the past two decades. Tours are offered Monday, Wednesday and Friday from 1:30 to 4:00 p.m.; reservations are required and must be made by calling at least two days in advance. There is a small fee for the tour. Don't bother visiting from late September through November, when the relics go on tour around the country.

Just outside Belmopan, at the intersection of the Western Highway and the Hummingbird Highway, **Guanacaste National Park** offers a splendid walk in the forest. Packed into these 50 acres of cool, damp woods are colossal trees that make you feel like you're wandering past nature's own highrises.

A guide from the visitor's center will be glad to join you, describing the abundance of life that exists along the leafy trails. Among the more interesting: armadillo houses, termite nests and logs lined with bulldog bats, who feed on fish as well as lizards and small mammals. Birdwatchers will be happy to know that blue-crowned motmots, collared aracaris, green-breasted mangos and other extraordinary, elusive birds are permanent residents here. There's also the imposing 300-foot-tall guanacaste tree, which the park is named for, laden with over 35 species of air plants, many as big as normal trees. If you're lucky, the guide will pluck a pod from a cohune palm and break it open so you can taste the coconutty flavor. Bring your swimsuit for a dip in the clear, fast-flowing Belize River, which cuts right through the park.

LODGING   If you're looking for a Belizean ranch experience, I highly recommend ✪ **Warrie Head Ranch** (Western Highway, six miles west of Belmopan; ceiling fans; moderate; 2-77185 in Belize City). Named for the spine-covered warrie, a type of wild boar that lives in surrounding forests, the ranch is draped across 137 pastoral acres, with grassy knolls, clear creeks and tropical fruit trees. Warrie Head Ranch offers nine cozy rooms decorated with Belizean tile floors, knotty pine walls and jalousie windows. A library exudes real warmth with its wildlife photos, board games and books on Belize. While you are here, you will be very lucky to meet Lydia, the lodge's virtuoso host and cook, who rustles up giant meals of steak, chicken and fresh vegetables (for vegetarians).

Despite its countrified name, the **Bullfrog Inn** (25 Half Moon Avenue; air conditioning; moderate; 8-22111, fax: 8-23155) is in the capital of Belmopan. The grounds are lush and filled with singing birds, but the rooms, though clean, carpeted and cooled by air conditioners, are rather featureless. On the positive side, the restaurant is the best in town.

Considered the business traveler's choice, the **Belmopan Convention Hotel** (corner of Bliss Parade and Constitution Drive, Belmopan; moderate; 8-22340, fax: 8-23066) is a gracious hacienda-style hostelry with a swimming pool. But don't expect Holiday Inn-style rooms; these are funky, featuring bright orange carpet, orange-striped bedspreads and hand-me-down furniture. Oh well, this *is* Belize!

RESTAURANTS   Checkered tablecloths, arched porticoes and fresh flowers lend real charm to the **Bullfrog Inn** (25 Half Moon Avenue, Belmopan; moderate; 8-22111). The most popular eatery in town, with politicians and visiting VIPs often gracing its tables, it has an open-air terrace that faces a tropical garden. Steaks, chicken, fish and hamburgers are standard fare, and there's an attached cocktail bar.

Across from the Belmopan bus station, the **Caladium Restaurant** (Market Square; budget; 92-22754) features a chalkboard menu of home-cooked fare. Fried fish or chicken, pork chops, T-bone steaks and thick, frothy milkshakes are local favorites. On Tuesdays and Thursdays, go for the escabéche and curried chicken.

SHOPPING   The **Market Square** in downtown Belmopan is comprised of stalls where vendors sell everything from copycat designer jewelry and radios to watermelons and chickens. Even if you don't buy, it's fun to watch. Open most days.

GETTING THERE: You'll have no problem driving to Belmopan from Belize City on the Western Highway. Or, take a Batty Brothers, Novelos or Z-Line bus from Belize City.

CAYO COUNTRY

South of Belmopan, the **Hummingbird Highway** is a part-paved, part-potholed path that resembles a collapsing sidewalk through the jungle. Bounding along in a beat-up jeep, with the feverish forest air pouring in through chattering windows, one expects to encounter a strange beast or an even stranger person. Instead, barefoot children dart out of the jungle clutching cups of corn kernels, so freshly cut that its sweet juice smell fills the air. If you ask where they are going, they will tell you to *madre*, so she can make her tortillas.

Even if you don't see the children, you will eventually spot the tiny signs for the **Blue Hole and St. Herman's Cave National Park** (on the Hummingbird Highway, 11 miles south of Belmopan). The latter is Belize's "other" Blue Hole, a pool of sapphire water as clear as air, with schools of fish scooting in every direction, buried deep in the rainforest. Sunlight filters through the treetops, changing the water into greens and blues and every shade in between. Swimming is excellent here. From this cool, enchanted spot, fern-lined trails lead off into a honeycomb of caves that last for miles. The caves are pitch-black and desolated, so bring a couple of flashlights, good walking shoes and a companion.

Twenty miles farther south, take the turnoff for Saint Martins Village. After about two miles on a gravel road, you will land at the crest of a vivid lake that glows phosphorescent blue and green. The lake is the reason **Five Blues Lake National Park** was christened on Earth Day 1992. Spanning 850 forested acres, it features a labyrinth of hiking trails and a small shelter where you can enjoy a picnic.

Back on the Western Highway, just west of Belmopan, take the turnoff for **Spanish Lookout** and you will soon feel as if you've left Belize. There, stretching to the edge of the horizon, is a scene right out of Pennsylvania's Dutch Country: folded green hills, wind-tickled fields of corn, and straw-hatted Mennonite farmers in horse-drawn buggies. Blond, freckle-faced Mennonite children race down the dirt roads and through the corn fields, and windmills churn against a bright blue country sky.

The Mennonites, who trace their roots to 16th-century Switzerland and Germany, began immigrating to Belize in the 1800s. Since then, they have slowly turned the unforgiving limestone ground into fruitful soil, and are now considered Belize's most prolific farmers. The remote Spanish Lookout is one of their largest greenbelts. If you drive there, take a truck. The road is very rutted and covered with rocks, and delivers a real beating to your vehicle.

From here to the Guatemala border, the Western Highway rises and falls through pine-clad mountain ridges and rocky pasturelands speckled with modest villages. This is the heart of **Cayo Country**, a region once rich with logging and chicle farming. Today, it boasts citrus groves and cattle ranches and an ever increasing ecotourism trade. The pulse of Cayo, as it's called around Belize, is **San Ignacio,** located 20 miles west of Belmopan. Draped along the banks of the Macal River and ringed with hills, San Ignacio is filled with restaurants, shops, businesses and nearly 9000 people who keep the town bubbling along. San Ignacio has long attracted a vast spectrum of humanity, from Maya and *Mestizos* to Guatemalan refugees, Lebanese entrepreneurs, Mennonite farmers, and adventure-seeking Americans and Europeans. Watching the various walks of life and listening to jungle tales told around town, one gets the distinct feeling that something exciting is about to happen.

After a stroll in San Ignacio, you may want to have a look at the minor ruins of **Cahal Pech** (Buena Vista Road; take the trail leading away from Cahal Pech Disco). Its name means "Place of the Ticks" and its first impression is not impressive, but if you wander the forested grounds you'll find the Preclassic city quite extensive. There are seven courtyards and 34 structures, including several temples, two ball courts and a sweathouse, sprinkled across two acres. The largest ceremonial structure is 77 feet high, with sharply tiered steps running up its face. Sadly, several buildings have been layered with concrete to slow down erosion.

San Ignacio is the headquarters for booking tours to surrounding Maya ruins and various sights, and for arranging horseback riding and hiking in the hills. It is also the place to arrange a canoe trip to **Ix Chel Farm** and the **Panti Mayan Medicine Trail** (check with Eva's restaurant, 22 Burns Avenue, San Ignacio; 92-2267). On the crest of a hill, amid five cleared acres of high bush country, the farm is owned by Americans Rosita Arvigo and Gregory Shropshire. The couple call it Ix Chel, after the Maya goddess of healing and of rainbows. On many summer afternoons, after the rain-gorged clouds have unleashed their showers on the forest, rainbows arch across the hilltop farm.

For several years, Arvigo and Shropshire have been collecting and researching the jungle vegetation that lies at their back door. So far, the husband-and-wife team have collected over 750 plant species, which are being catalogued by the New York Botanical Garden. The garden, along with the National Institute of Health, Metropolitan Life Insurance and other organizations, have provided grants for research at the farm. Already, the world's jungles have produced

Keel-billed toucan

treatments for ovarian cancer (a substance called taxol, derived from the yew tree) and Hodgkin's disease (substances from the periwinkle). It is hoped that the forest holds cures for other cancers and for AIDS.

The **Panti Mayan Medicine Trail,** which begins near the couple's house, helps visitors learn about their research here. You can take a self-guided tour, but it's far more enjoyable to hire a bush guide, available daily from 7 a.m. to 5 p.m. With his descriptions of jungle healing secrets, a guide makes the trail come to life. Sunlight and dewy rain filters through the jungle ceiling as he reveals such cures as cowfoot, cocol mecca, negrita, grapevine and bullhoof vine—foliage that to the untrained eye seems no different than any other forest specimen. Bullhoof, he says, will stanch internal bleeding, and grapevine conceals a fountain of fresh water. For more than an hour he goes on like this, explaining mysteries and relating healing stories that make life here seem even more mysterious.

The trail is named for Don Eligio Panti, one of Central America's most revered bush doctors. Now in his late 90s and nearly blind, the Maya shaman still practices natural healing in a nearby village. For several years, Arvigo has been Panti's apprentice—a rarity, as she puts it, "for a gringo and a woman."

Panti's great nieces, Belize's famous Garcia Sisters, practice their own style of Maya education a few miles south of San Ignacio in a picturesque farm village called **San Antonio.** The way to San Antonio is on a bumpy dirt road that leaps and dives among hills cascading with cohune palms and jungly pasture, a roller coaster ride through neotropical scenery with a slim possibility of meeting another vehicle. Once you arrive, you are met by freshly painted farmhouses, horses grazing on velvet green knolls, a teeny clapboard barber shop, and a one-room schoolhouse that throws its door and windows open to the warmth of day.

Not far from the school, at the **Tanah Mayan Art Museum** (for information, call 92-3310 in San Ignacio; admission), you will be met by one or more of the five smiling, engaging Garcia Sisters. In their teens and 20s, Sylvia, Carmelita, Aurora, Piedad and Maria will greet you in their *huipiles*, beautiful embroidered dresses traditional of their Yucatecan Maya heritage. They will take you through the many artifacts and artworks of their warmly arranged museum, from the welk shell jewelry, cedar violin and slate carvings to the 100-year-old butak chair handcarved from local santa maria wood by their great-great-grandfather. They will show you the cedar baby tub, carved from a single log with a machete and an axe, that their great-grandparents were bathed in, and that their grandparents bathed *them* in. And they will tell you the story of how their museum came to be.

"In the early 1980s, their father, a village farmer, met a little piece of black stone while working in the field," explains Piedad. It was so smooth and glossy he brought it home, and Aurora instinctively started carving it. When she was done, she had lured from the stone the image of a whale she had seen in a dream. Local villagers pronounced it a grand omen, saying that God had given them the stone to bring back the Maya art and culture that is so quickly disappearing today. Soon Aurora was carving more slate and needed a place to display and sell it. In 1985, in a loosely thrown up wood building, the sisters opened the Tanah Museum.

Since then, the museum has more than tripled in size, and carries many local artworks and handicrafts. Among the exhibits is Aurora's original whale, and though it reveals obvious talent, it is neither as detailed or compelling as the images she has gone on to resurrect from local slate. Younger sister Maria has also proven to have a knack for the ancient Maya art. The talent, Piedad says, is no doubt traceable to their *padre*, who, before he met that little black stone, used to carve limestone bowls and trade them to the neighbors for chickens.

LODGING   There's not a whole lot going on between Belmopan and San Ignacio, unless you visit ✪ **Caesar's Place** (Mile Post 62, Western Highway; ceiling fans; moderate; 92-2341, fax: 92-3449). The roadside scattering of buildings and bougainvillea is a friendly place to stop for a cold Belikin, hot home cooking or a room for the night. Four large rooms feature cedar paneling, Mexican tile floors and private baths with hot water. Out back, you can take a dip in Barton Creek.

In Cayo, the **San Ignacio Hotel** (18 Buena Vista Road, San Ignacio; rooms have either ceiling fans or air conditioning; moderate to expensive; 92-2034, fax: 92-2134) is as close as you get to a real hotel. Its hillside venue offers lovely vistas across Cayo and the Macal River, and there's a pretty swimming pool decorated with tropical planters and wrought-iron furniture, where one could easily lose an afternoon sampling Belizean rum (the margaritas are memorable, as well). Rooms are spacious and contemporary, adorned with Honduran mahogany furniture and offering private balconies.

Just uphill from the San Ignacio Hotel, the **Piache Hotel** (18 Buena Vista Road, San Ignacio; ceiling fans; budget; 92-2032) is the thrifty traveler's choice. The grounds, sprinkled with plants potted in an assortment of tin cans, tubs and tires, reflect the style of a friendly eccentric. That would be Godsman

Ellis, a gregarious Garifuna who can tell you much about San Ignacio and about Belize, preferably at his thatched cabana bar. Just off the bar, in a cinder-block building, are 17 extremely basic but basically clean rooms, with rummage-sale furnishings and curtained bathroom doors. Some rooms here have air conditioners that more or less work.

At ✪ **Mida's Resort** (Branch Mouth Road, one-quarter of a mile north of San Ignacio; budget for campsites and rooms with shared bath; moderate for cabanas with private bath; 92-3172, fax: 92-3845), you can pitch a tent or string a hammock between the trees and sleep under the stars. Most people, however, prefer to stay in one of the four cabanas, even if they are primitive with their cement walls and open windows. Two of the cabanas are duplexes with shared baths. The setting is homey and pure country, five riverside acres of former pastureland owned by Englishman Mike Preston and his wife, Maria Preston, who was born in San Ignacio (Maria's father's cows grazed on the property until a 1990 flood wiped out most of the vegetation). Among their many ecotourism projects, the couple and their two sons are working to restore the land.

Popular with backpackers, hikers and naturalists, ✪ **Maya Mountain Lodge** (on Cristo Rey Road, three-quarters of a mile from the Western Highway, near San Ignacio; moderate; 92-2164, fax: 92-2029) is an ecotourism retreat set along a verdant green hillside with tropical gardens and chirping cicadas. There are comfortable cottages, as well as very basic rooms with vinyl floors, plywood walls and curtained bathrooms. The real highlight is the lovely indoor-outdoor dining room, with a mango tree growing right through the middle. An extensive schedule of day trips and cultural programs is offered here, including the ever-popular "Belize Night" held every Friday and featuring a presentation on local topics.

Rubble from Maya ruins sprinkle the grounds at the remote **Clarissa's Cottages** (off the Western Highway, about three miles from San Ignacio; budget; 93-2462 or 92-2424). Like glorified camping, the three basic cottages have concrete floors and bamboo walls. But they reside in a most coveted spot along a bubbling creek, where iguanas and bromeliads decorate the trees. A thatched-roof restaurant serves tasty food.

In a stunning hillside setting overlooking the Macal River, ✪ **Chaa Creek Cottages** (on the Macal River, about eight miles outside San Ignacio; expensive to very expensive; 92-2037, fax: 92-2501) gives the feeling of being pampered—in the jungle. Unsurpassed for service and deep woods surroundings, its adobe cabanas are warm and inviting, with chestnut-colored Mexican tile floors, mahogany beds, Guatemalan blankets and thatched roofs soaring above the trees. By far the most coveted room is "The Screamer" (supposedly named for the screams of newlyweds who've stayed here), a voluminous 12-sided cabana propped high atop a water tower and affording views of the mountains and jungle. None of the cabanas have screens on the windows, but not to worry: there are few mosquitoes, only dazzling butterflies that float in one window and out the other. Around dinnertime, you'll be welcomed by the owners, a gregarious couple named Mick and Lucy Fleming (he's English, she's American) who are well-known around Belize. The indoor-outdoor dining room is a romantic affair offering tasty, local-grown cuisine. Before dinner, everyone gathers on the birdwatching deck, near the elegant wood bar, to trade "You wouldn't believe it..." stories of the day.

Downriver from Chaa Creek is ✪ **duPlooy's** (about nine miles outside San Ignacio; ceiling fans; moderate to expensive; phone or fax 92-3301, or 803-722-1513 in the United States). Though not as fancy as its neighbor, du-Plooy's offers the same feeling of rural peacefulness. Accommodations range from cottages with stone floors and screened porches to basic rooms (some with shared bath) in a main building. Co-owner Ken duPlooy, originally from Zimbabwe, is an avid birdwatcher who will point out the many species camouflaged in the foliage.

Getting to ✪ **Black Rock Lodge** (on the Macal River, outside San Ignacio; expensive; for reservations, call 92-2341) takes much stamina and motivation: First you trek eight miles down a bumpy, stony road, then hike 30 minutes through the jungle. But the scene that awaits you is more than worth it. Perched on the edge of a sheer wall of limestone, peering across the swirling river, is a cluster of fancy, thatched-roof tents engulfed in banana plants and surrounded by 250 acres of thick forest. Water from the river is pumped up for drinking, bathing and cooking, and rays from the sun are used to make all the lodge's electricity. Meals are prepared by a friendly staff, and there's a bar on-site. This is camping at its best. The rates include three meals daily.

Easy access makes ✪ **Windy Hill Cottages** (Western Highway, about one mile west of San Ignacio; ceiling fans; moderate; 92-2017, fax: 92-3080) a good choice for accommodations. It's one of the few country lodges that doesn't require a marathon trek down a rocky road, and it's the only with a swimming pool—but don't expect the Taj Mahal. What you can expect are picturesque, comfortable surroundings and congenial, knowledgeable innkeepers who tend to your every need. Lourdes Hales, a registered nurse and native of San Ignacio, and her husband, Bob Hales, a 20-year resident of Belize, will also introduce you to local sites and customs and history. Every cottage has a private bath with hot water and a veranda for enjoying the hillside views. There's an informal dining room and even a thatched-roof game room with a pool table.

RESTAURANTS   That sparkling new, tin-roofed, bilevel wood building on the way to San Ignacio is **Mike's Paradise Club** (Mile Post 58, Western Highway; budget). Opened in 1993 by a fellow named (what else?) Mike from Illinois, the open-air bar and grill serves big burgers and satisfying portions of chicken, fish and steak. Serving hours are officially from 10 a.m. to 6:30 p.m. After that, the band starts playing and you take your chances on getting anything more than a cold Belikin or cocktail.

Some people claim you haven't been to Cayo if you haven't been to **Eva's** (22 Burns Avenue, San Ignacio; budget; 92-2267). The central nerve of jungle comings and goings, Eva's is where you go to book tours, meet fellow Americans, buy postcards, and hear various tales that get taller as the night (and the beer) wears on. The food is strictly a side attraction, but it's cheap and not half bad. Among the choices: chicken curry, stew chicken, rice and beans, tamales and hamburgers.

Few places in Belize remind one of the United States. An exception (and a good one, after you've been in the jungle a few days) is the **Red Rooster Inn** (2 Far West Street, San Ignacio; moderate; 92-2506). Like a happenin' sports bar, its ceiling is strung with pennants of U.S. teams and its glossy wood booths accommodate patrons holding mugs of frothy beer. Pizza is the order of the day, and the cheesy, thin-crusted, bubbling discs taste a lot like home.

In San Ignacio, there are two possibilities for Far Eastern fare. You'll easily spot **Serendib** (27 Burns Avenue; budget to moderate; 92-2302) by its yellow clapboard storefront. Inside are wood-paneled walls and whirring ceiling fans, and a menu of fried rice, chow mein, Sri Lankan curries and shrimp, as well as burgers and salads. More run-down, but still praised around town, is **Maxim's** (Far West Street; budget; 92-2282). In a tiny, dark cinderblock building decorated with wildlife murals, it serves sweet and sour dishes, chop suey, curries, fresh fish and burgers.

SHOPPING   Prices are kind of high but the selection is good at **Caesar's Place** (Mile Post 62, Western Highway; 92-2341), a new-in-'93 boutique of local artwork, jungle healing potions, T-shirts and other high-quality Belizean gifts.

San Ignacio has a handful of interesting shops. If you're in need of inexpensive tennis shoes or leather sandals, duck into **K. K. Store** (23 Burns Avenue; 92-3418). Foremost among the tourist stores is **Farmer's Emporium** (24 Burns Avenue; 92-2253), which seems to carry every souvenir of Belize. Alongside these quality goods are handy items like spray paint and fresh black beans.

Toucan Gift Shop (41 Burns Avenue; 92-2211) has beach towels with vivid Maya designs. At **Arts & Crafts of Central America** (1 Wyatt Street; 92-2823), there's a good selection of Guatemalan woven rugs and blankets and handcrafted jewelry.

NIGHTLIFE   In downtown San Ignacio, the **Blue Angel Club** (Hudson Street; 92-2431) is a second-floor roost with an enormous wood dancefloor outlined in chainlink fence. Crowded most every night, but wildly popular on weekends, when bands churn out reggae and soul music. Cover on weekends.

A giant longhouse offering fantastic views across Cayo, **Cahal Pech Disco** (Buena Vista Road, San Ignacio; 92-3380) is named for the nearby Maya ruins. Easily the most popular nightspot in Western Belize, it pulses to reggae and punta rock, compliments of top-notch local bands. Cover for men only.

GETTING THERE: I recommend driving a rental car to San Ignacio, though regular bus service is available from Belize City on either Batty Brothers or Novelos.

MOUNTAIN PINE RIDGE AND CARACOL

South from San Antonio, the dirt roller coaster ride called the Chiquibul Road transforms into a clay trail that plunges into an enchanted forest known as **Mountain Pine Ridge** (from the Western Highway, take the turnoff at Mile Post 65 at the town of Georgeville). Were it not for the pockets of cohune jungle and broadleaf forest, you'd think that you had been transported from the jungle to the Great Smoky Mountains. Only these mountains are marbled with greens of every tropical shade and creased with rivers as clear as air. Chilly streams swirl around polished black boulders glinting in the sun, then disappear into networks of caves that have no end. Hardwood trees drip with ferns and giant bromeliads and orchids, perfuming the cool breeze that trickles through the leaves. Gone is the oppressive jungle humidity one has come to expect in Belize; here in Pine Ridge, as it's called locally, bonfires and fireplaces are the companions of evening.

Trails of clay, grassy dirt and limestone are the parkways of Pine Ridge. The trails are often muddy and flooded in the summer rainy season, so it's best to travel them any other time. In some places along the trails, leaves, vines and trees suck up every inch of space, though even here one can spot the toucans that decorate the treetops and the blue and orange butterflies that dance in and out of shadows. Ocellated turkeys dash in and out of the forest, and a brocket deer, frozen in the bush, aims his charcoal saucer eyes at a visitor. Green parrots poke their heads out of holes in a cohune palm, nests conveniently carved by a woodpecker. Allspice trees provide showers of pungent leaves; pluck one and smell it, and be reminded of pumpkin pie and holidays. Belizeans, however, are reminded of the spicy coconut milk their mothers gave them.

Much of Pine Ridge lies within the **Mountain Pine Ridge Forest Reserve,** which means logging is legal but regulated to allow the felling of only certain trees. In recent centuries, widespread logging stole plenty of the primary forest, though abandoned logging camps and sawmills are slowly being swallowed by the vegetation they tried to destroy. Headquarters for the reserve is in the village of **Augustine,** where tiny white tin-roofed houses gather beneath cathedrals of slash pine trees. Here, an old frame building set in the woods acts as the **Forestry Department station** (for information, call the main forestry office in Belmopan, 92-23629), which can direct you to various sites in the area.

One you won't want to miss is **Río Frío Cave** (about a mile west of Augustine), reached by a pebbled path that ambles down from the road into a dark den of trees. It is not a cave in the normal sense, but an overwhelming tunnel of stone that arches to the heavens, with a mouth that shelters a white sand beach dotted with boulders the size of houses. Water rushes in one end of the cave and out the other, coursing the half-mile length of this stone vault. Dim light filters through the cave, illuminating razor-sharp stalactites and walls smoothed by eons of water. One-hundred-foot-long vines dangle, confetti-like, from the ceiling. As you leave Belize's largest known river cave, notice the steps angling into the cave's mouth: They are stone keepsakes from the nearby ancient city of Caracol.

There is nothing dark or mysterious about **Río On Pools** (about two miles north of Augustine), just a sense of not being able to get enough of the view. Like a great basin of Alka Seltzer, it is a hillside panorama of marbled brown rocks washed by fizzing water traveling in every direction and framed in giant slash pine trees. Where the rocks corral the water are mini swimming pools, with water that's invitingly cool and clean. The best swimming is reached at the very top; the best views are toward the bottom.

Farther north and east lies Belize's most famous waterfall, **Hidden Valley Falls**, also called the Thousand Foot Falls because it thunders down 1000 feet from a granite ledge, disappearing into the misty jungle below. The falls are not viewed from close up, but from an overlook across a great ravine enveloped in a panorama of delicious green mountains and mystic haze that heightens as the sun takes leave. Here, on a platform that begins to jut into the ravine, with the wind whispering through pine needles, you can fixate on the scenery: mistletoe curled atop a slash pine tree, an orange-breasted falcon perched on a dead limb, visual lines between the broadleaf jungle and pine forest etched across the mountains. To make the views last, have a picnic on the nearby covered tables.

Not far from the overlook is a small tin-roofed frame building with a sign that says **Hidden Valley Institute for Environmental Studies**. Inside, it has the beginnings of a forest laboratory, with shelves lined with specimen bottles, but as of late 1993 the fledgling operation had no researcher. The institute is the hopeful creation of a Floridian named J.C. "Bull" Headley, who owns the 18,500-acre Hidden Valley Reserve, located within the Pine Ridge Reserve. The Hidden Valley property includes the Thousand Foot Falls as well as the Hidden Valley Inn, which publishes a map to the myriads of lesser known overlooks and sites in the area. There's the scenic **Lake Lollyfolly** and **Bull's Point**, which looks across a shimmering green valley, and **Butterfly Falls**, a forested haunt where butterflies float across a creek and travel *up* a waterfall. There's also **King Vulture Falls**, where a mountain is etched with trenches of waterfalls ruled by king vultures. To really see the throngs of eerie black creatures, you'll need strong binoculars (preferably 80 power) or a telescope.

CARACOL South of here, the cool Pine Ridge slowly slips into a deep, dense forest called the **Chiquibul Wilderness**. Here, set atop the Vaca Plateau in the foothills of the Maya Mountains, is the place everyone is talking about.

Caracol, it seems, was a supreme Maya city, surpassing even the mighty Tikal. It says as much on an marker, discovered on a Caracol ball court, that
proclaims the victory of the Lord Water of Caracol over the warlords of Tikal.
The year was 562 A.D., and Caracol reigned sovereign for the next century.

Caracol slept, consumed by jungle, until 1937, when it was discovered by
a mahogany logger named Rosa Mai. Mai reported his find to the Belizean
government, which dispatched then-Archaeology Commissioner A.H. Anderson. During a two-week visit in 1938, Anderson logged numerous structures,
altars and massive intricate stelae, many of which were painted and stuccoed.
He also bestowed the name Caracol, meaning "snail," for a road that coils
through the hilly terrain, though it could just as well have been named for
the mounds of snail shells found here.

Rumors of Caracol's fabulous stelae spread, but it wasn't until the early 1950s
that epigrapher Linton Satterthwaite went in search of the great stone monuments. He did indeed find them, and carted some back to the University of
Pennsylvania. During the next 30 years, various recovery teams visited Caracol, but they only stayed long enough to extract more of the beautiful stelae.
Finally, in 1985, two archaeologists from the University of Central Florida
launched a full-scale excavation. What Drs. Diane and Arlen Chase found—
and are still finding—is a glorious city and culture that is reshaping current
thinking about ancient Maya existence.

Caracol, it seems, had a big middle class. In fact, most of its 187,000 residents—nearly as many people as live in all of Belize today—were probably
middle class, enjoying all the wealth and perks historians had thought were
reserved for nobility. Throughout the metropolis are elite neighborhoods
whose homes are spacious and elegantly arranged, with bedrooms boasting
large slabs of sleeping stone—in effect, king-size beds. The extraordinary
causeways that run out from the city center would have afforded scenic views
of Caracol's splendorous buildings—not something city planners would have
designed for a population of peasants. And though the Maya supposedly entombed only rulers and priests, many of Caracol's tombs held middle-class
families and their painted vessels, gems and other valuables.

Indeed, Caracol's myriad tombs tell much about the city, and perhaps about
Maya life. As of late 1993, a staggering 55 tombs had been discovered—more
tombs than have been found at any other Maya site. Caracol's "tomb culture"
suggests that ordinary citizens buried their dead in specially made chambers
in their homes, not in outlying cemeteries as previously believed. The Chases
speculate that the dead may have even played a role in rituals conducted by
their living descendants.

Two of the most exciting tomb finds, however, did not reveal middle-class
members. Rather, the crypts uncovered by the Chases in 1992 held a king
and a woman, likely his wife, and a royal family of four. The king's tomb,
which dates to 480 A.D., was embellished with 17 elaborately painted vessels,

obsidian earflares, and jade and shell necklaces (though only fragments of these remain). In the second tomb, the floor was dusted with jade flakes. There were two men here, including one wearing a necklace of human teeth, a woman, and a fourth person of unknown sex. There was also a painted text indicating the tomb was built in 686 A.D., about four years before it was sealed.

Arriving in the jungle mantle of Caracol today, it is difficult to appreciate the true scope of this Classic city. But as the Chases and their excavation team continue to peel back thousands of years of nature's shroud, they are discovering a place of staggering size, brilliant design and stylish architecture. At least 4000 structures are spread across 55 square miles, making Caracol 80 percent more dense than the great Tikal. Work here could well continue for many decades; the Chases say that "by the year 2003, we don't even see ourselves out of the major plazas."

Much of their work, which includes "stabilizing" or securing the structures, is concentrated in the city's nucleus, where they have discovered stucco and plaster palaces, pyramids and temples that were painted dazzling shades of red and blue, and even red and white stripes. Those that weren't painted were silvery white, their marbleized limestone catching sunrays by day and moonlight by night. Among the grand buildings are several low-lying structures that were perhaps ancient fast-food stands.

From the administrative hub, causeways from nine to thirty feet wide fan out like the spokes of a wheel, reaching out at least five miles all around into Caracol's sprawling suburbia. These were not only footpaths but crucial routes for transporting food and water throughout the region. Where some of the causeways culminate are mini plazas whose designs suggest markets and way stations for crops and merchandise. The crops likely came from Caracol's vast agricultural fields, evidenced by thousands of terraces found by the Chases. The terraces indicate not subsistence farming but cash crops—further proof of a sophisticated middle class.

To irrigate the fields and provide drinking water for residents, Maya engineers created a complex reservoir system that funneled water to crops and homes. It was a necessary system, since, strangely, the Maya had chosen to build their city far from a good water source. Now, nearly 2000 years later, that same reservoir provides bathing water for Caracol's current residents—the excavation team that includes the Chases, nine University of Central Florida undergraduates, five post-graduate supervisors and about 45 Belizean bushmen, some of whom are descendants of those ancient Maya.

Actually, the entire team is only in residence from mid-February through May each year (minus a break for Easter week), and this is absolutely the best time to visit Caracol. Not only can you see how archaeologists live (in meager huts next to banana groves) and work (in musty, dusty excavation pits), but a visitor will enjoy an extensive guided tour by an enthusiastic, knowledgeable student. Everyone who comes to Caracol is assigned a guide; visitors are not allowed to wander the site alone—a necessary rule, considering the extent of ongoing excavation and preservation. Try to arrive shortly before 10:30 a.m. or 1 p.m., when scheduled tours are offered daily.

If you travel to Caracol between the end of May and mid-February, one of the Belizean caretakers will escort you through the ruins. No matter when you come, you must obtain a visitor's permit beforehand, available from the Forestry Department Station in Augustine, 30 miles north of Caracol, or from the Department of Archaeology in Belmopan (8-22106). The Belmopan office can also provide current road conditions; roads sometimes flood in the rainy season and are closed for up to 24 hours. This is a minor inconvenience, considering Caracol only became accessible year-round in early 1993. Before that, most of Caracol's few visitors came on horseback. The first two months the new roads opened, however, more than 2000 visitors streamed in.

The Caracol tour begins in the epicenter, just off the archaeologists' camp. Here looms the lofty **Caana**, Belize's tallest manmade structure, emerging 139 feet from the floor of **Plaza B** and crowned by three temples, several pyramids and a courtyard. It is also known as **Sky Place** and **Sky Palace**, the latter being bestowed by students, who love to sleep atop its summit on full moon nights. Caana is so stupendous that its temples are not fully visible from the plaza floor. But ascend its steep steps and you will discover many quadrants and rooms and sleeping benches. One of the chambers, nicknamed the "dwarf room," has inexplicable two-foot-high doorways and teeny benches.

One of Caana's pyramids, number **B18**, reveals a well-preserved staircase flanked by a stone mask. Between structure **B18** and **B19** are remnants of a decorative baseboard, painted such a deep red that the color remains almost as vivid today. At the top of B19 is a massive plaza and Caana's peak. Here is where you should take time to look down on the jungle, whose ten-story trees are dwarfed by this proud view. Then stroll next door to **temple B20**, where looters tunneled into three tombs, taking whatever valuables were there and destroying a painted text on a plastered wall. The Chases spent most of their first season, in 1985, cleaning up the damage and salvaging broken vessels and bones.

Situated conveniently near the great Caana is the elite **Barrio Group**. Like an uptown Manhattan, the posh residential area enjoyed easy access to Caracol's epicenter, or downtown. Likewise, the **South Acropolis**, across the city center, was an upscale area situated right next to the reservoir. Several tombs were uncovered among these homes, including a vertical vault harboring a woman and a man. The capstone, or tomb lid, was not painted red as traditional for nobility, indicating the couple may have been buried in their own house.

The South Acropolis residents no doubt watched a lot of *pok-ta-pok*, or Maya ballgames, in the neighboring **ball court**. They also likely witnessed the recording of their ruler's victory over the lords of Tikal. The triumphant battle between Caracol's Lord Kahn II and his Tikal enemies is recorded on a **ball court marker** that today is sheltered by a piece of thatching. Several years ago, the marker was, incredibly, crushed by logging trucks. It has been reassembled but its 1400-year-old features are, unfortunately, very vague. The best way to admire its hieroglyphs is with a flashlight at night.

Across the epicenter, in **Group A**, some of Caracol's most influential figures lived, conducted business, and were eventually buried. Nine stelae and six altars were found here, as well as numerous crypts that belonged to the elite. You can climb into the deep tomb of **building A3**, where the Chases discovered 9000 pieces of jadeite, 13 quail skeletons, and the badly decomposed body of an adult. Glyphs on the tomb's capstones record a date of approximately 695 A.D. and describe a person of royal lineage.

Presiding over Group A is the **Temple of the Wooden Lintel,** or **structure A6**, which, amazingly, has its original sapote wood door lintels. Steep short steps run down the temple's face, but a determined person will want to scale them to explore the temple's myriads of floors and rooms. Beneath the lowest floor, researchers found a tomb where an urn was filled with a cache of mysteries: stingray spines, sharks' teeth, fish vertebrae, pumpkin seeds, pine needles, seaweed, and even a beehive that has survived, virtually intact, all these centuries.

There is much more to see and learn at Caracol, even as researchers make new discoveries every day. And now that the roads are open year-round, researchers expect this extraordinary place to become Belize's premier inland destination.

With that in mind, the Chases are rallying the Belize government to hire wardens—not easy in a country too poor to excavate the ruins in the first place.

XUNANTUNICH   From Caracol back to San Ignacio is about four hours of rough and tumble roads. You'll be so glad when you feel the smoothness of the Western Highway again, you'll want to stop off for a drink (highly recommended: the poolside terrace at the San Ignacio Hotel). Afterwards, head west on the Western Highway to the village of San José Succotz, where you can take the hand-cranked car ferry across the gurgling Mopan River (notice the women washing their clothes). From here, a dirt road leads to **Xunantunich** (admission). One of the few Maya cities built atop a hill, Xunantunich (Shoo-NA-tu-NISH) is a stirring place looming along a limestone ridge in the Belize River Valley. Its name means "Stone Woman," a modern-day moniker alluding not only to this rocky plateau but to the erotic female images that could be conjured from the sleek, shapely temples.

Xunantunich flourished 1000 years ago, during the Classic Period. More than a century ago, amateur archaeologist Dr. Thomas Gann first explored the site, but did no excavations until he returned in 1924. At that time, he uncovered caches of burial items as well as hieroglyphs that were circling a main altar. He took them with him, and their whereabouts are a mystery today.

Over the years, excavations at Xunantunich have been piecemeal. In 1938, British archaeologist Eric S. Thompson unearthed a residential group, while in 1949, then-Archaeology Commissioner A.H. Anderson discovered the remnants of a stucco frieze. In 1952, an amateur British archaeologist named Michael Stewart discovered burials and offerings. Seven years later, a Cambridge University researcher named Euan Mackie uncovered evidence in one of the temples that Xunantunich had been wrenched by an earthquake in about 900 A.D. It was at least one possible explanation for why the city was abandoned at this same time.

During the 1970s, various teams worked to excavate and preserve Xunantunich's greatest structures. Today the site is small but immensely scenic, a one-mile oasis of emerald grasses speckled with cohune palms and limestone outcroppings. The city's buildings encase three plazas fashioned in north-south design and its outskirts are sprinkled with house mounds. The structures go from grand to comfortable to tiny, no doubt accommodating a spectrum of Maya classes.

Attention is naturally focused on where the elite spent their time. That would be **Group A,** where several temples gather around two grassy plazas. Dominating **Plazas A1** and **A2**—and all of Xunantunich—is 130-foot **El Castillo,** a terraced palace with a toothy contour and a skirt of velvety green grass. In Belize, it is second only in height to another great Maya palace, Caana, in the nearby city-state of Caracol. Climb the face of El Castillo and—when you've recovered from the overwhelming view of the countryside—notice the platform topped with two temples. The temples are famous for their elaborate bone-colored friezes, including an astronomical frieze and a frieze portraying a headless man. The palace's exposed blue-and-white limestone, glinting in the sunlight, takes on haunting shapes.

Like many Maya temples, Castillo is actually a series of buildings superimposed upon each other over the centuries. You can see evidence of earlier levels and layers everywhere; notice the wide terrace, about 35 feet up the north side, that at one point had buildings lining its edges. And if you look closely at the two upper temples, one resting upon the other, you'll see that the Maya originally covered the lower temple to make a foundation for the higher one. Only now, after archaeologists have cleared away debris and centuries of vegetation, is their construction so obvious.

Smaller temples congregate around Plaza A, one of the most interesting being **structure A15,** which has a stone bench. Just off Plaza A is a small **ball court,** which now resembles a grassy alley. Nearby, the structures around **Group B** are thought to be upper- and middle-class homes, hinting that Xunantunich was once occupied by a cultured, elite society.

The ruins are an excellent place to have lunch, but bring your own. The closest refreshments are in San José Succotz, back across the Mopan River.

West from Xunantunich on the Western Highway, the last place before Guatemala is **Benque Viejo**. The small border town is a peaceful place with two-story clapboard homes painted in crayon colors, wash strung across the porches, and chicken-wire fences (and chickens) running all over the place. There are no real sites here, other than the friendly residents, *Mestizos* and Mopan Maya, who tip their hats to you as you stroll down the dusty streets.

When you're exploring, notice the sign on **Dr. Jorge L. Garcia's Office** (George Street near Liberty Street): "Consulta Diaria, 3 p.m. to 6 p.m." One assumes this would be the best time to be stricken by the dastardly illness.

After Benque Viejo, you can turn back into the familiar terrain of Belize or make the adventurer's choice and cross into Guatemala. What awaits beyond the border is some of Mesoamerica's most spectacular rainforests and truly its most sensational Maya city. The 2500-year-old kingdom of Tikal still rules the vast jungles of northern Guatemala, known as the Peten, drawing more than 100,000 visitors each year. Tikal is only about 40 miles from the Belize/Guatemala border, but it's one long hellacious ride down a body-battering dirt road, with possibilities of bandits hiding in the roadside bush. The border crossing, however, is not so much a test of courage as of patience.

One the Belize side, you will surrender your tourist card, have your passport stamped and pass through with relative ease. On the Guatemala side, at Melchor de Mencos, you must show your passport and visa (obtained ahead of time in the United States; there is no Guatemala embassy in Belize) and, depending on the time of day and mood of the border officials, pay a small fee, or *propina*. Several officials may also have to "review" your documents before allowing you to pass.

Despite ongoing political conflicts within Guatemala and its tenuous relationship with Belize, it is unlikely you will encounter problems at the border or while traveling around Guatemala, especially in the Peten, where the government is focusing its tourism efforts. For more on traveling into Guatemala, see Chapter Eleven.

LODGING   Since 1991, four lodges have opened in Mountain Pine Ridge Forest Reserve, offering travelers easier access to this vast wilderness and to the exciting Maya city of Caracol.

Only 30 minutes from civilization but three-and-a-half hours from Caracol, **Maya Ranch** (Pine Ridge Road, four-and-a-half miles from the Western Highway; moderate; fax: 92-2060) enjoys a location so agreeable one is tempted never to leave. Set on a resplendent hill dotted with Maya house mounds, the ranch house looks across boundless emerald pastures where Brahma cattle graze. American owners Beth and John Roberson raise 800 of the cattle on half of their 4700 acres; the other half is dense forest. Both are devoted Belize transplants; John has lived here more than three decades, while Beth arrived as a Peace Corps volunteer on Valentine's Day 1973—and never left. The couple offers accommodations in an immaculate two-bedroom, one-bath guest house fashioned from beautiful mahogany and santa maria woods. A modern kitchen, well-stocked library and washer and dryer (though electricity only runs three hours daily) make guests feel right at home. For those who don't want to cook, meals are served in the Roberson home just a short stroll away.

If you want to feel as if you've retreated to some secret mountain hideaway, stay at ☻ **Hidden Valley Inn** (about two hours from the Western Highway, take the turnoff at Georgeville; very expensive; for reservations, call 8-23320 in Belmopan, fax: 8-2334, or 800-334-7942 in the United States). Here, a cluster of lovely stucco cabanas huddle under sky-reaching pine trees surrounded by cushiony trails of pine needles and brilliant impatiens that grow like weeds. Inside, Mexican tile floors, Guatemala throw rugs and high angled ceilings create visual warmth, while wood-burning fireplaces provide physical warmth on nippy winter nights. Cocktails and tasty meals are served in a big elegant ranch house that feels like something out of the American Southwest. But you'll know it's not when you hear what sounds like a Chihuahua yapping— only to learn it's a barred forest falcon calling to its mate. Rates include breakfast.

Around the corner, the less fancy ☻ **Pine Ridge Lodge** (moderate to expensive; 92-3310 in Belize or 216-781-6888 in the United States) offers wooded cottages ranging from primitive to quite comfortable. The primitive "Forest" cottages are dark and dreary and moderately priced, so opt for the "Mayan" cottages that are open, airy and still in the moderate range. For an expensive rate, you can have a secluded, spacious "Riverview" cottage with a screened porch along a scenic creek. There's no electricity (kerosene lamps provide light), but the cook manages to turn out good food with a gas stove and generator-powered refrigerator.

Upon arriving at ☻ **Blancaneaux Lodge** (Mountain Pine Ridge; expensive to very expensive; phone or fax: 92-3878), one senses the place is vastly different from any other in Belize, having tremendous warmth and flair in its design, and yet set so far up here in the jungle mountain wilderness. Planters gush with exquisite flowers and frilly ivy masks a stone fireplace. A curved dining room is suspended above the forest, and cabanas are adorned in a sensual African style. It all reflects the tastes of Francis Ford Coppola and his wife, Elsie, who own the lodge. In 1981, the famed movie producer and director fell in love with Belize and bought the lodge—the oldest jungle lodge in Belize—and this exquisite piece of secluded forest. Belize, being Belize, didn't pay much attention back then, nor when Coppola opened the lodge in early 1993. What has been making waves is Coppola's espresso machine, purported to be the only one in Belize, and his pizza oven imported from Italy ("Imagine!" locals say, "A *real* espresso maker!").

Coppola's special touches don't end in the kitchen or in the lodge surroundings. As of summer 1993, he installed his own hydroelectric plant using water from the river that flows just beneath the lodge. He has a private airstrip that eliminates the four-hour drive from Belize City (though chartered flights are expensive—about US$360 round-trip, minimum three passengers). And he is remodeling 12 existing rooms and cabanas and adding 12 new ones. Several of the new cabanas are already open, and they are without doubt the most lavish digs. *Note:* Generous discounts (up to 50 percent in the off-season) are available for Belizeans and employees of the government and Hollywood movie studios.

RESTAURANTS   When movie director and producer Francis Ford Coppola opened his **Blancaneaux Lodge** (Mountain Pine Ridge, about two hours from the Western Highway; expensive; reservations required by calling 92-3878) in 1993, he flew an espresso maker and pizza oven over from Italy. News of the two unheard-of-in-Belize items spread across the country, and requests for a seat at Coppola's table have been pouring in. He is happy to oblige, provided guests make reservations. The menu, of course, leans toward Italian, which the lodge's Belizean chef has become adept at preparing. For lunch, there are speciality pizzas such as Neapolitan with fresh mozzarella, tomato and basil; for dinner, the five-course menu focuses on pasta, smoked meats and local seafood.

GETTING THERE: There is no bus service to Mountain Pine Ridge. However, it is quite easy to find your way in a rental car to the Mountain Pine ridge lodges (which I did solo), and certainly possible to drive all the way to Caracol (though I hired a driver). Because of its extremely remote locale down miles of unmarked dirt jungle roads, I recommend hiring a driver to take you into Caracol your first time; there's no need to hire a tour guide, since guides are provided at the ruins. All area lodges, including those in San Ignacio, will arrange a driver.

You can easily drive to Xunantunich and to Benque Viejo del Carmen, though you can't take the car across the Guatemala border. There's no bus service to Xunantunich, but you can take a Batty Brothers or Novelos bus to Benque Viejo from nearby San Ignacio.

CHAN CHICH

If you drive to **Chan Chich,** you will think you've accidentally exited the earth into some planetary jungle, like when Star Trek's Captain Kirk gets unexpectedly beamed to a strange Eden. The extraordinary lodge and Maya ruin is flung way out in Belize's northwestern hinterlands, almost to Guatemala, nowhere near civilization, and at least a four-hour drive from Belize City in the dry season. Forget the rainy season—all the roads are washed out.

But most people who visit Chan Chich do it in a small charter plane, flying low over a wheat-colored plateau that explodes into emerald jungle, then nosing down into a pinpoint clearing called **Gallon Jug.** An old logging camp turned farm center, the Jug is owned by American entrepreneur Barry Bowen, who in 1984 bought 125,000 surrounding acres and made them a nature reserve.

What Bowen and his crew found when they first arrived were lots of marijuana fields, numerous Maya temples that had been looted, and leftovers from poachers who were hunting with abandon. Indeed, under a single tree, in a bloody, feathery heap, were the bodies of 24 ocellated turkeys. Bowen's solution: build a lodge that would break even, but whose primary goal was to protect the forest by having year-round visitors. In 1988, he opened 12 hardwood cabanas, constructed entirely from local materials and set in the plaza of an unexcavated Maya ruin. The ocellated turkeys found today at Chan Chich preen around the grounds, fearing only rejection by a mate.

With virgin rainforest running for miles in every direction, the lodge offers visitors a window on the wildlife of Belize. Howler and spider monkeys navigate the trees overhead, while toucans nest near your room. Nighttime brings the chilling roars of howler monkeys; come dawn, you will think you awoke in nature's own amphitheater, flooded with a symphony of purrs, screeches, whishes, rattles and even pop-pop-pops. After a day or so, you learn the rhythms of the jungle, and they become your own.

In fact, because it is cushioned by protected lands—to the west lies the 1.7 million-acre Maya Biosphere Reserve; to the south, 200,000 acres owned by Programme for Belize—Chan Chich enjoys a spectacular abundance of wildlife. Birders, naturalists and lovers of archaeology are among the lodge's most devoted clientele, though its secrets are lately being divulged among mainstream travelers.

Lest you think building a lodge on a Maya ruin is sacrilege, Bowen points out that since he opened, problems with looting and marijuana growing have ceased. He has his opponents, but Bowen is proving himself an ecotourism advocate, taking care to protect the ruins while guests enjoy them and refusing to interfere with wild life (even bird feeders are not allowed).

Ocellated turkey

LODGING   For the ultimate Belize jungle experience, spend the night in a 1700-year-old Maya city. It's possible at ✪ **Chan Chich Lodge** (ceiling fans; very expensive; for reservations, call 25-2321 in Belize City or 800-343-8009 in the United States), whose lovely thatched cabanas rest atop a Classic plaza encased in ancient temples and tombs.

But living in this jungle doesn't mean roughing it. Chan Chich's 12 bungalows are attractive and entirely comfortable with their hot showers, downy linens and spacious quarters. Fashioned from gleaming local woods and crowned with soaring thatched roofs, the cabanas feature louvered windows and big screens parked near the ceiling for maximum coolness. Spacious wrap-around verandas are ideal for wildlife watching and for admiring the lodge's luxuriant landscaping. There's a restaurant where everyone meets for outstanding meals, as well as a bar where nightly stories sound like something out of turn-of-the-century Africa. Here's where you'll get to know Chan Chich caretakers Tom and Josie Harding, former Californians who are responsible for this extremely well-run facility.

Guests are provided maps of the many trails that radiate out from the lodge, or they can purchase the invaluable *Exploring the Rainforest, Chan Chich Lodge* guide by Carolyn M. Miller and Bruce W. Miller. Local guides, who are not only knowledgeable but really love the jungle, conduct tours of the trails and ruins, including burial chambers painted with friezes, several times daily and one some nights. Horseback riding, canoeing and local sightseeing excursions are available, as well.

During holidays and peak seasons (January through March), book at least several weeks in advance. Prices include all meals and complimentary beer—one of the best deals at absolutely one of the best lodges in Belize.

GETTING THERE: Because of its extreme remoteness, Chan Chich provides charter flights in small planes from Belize City to the nearby outpost of Gallon Jug—a fantastic way to see the wilds of northern Belize.

Southern Belize

0   20 kilometers
     20 miles

GUATEMALA

Belize City

Western Hwy.

Belmopan

Coastal Rd.

NORTHERN LAGOON

Bird Caye Bird Sanctuary

SOUTHERN LAGOON

Gales Point

Hummingbird Hwy.

Melinda Forest Reserve

N

Dangriga

Hopkins

Victoria Peak (el 3675 ft.)

Cockscomb Basin Wildlife Sanctuary

Maya Centre

MAYA MOUNTAINS

Big Creek

Placencia

Southern Hwy.

NIM LI PUNIT

Monkey River

LUBAANTUN

San Pedro Colombia

San Antonio

Blue Creek

Punta Gorda

GULF OF HONDURAS

SARSTOON RIVER

GUATEMALA

TEN

Southern Belize

The least populated, least visited and most rainy region of the country, southern Belize takes in the chunk of land south of Belize City to the Guatemala border. There are only three real towns—Dangriga, Placencia and Punta Gorda—all nestling against the Caribbean Sea, with primitive coastal villages scattered in between.

Inland is a different story. Here are the Maya lowlands and their foothills, looming as a deep, dark, forbidding chasm of rainforest punctured by jagged peaks of limestone and drop-off granite walls. Rising above all other peaks is Victoria Peak, Belize's highest at 3675 feet, whose "great cone of solid rock (shoots) perpendicularly skyward, seeming to float on the very roof of the forest," or so it was described by a member of the 1927 Grant Expedition, which, like many other teams over the years, failed to reach the summit. Thirty-nine years earlier, a team organized by British Honduras Governor Roger T. Goldsworthy did scale the peak and named it Victoria. Team member J. Bellamy, in a report to the Royal Geographical Society, said the whole area was "enveloped in a cloud of mystery."

"Karstic" is what geologists call the porous rock jungle of southern Belize, where bottomless fissures have been chiseled by eons of incessant rain. In the deepest recesses, the landscape is so dense and threatening, it is thought to be unexplored by humans, at least in modern times. Maya ruins are still being discovered, some of which have not seen humans in more than a thousand years. Those areas that have been explored exact respect from their explorers, for here are more poisonous snakes than anywhere else in Belize, and more drug runners. Abandoned logging camps dot inland rivers, their names—"Go to Hell" and *Sale Si Puedes* (Leave While You Can)—reminding one of the tenuous thread of life in these jungles.

Visitors to southern Belize shouldn't venture into these risky wilds, even with a bush guide. During more than ten years of research in southern Belize, one American archaeologist has dodged bandits' bullets and worked in areas that were "loaded with poisonous snakes." Chances are good you, too, would cross paths with a deadly snake, drug runner or looter, or with the Royal Highland Fusileers who patrol these frontier forests. The latter would ask for your government permits (several are needed to travel these jungle reserves) and purpose for being there ("simply having a look around" is *not* good enough).

However, there is much to see in less remote areas (which, incidentally, will seem *very* remote to many people), and you can take forays to several forested Maya ruins and a dense wildlife sanctuary. The worn, washboard Southern Highway provides access to these sights, though its poor condition prevents most people from venturing all 202 miles from Belize City to Punta Gorda, the end of the line in southern Belize. In fact, the trip is considered a measure of prowess, and if you want to earn a bit of Belizean admiration, wait until a night when the group rum bottle is near empty and announce that you drove "all the way to P.G.," the nickname for Punta Gorda.

Of course, *not* going all the way to Punta Gorda is one way to experience the Southern Highway and not get too physically and mentally mangled. Dangriga, the first major town, is only about a three-hour drive in the dry season; four to five hours in the rainy season. The next big stop, Placencia, is another hour and a half in a rattling car with dust and dirt flying behind you. But it's great adventure, and the tight web of jungle that clutches much of the road makes for a thrilling backdrop.

If you're pressed for time and energy, the best way to visit this region is to fly. Local airlines offer service to airstrips in Dangriga, Placencia and Punta Gorda. (Note the emphasis on *airstrips*. The closest thing to an airport is a palm tree and grass worn down by passengers waiting with their luggage.) Flying is not only much faster and also quite scenic, it costs the same as renting a car. Plus, you get to ride in a small tinny plane that feels like an old jalopy with wheels, usually piloted by a polite, clean-cut fellow fresh out of flying school (beverage service is *not* available, in case you had any doubts).

DANGRIGA

The largest town in southern Belize. **Dangriga**, with its downtown hubbub and harborfront vistas, feels like a miniature Belize City. It's not particularly scenic, just smaller and therefore less crowded and dirty. A walkable grid of paved and dirt streets is lined with clapboard hovels and businesses, highlighted by the Burger King (no relation to the one you're thinking of); the Sunrise and Starlight Chinese restaurants (just two of many); and Pepito's Store, which sells breadfruit on Breadfruit Road.

But beneath the drab, simple facade is a strong people with a rich, mysterious, tightly protected culture. Most of Dangriga's 8000 residents are Garifunas (pronounced Ga-RIF-unas), who came to Belize in the 1800s from the Caribbean island of St. Vincent. Two hundred years earlier, a ship carrying West African slaves ran aground in St. Vincent. No one's sure whether the survivors became slaves or citizens on the island, but what is certain is that they eventually intermarried with the native Caribs and created the Garifuna. Freedom was the foundation of their culture, and it caused them to rebel against British colonization of St. Vincent in the 19th century and flee to Central America. Freedom is still integral to Garifuna existence today, specifically the freedom to practice their centuries-old farming and cooking methods, their painting, woodworking and music, and their enigmatic religion. Only in recent years have visitors to Dangriga been invited to observe some of the Garifuna ways.

One place to learn about both Garifuna art and the art of cooking is at the **home of Austin Rodriguez** (32 Tubroose Street; 9-2308; call ahead for an appointment). Amidst a gathering of clapboard shacks with chickens pecking around the dirt floors, Rodriguez fashions drums from mahogany, cedar and maple woods, stretching deerskin across the tops. The self-taught drummaker and Dangriga native has been carving congo and other drums for more than 30 years. His customers span several continents, and his drums have been played in many a *dugu*, the all-important Garifuna ceremony and feast for reconciling with dead ancestors.

While Rodriguez makes drums, the women and children of his extended family are usually busy making cassava bread. You can witness various stages of this day-long process, which includes peeling dozens of the white glistening root vegetables, feeding them into an electric masher (they were all mashed by hand until a few years ago), then stuffing the mashed mixture into a woala. Named for the big local snake, the woala is a six-foot-long rattan strainer that, when hung from a tree by several sturdy women, causes cassava juice to drain into buckets. After several hours, the juice is taken away to harden overnight (unhardened, it is poisonous), after which it will transform into starch. Meanwhile, the mashed and juiced cassava root is baked into a thin, white flatbread called *ariba*. To unaccustomed taste buds, it has about as much flavor as a paper towel, which is sad considering the amount of work involved. But to locals, a fresh-baked batch of *ariba* is a treasured thing, and those who receive it are very lucky indeed.

Nowhere is this cassava tradition better captured than on the canvases of **Benjamin Nicholas**, whose colorful and compelling portrayals of local life have gained national and international attention. "These are the people in my head. I've been painting them every day, nonstop, all my life," Nicholas will explain if you drop by his house and studio at 25 Howard Street (before you go, call 5-22785 for an appointment). The 62-year-old man with a pushbroom mustache and pointy goatee fills his days and his canvases in a dim, concrete-floored room that looks out to sea through barred windows. His paintings, many unfinished, surround him with scenes of pensive-eyed Garifuna women toiling over their cassava, and of happy children playing by the sea.

Artist **Mercy Sabal** (55 Citron Street; 5-2651; call in advance for an appointment) preserves her native culture not with a brush and oils but with flowing quilts embroidered with vivid pictorials. One series, "Woman of the Soil," portrays her Garifuna sisters sweating in the fields as they dig up cassava and other vegetables—still part of their daily routine. Another shows them gathering coconuts and firewood and balancing *fania* baskets on their heads. For those wondering about a Garifuna woman's role in society, Sabal (and many others) will point out that she shoulders not only the household chores but is also responsible for gathering food, delivering babies, treating the sick and making clothes for her extended family.

From Dangriga, there are numerous possibilities for day trips, including nearby islands such as **Tobacco Caye** and **South Water Caye** for snorkeling and picnicking, and **Man-of-War Caye** for watching the frigate birds and brown boobies that swarm the island. Or you can head inland.

If you head north for six miles down a bumpy clay marl road, past hillsides masked in citrus and banana groves and vultures perched atop spindly trees, you will discover a real out-of-the-way but very important place. Here, from a humble little building surrounded by weeds comes millions of bottles of Marie Sharp's Hot Sauce. *The* hot pepper sauce of Belize, gracing the top of nearly every restaurant and home cook's table, it is made with habañero peppers, the world's hottest chile peppers, measuring between 200,000 and 300,000 on the Scoville Chart, the Richter scale of chile peppers (jalapeños measure 5000). This tiny "factory" and the surrounding 400 acres are called **Melinda Farm** (call 8-22370 for directions and an appointment), and is the birthplace of Marie Sharp's Hot Sauce, formerly called Melinda's Hot Pepper Sauce.

There are many stories surrounding this pepper sauce, one being that it was named for a woman called Melinda, which it is not. Rather, it is named after the Melinda Forest Reserve within which it lies. Another misnomer is that the sauce is made from peppers grown on Melinda Farm, when, in fact, the soil here is not suited for habañeros but for citrus. Farms in the surrounding Stann Creek Valley provide all those peppers for Marie Sharp's Hot Sauce.

Melinda Farm is owned by Marie and Jerry Sharp, who called their sauce Melinda's until they had a falling out with their United States bottlers and distributors (distant relatives in New Orleans), who purportedly put the Melinda label on inferior sauces made in other countries. Now the only bonafide Melinda sauce is that labeled Marie Sharp's (bottles in the U.S. still say Melinda's, but owning one in Belize is tantamount to treason).

Depending on the time of day and year, you can walk around the factory and watch the Belizean women giggling in their baker's hats while they stir up a batch of the tasty sauce. Amazingly, every batch goes into a 60-gallon trough with only three spigots, which fill 1536 bottles in just 90 minutes. During an average eight-hour day, close to 8000 bottles are filled. And that's just the hot pepper sauce. This tiny factory turns out many other unusual, delicious concoctions, including mango chutney spiked with ginger and brown sugar, guava, papaya and banana jams, and a hot pickle relish called *curtido*. If you're wondering what all those good smells are in each vat, food chemist and quality control manager Ivan Joseph can tell you the *basic* ingredients—detailed recipes are, of course, top-secret.

Joseph will take you outside the factory and show you a habañero plant (there is a small experimental field here), its satiny red lanterns dangling from a leafy bush. He will also take you through groves of citrus and papaya, and the tiny cemetery wherein resides the Burns Family, who originally owned the farm.

North from the farm about 12 miles, at the tip of a skinny peninsula that pokes into the wide Southern Lagoon, is a locked-in-time fishing village called **Gales Point**. There are only about 300 people here but many more manatees, who are drawn to the warmth and safety of the lagoon. You can hire a boat (just ask around the village) to take you "manatee watching" through the picturesque Southern Lagoon and up into the Northern Lagoon, with a stop at the **Bird Caye Bird Sanctuary** for glimpses of ibis, herons and egrets.

LODGING   As befitting a last frontier, the lodging in southern Belize is low on comfort, high on funkiness—and character, if you're lucky. Elegance exists only in the seaside sense, and only in Placencia at a place called Rum Point Inn (see Placencia Lodging section later in this chapter).

In Dangriga, the best place on the sea is the ◎ **Pelican Beach Resort** (north end of town; ceiling fans; moderate; 5-22044, fax: 5-22570), where several old houses are strung together beneath the palm trees. Checking into one of the spacious, timeworn rooms is like climbing into an old bathrobe: vinyl-covered floors creak beneath your feet, a stuffed vinyl chair invites you to rest your body, and a rare-in-Belize bathtub lets you soak off the film of the jungle. Constant sea breezes and strong ceiling fans keep things cool, so you only miss the air conditioning on hot summer nights. Resort owners Therese and Tony Rath are members of the Belize Audubon Society and are well-known conservation pioneers around Belize. Tony's wildlife photos grace the walls of the lobby and dining room, the latter being the best restaurant in town.

Dangriga's most modern digs are at the **Bonefish Hotel** (15 Mahogany Street; air conditioning; moderate; 5-22165; fax: 5-22296), a two-story cinderblock building washed in seafoam green and situated across from the sea. A 1992 remodeling gave the place an airy ambience, and most of the rooms are freshly painted and spacious. The views aren't great but there is cool air conditioning (go for it—it's *hot* in Dangriga!), big bathrooms with brand-new tubs, and cable television. The lobby is small and fashioned like a comfortable living room, and there's a cozy dining room where home cooking is the order of the day.

RESTAURANTS   Listen to the waves roll ashore at the **Pelican Beach Resort** (north end of town, Dangriga; moderate; 5-22044), where an entirely pleasant dining room is decorated with wavy Belizean tiles, louvered windows and pink linens. There are usually three choices for dinner, including some type of steak, chicken and grilled catch of the day. Side dishes of baked plantains and tomato pasta are just as delicious.

Chinese restaurants seem as plentiful as palm trees in Dangriga. My favorite is the **Sunrise** (96 Commerce Street; budget; 5-22482), where the dining room is neat as a pin. Besides chop suey and curries, you can order fried conch or fried chicken, and choose from more than ten soups, including lobster noodle and chicken and shrimp.

There are only three tables and a television that blares all day in Creole and Spanish, but the food is tasty and plentiful at **Ritchie's Dinette** (Commerce Street, near the police station; budget). The blackboard menu is short and simple: saucy stew chicken, beef or fish, with a side of rice and beans.

For hearty, homestyle food in a casual dining room with one big vinyl-covered table, stop by the **Bonefish Hotel** (15 Mahogany Street, Dangriga; moderate; 5-22165). Depending on what the cook's cooking, you may have pork chops, fried chicken or T-bone steak, accompanied by potatoes, rice, whipped cassava with coconut milk (a Garifuna specialty), and a green salad. For breakfast, there are eggs and bacon and pancakes.

NIGHTLIFE   In Dangriga, try **The Blue Horizon**, also known as the **Round House** (north end of town, across from the Pelican Beach Resort; 5-23112). The big, round thatched-roof cinderblock building sits along the sea, offering rum drinks and the best punta rock concerts around.

GETTING THERE: Maya Airways offers the most frequent service to Dangriga from Belize City and other points around Belize. However, you can also catch a flight from Belize City to Dangriga on Tropic Airways. Bus service from Belize City to Dangriga is offered by Z-Line.

If you're flying in, as the toucan flies, Dangriga is 37 miles south of Belize City. But as you and your car travel, it is either 77 miles or 107, depending on the time of year. In the dry season, you can take the shorter route: the Western Highway from Belize City to Mile Post 31, then south on the new dirt Coastal Road to Gales Point and then Dangriga. In the rainy season, you'll have to follow the Western Highway all the way to the Hummingbird Highway near Belmopan, then turn south for four hours of potholed trails that most resemble the site of a recent bomb explosion. The jungle scenes, however, are like something out of a banana republic postcard, and there are places where you can swim in clear pools and explore cool caves clouded with mist.

PLACENCIA

After exploring the area north of Dangriga, head south, preferably on a different day, since the roads are rough and by now will seem endless. The first southern stop is **Hopkins**, a Garifuna fishing village where 20th-century life has barely begun to trickle in. It's best to arrive by boat; it's not only faster and less stressful on the body but affords a striking view of the village as you approach the gathering of seaside stilt huts framed by the luscious green Maya Mountains.

There's no electricity in Hopkins, though the phone lines that arrived recently do feed the village's handful of telephones. Garifuna families cling to the traditions of their ancestors, shunning the trappings of modern life. In fact, before villagers opened several very primitive lodges, the only visitors were infrequent drifters who themselves knew little of the outside world. No matter who seems to wander into their sheltered outpost, the villagers are more than friendly, inviting you to dine in their homes (for a small fee, of course; there are no real restaurants in Hopkins) and learn about their way of life. That might include accompanying a fisherman in a dugout canoe or joining a punta rock party with its feverish beat and fast, sexy dancing. Or, you can explore local waters on your own with a kayak, available for rent at the village docks.

South of Hopkins, a grinding ride down the clay washboard Southern Highway will bring you to **Maya Centre**. This is the gateway to the **Cockscomb Basin Wildlife Sanctuary** and home to an ever-expanding group of Mopan Maya, many of whom gave up their homes and *milpa* farms to make way for the sanctuary. If you patronize the village's one-room **crafts center**, which carries attractive slate carvings and woven baskets, you will be fueling the local economy with tourist dollars and therefore discourage the need for poaching and looting.

From Maya Centre, it's six miles into the jungle before you reach the sanctuary's **Visitors' Center**, where there are picnic tables, primitive camping huts and trailheads that disappear into surrounding forest. There's also brief information on Cockscomb and its beginnings, though if you really want the big picture, read Alan Rabinowitz's book *Jaguar*. The fast-moving adventure recounts Rabinowitz's field research in Cockscomb during 1983-84, trapping, tagging and tracking jaguars, living with Maya villagers, surviving a plane crash, battling poachers and arrogant, wealthy American hunters flying down for a quick kill, enduring various jungle parasites and ailments, and dodging drug dealers and snakes (though one of his Maya assistants, while chasing a jaguar, was bitten by a fer-de-lance and subsequently died).

Most of the jaguars Rabinowitz tracked died as well, either by poachers, injuries obtained during capture, or reasons unknown. But the New York zoologist did prove one thing: That despite considerable poaching and wrecking of the forests for farmland, the jaguar still has a chance in Cockscomb, and indeed in Belize itself. Compared to Belize, most other Central and South American habitats are rapidly dwindling. Even in Costa Rica, Rabinowitz found "only a few places...where jaguars might still roam in their natural state."

In late 1984, after much work and support by the Belize Audubon Society, the Forestry Department and local Maya families, Cockscomb was declared a National Forest Reserve where hunting was banned. In subsequent years, it was upgraded to a sanctuary to protect all animal and plant life, and now logging is banned. Today, it is the world's only jaguar preserve, boasting the densest population of jaguars ever recorded. It lies in a 100,000-acre bowl of forest, ringed on three sides by ridges and mountains, including Victoria Peak, which appears as a shard of rock looming in the distance.

A honeycomb of trails coils through portions of the sanctuary, offering hikes ranging from one hour to several days. Many of the trails are former logging roads carved as recently as the early 1980s. The jaguars and other cats of Cockscomb, including pumas, ocelots, jaguarundis and margays, use these roads to travel and stalk their prey. However, it's doubtful you'll see a jaguar unless it's dark, since it is a nocturnal beast and, despite its ferocious reputation, avoids prey larger than itself, specifically people. The other cats are just as elusive, preferring to watch *you* from their safe hiding place in the bush. It *is* likely that you'll encounter the jaguar's telltale signs—feces and scratch marks—and then you will know he or she is not far away.

Many other Cockscomb inhabitants are less shy about showing themselves. More than 290 species of birds light up the trees with song and color, including keel-billed toucans, scarlet macaws, great curassows and king vultures. You may also encounter a boa constrictor or red-eyed tree frog, or even a tapir (mountain cow), a creature who loves the dense, dewy foliage kept cool by triple canopies of trees.

Along the **Curassow Trail**, phosphorescent butterflies float across footpaths carpeted with silky ferns, and vines seem to drop out of the sky. Palm fronds stretch three stories high, and fungi grow as big and brilliant as lacquered seashells. A trail of pebbles beckons down to a swimming hole with water so clear you can drop a coin 25 feet to the bottom and tell if it lands heads or tails. Overhead, waterfalls plunge down from the boulders.

Scattered throughout the basin are the ruins of ceremonial centers and house mounds that belonged to the ancient Maya, perhaps the first humans to call Cockscomb home. But far greater than these small reminders are **four Maya sites**—just discovered in 1993—entombed deep in the perilous rocky rainforests southwest of Cockscomb. After ten years of research in southern Belize, including excavations at Lubaantun and Nim Li Punit near Punta Gorda, archaeologist Peter S. Dunham found the sites in terrain so dense and precipitous it was thought no humans could have survived there. But the Maya not only survived, they created thriving communities more than a thousand years ago on what Dunham believes may be "the only volcanic and metamorphic deposits of their kind in the Maya area." For this land of 1000-foot limestone cliffs and hammocks seething with fer-de-lance snakes is also super-rich in minerals, which likely drew the Maya. Dunham, assistant professor of anthropology at Cleveland State University, suspects the Maya were mining hematite for red ochre, pyrite for mirrors, granite for grinding stone, and other minerals that "underwrote the Maya economy."

Although each of these ancient communities had a "downtown" area with pyramids, there are no grand buildings to indicate a "New York" or an "L.A." This is like finding a Denver mining town or a Houston oil town," explains Dunham. The archaeologist and his team of five students, a biologist and a geologist located the sites on tips from hunters. After setting up camp, the Royal Highland Fusileers who patrol the jungles brought the team supplies, and hence they named one of the communities RHF. They call the other three Tiampiha, the Yucatec Maya word for "between two waters;" Tzimin Che, which is Mopan Maya for tapir; and Ekxux, Mopan Maya for the rare red extremely poisonous fer-de-lances who live at the site.

Dunham's research here will continue for years, though it is unlikely that the sites will ever by accessible to the public. He cautions anyone who even thinks of visiting: "Don't do it. The area is very rugged and very dangerous, full of looters and drug runners. I've been shot at."

Tours to the Cockscomb sanctuary, however, are highly recommended and can be arranged in Dangriga through **Pelican Beach Resort** (north end of town, near the airstrip; 5-22044). Or, from the southern town of Placencia, contact **Junior Burgess** (6-23139), one of the best bush guides in Belize. Cockscomb is about half-way between Dangriga and Placencia. For information on camping in Cockscomb, contact the Belize Audubon Society at 2-77369 in Belize City or write to the sanctuary at P.O. Box 90, Dangriga, Belize.

Many travelers find **Placencia** the most desirable place in southern Belize. Its sands are whiter and deeper than most cayes' sand, and its seaside resorts are instantly captivating. True to its name, the area forms a peninsula where a lagoon meets the Caribbean Sea. The peninsula's northern end is a wild and windswept coast with occasional resorts. The southern end is a jumble of weathered stilt buildings perched in the sand and edged by a concrete sidewalk. There are many palm trees, but no road. Could this be the town? Remembering you are in Belize, you realize that, of course, it is!

Spend a few hours in Placencia, and you'll meet half the village (the other half comes out at night, when seaside watering holes are alive with music and rum). Young Anglos adore Placencia, and give the sleepy village a bohemian edge. Though still remote and primitive, Placencia is quickly gaining a reputation as a savvy ecotourism destination. Surrounding jungles welcome exploration and dazzling, little-explored offshore reefs beckon to divers.

On the mainland across the Placencia Lagoon is **Big Creek,** whose pebbly clay airstrip brings visitors to the area (outgoing passengers, please wait under the palm tree next to the runway). The town is a hot, bustling place crowded

Jaguar

with wood shacks and one bright spot called the **Bill Bird Lodge & Restaurant** (next to the airport), where you can have a cool drink at the air-conditioned **Thirsty Toucan** bar.

LODGING   In the primitive village of Hopkins, several ultra-basic spots open their doors, the best being **Sandy Beach Lodge** (seaside on the south end of the village; budget; for reservations call 5-22033). It's run by the Hopkins Women's Cooperative, the only women's cooperative in Belize, and it features 22 rooms. There's no electricity or hot water, but the sheets and bathrooms are clean (some rooms have shared baths). Best of all, the gregarious women who run this place are great cooks!

Along the sea in the village of Placencia, five charming cabanas rest right in the sand at **RanGuana Lodge** (mounted fans; moderate to expensive; 6-23112). Brightly painted on the outside, the interiors feature wood walls and barrel ceilings, bathtubs and coffeemakers. Ask for a cabana facing the sea.

Near the tip of Placencia's point, a scattering of mobile homes and cabanas have been freshened up and planted in the sand. Odd as they may seem, the six mobile homes at **Sonny's Resort** (moderate; 6-2046) are not bad considering the amount of space and the screened porch, though for a slightly higher price you can have a fancier cabana with a mini-refrigerator, coffeemaker and ceiling fan.

Placencia's choicest lodging is found on the north end of the peninsula, away from the village. The ✪ **Turtle Inn** (one mile north of Placencia Village; very expensive; 6-22069) looks like a place where you could wash ashore and be happy for a very long time. Hammocks are strung between palm trees and an old canoe is parked in the sand. Six cozy cabanas, built by owner Skip White, have bamboo walls, thatched ceilings and private baths. White, known as an excellent bush guide, offers excursions to surrounding jungles. Rates include three meals daily.

Twin chocolate-brown buildings along the sea signify you've reached **Kitty's Place** (1.5 miles north of Placencia Village; moderate; 62-2027). It's a comfortably worn spot with warmth and character, thanks to American owner Kitty Fox. Choose from apartment-style rooms with private bath and kitchen or smaller quarters with shared bath. A good restaurant and little bar are also here.

Foremost among area resorts, and one of our very favorite Belize lodges, is ✪ **Rum Point Inn** (two miles north of Placencia Village; very expensive; 6-23239, fax: 6-23240, or 800-747-1381 in the United States). From the local airstrip, getting to the inn is a rewarding experience: a 20-minute boat ride through silent, shimmering mangrove canals. At the inn, you'll meet delightful owners George and Corol Bevier, former Americans who are Belize aficionados. George is a medical entomologist who has recorded the daily weather for 20 years, only to report there are no weather patterns in Belize! The inn consists of several unusual, podlike cabanas right on the beach, decorated with indoor gardens, Guatemalan sling chairs and comfortable beds. The ceilings are high and round and give the feeling of being in a rotunda. Meals are served family-style, with lively conversation on ecotourism. Numerous day trips are offered here, including dive excursions through the lodge's dive shop.

Toward the north end of the peninsula, **Singing Sands Inn** (seven miles north of Placencia Village; expensive; 6-22243) is as pretty as can be. Opened in 1992, the inn is landscaped with luxuriant flowers and features a tropical restaurant. Six cabanas line the beach, each with attractive wood furniture, wood paneling and porch overlooking the sea. A quiet, relaxing place.

RESTAURANTS   In Placencia Village, locals and visitors gather to swap fish tales and feast on fish at **Kingfisher** (moderate; 6-23175). The big, weathered clapboard building rests right on the sea, and also serves steaks and pork chops.

Jene's (Placencia Village; budget; 6-23112) is classic Belize. Punta rock blares from a little radio, beads dangle in the window, and a picture of a marijuana leaf proclaims: "Nature's Way of Saying Hi!" Oh, and did we mention the dust-caked fan and year-round Christmas garland? Open from early morning to late at night, Jene's serves eggs, hamburgers, fried chicken, fish sandwiches and conch steaks.

Great Placencia meals come not only from restaurants but from backyards. At **Brenda's Place** (near the post office, Placencia Village; budget; 6-23137), backyard picnic tables are where terrific Belizean home cooking (compliments of Brenda, of course) is served in plates that runneth over. The menu changes daily, depending on local offerings and Brenda's mood. But count on Caribbean-style seafood, chicken and steaks. Brenda's pies are legendary.

Across the lagoon from Placencia, next to the Big Creek airstrip, is the bright, breezy **Bill Bird Lodge & Restaurant** (budget to moderate; 6-22252). Even if you aren't hungry enough for a hot dog, hamburger or stew chicken, you can cool off with a sweet limeade or homemade ice cream on the airy screened porch draped with hanging plants.

SHOPPING   A few funky shops in Placencia are worth a stop. Local handiworks are mainstays at **Made in Belize** (Placencia Village), where shelves display crafts, jewelry and hand-painted T-shirts. **Miss Lizzies** (upstairs from Jamie's Restaurant, Placencia Village) offers a mixed bag of homemade preserves, crochet, wine and used books. The local grocery, **Wallen's Market** (near the soccer field, Placencia Village; 6-23128) stocks household items as well as postcards.

The T-shirts, cotton dresses and other last-minute items at **Rum Point Inn's** gift shop (two miles north of Placencia Village; 6-23239) are attractive and well-designed.

NIGHTLIFE   It's never a bad time for a drink at the **Kingfisher** (seafront, Placencia Village; 6-23175). Boisterous and seaworn, it's always crowded.

Everyone's talking about **Cozy Corner Bar & Disco** (Placencia Village), a shuttered white house where you can dance and meet fellow travelers. Wednesday nights feature famous "chicken drops" (guess what the chickens drop).

The bar at **Tentacles** (on the water, south end of Placencia Village) is fine for a drink *before* the disco. The crustacean-shaped building looks like it's crawling out to sea.

GETTING THERE: Maya Airways offers regular flights from Belize City to the Big Creek airstrip, usually with a stop in Dangriga along the way. Tropic Air also services Big Creek. From there, your lodge will provide boat transfers across Placencia Lagoon to Placencia. Or, ask about boat service next to the airport at the Bill Bird Lodge and Restaurant. Bus service from Belize City to Placencia is available on the Z-Line.

By car or bus, Placencia is about an hour and a half to two hours south of Dangriga on the Southern Highway, a dirt road that's usually in fair condition. In the rainy season, portions of the road may be closed, so check road conditions in advance.

PUNTA GORDA

On the Southern Highway, about 25 miles north of Punta Gorda, you'll see a sign for **Nim Li Punit**. This Late Classic site lacks the scope and architectural intrigue of Lubaantun, but boasts at least 25 intricately sculpted stelae. One measures more than 30 feet, making it one of the tallest along the Maya Route. Nim Li Punit means "Big Hat," likely referring to its location along a ridge overlooking coastal plains.

Perhaps no town in Belize is quite so edge-of-the-world as **Punta Gorda.** Just before the Guatemala border, it's about as south as you can get on the Southern Highway. Given the sad state of the road, it's understandable that few Belizeans ever travel to P.G. (as Punta Gorda is known in Belize), though they spend a lot of time talking about it. Indeed, there's a certain mystique about this place where Garifunas still practice sacred ceremonies, pounding on drums, shuffling their feet and calling to dead ancestors. But only rarely are outsiders permitted to witness these impassioned rituals.

What visitors to Punta Gorda will see is a quirky outpost where chickens sprint across the streets and filmy store windows advertise five-gallon buckets of pigs' tails. There are a handful of Americans here, people like Gary, who works for the local Voice of America station. Gary related how, in the last 28 months, he survived a near-fatal attack of dengue fever and two plane crashes in the swamps. He smiles, then says even though his company will transfer him, he wants to stay another year. Life in this banana republic, he points out, is a big adventure. And really, if he ever needs to "get away from it all," he can take a skiff to nearby deserted Moho Caye, sit on the beach, and drink a beer.

Punta Gorda itself is pretty much "away from it all," and there's not much to do in town. However, the lush jungles outside town harbor several sightseeing treasures. Tours to these areas can be arranged through the **Toledo Visitors Information Center** (Front Street at the wharf; 7-22470).

Heading west from Punta Gorda, a dirt road climbs through dense rainforest, skirting Maya villages where cacao beans are drying next to thatched huts.

In the village of **San Antonio,** the **San Luis Rey Church** was built in 1954 with stones from surrounding Maya ruins. No doubt some came from **Lubaantun** (five miles west of San Antonio, just past the village of San Pedro Colombia), a late Classic ceremonial center hidden in undergrowth. This isolated ruin sees few visitors, but those lucky enough to come will find Santiago Coc, the Maya caretaker who gives enthusiastic tours. Coc should know the area; in 1970, he assisted archaeologist Norman Hammond, then a doctoral student at Cambridge, with excavations.

Lubaantun means "Place of Fallen Stones," and that's just what it looks like. Within a mile of cleared jungle are mound upon mound of stones, some masked in fungi and others sprouting big trees. Eleven major buildings are set in five plazas, built atop a ridge similar to western Belize's Xunantunich. But unlike any other Maya site, the structures here were built without any mortar. Instead, each stone was painstakingly cut to fit another—yet the only tools found were pieces of flint. Archaeologists also found grinding stones for corn and an open chamber with a human jawbone and 1000 mollusk shells, though their purpose is unknown.

But the most astonishing find was a crystal skull, perfectly carved from a single cube of rock crystal. Void of tool marks, its construction seems impossible. In 1926, Canadian Anna Mitchel-Hedges discovered the skull in a temple vault and took it to Canada, where it resides today. Belizeans, rightfully perturbed, believe the skull should be returned to Belize.

A little farther down the dirt road, a path winds through cool jungle to **Blue Creek.** There's no sign for this marvelous swimming hole and local secret. A tangle of vines sway overhead, and schools of fish dart through the lucid water. Water gushes down from the jungle hills, creating many small falls. A quarter-mile farther on the trail are several caves and a wood shed for camping.

Back on the dirt road, and heading east, a sign on an abandoned, weed-choked clunker advertises **Dem Dats Doin** (admission; for information, call 7-22470). It's owned by a Hawaiian couple who call their spread a "Self-Sufficient Integrated Farm System." A guided tour introduces you to their "biogas digester," which uses pig manure to create methane gas to run their lights and refrigerator. The manure also fertilizes their gardens, which provide food (the pigs are for sale, by the way). You'll see a "solar oven," a foil-lined box that even bakes cakes, and vials where jungle plants are being converted to perfumes, rums and oils. If this weren't Belize, it would seem a very strange place!

Once you've seen the jungle side of Punta Gorda, you can head out to sea. Day trips to the **Snake Cayes** and **Moho Caye** (for information, visit the Toledo Visitors Information Center, Front Street at the wharf; 7-22470) offer snorkeling and fly-fishing in pristine, remote waters. One of the most exciting excursions from Punta Gorda is a three-day trip down the **Río Dulce River** to **Livingston, Guatemala** (also arranged through the visitors center). For more on visiting Guatemala, see Chapter Eleven.

LODGING   Punta Gorda has many older, sad-looking lodges whose rooms are sporadically occupied. Which means if you don't mind slumming it, you can stay here for low budget prices, especially if the hotel is empty and you wrangle a good deal (like from US$15 to $20).

No doubt the best deal for an ecotourist is to stay outside Punta Gorda in a remote Maya village. As part of a new, experimental ecotourism program, several Maya and Garifuna villages are welcoming visitors. In one of the best programs, called the **Maya Guest House Program,** travelers spend two days with the 225 residents of Laguna Village, tucked in the rainforest ten miles west of Punta Gorda. During a stay, guests can help village women grind corn for tortillas, watch basket weaving and pottery making, help the men cut sugar cane and explore a local cave that has 1000-year-old Maya paintings. At night, there's barefoot dancing around a bonfire.

Accommodations are in one-room thatched huts with concrete floors and bunk beds, a slight step up from the villagers' own mud-floored huts strung with hammocks. There's also a separate building with a shower and outhouse. Guests get a basket with their eating utensils, which they carry to various homes for meals, as local families share the responsibility for feeding visitors.

In case you're wondering about a language barrier, more than half of the villagers speak English, including many giggling children who become elated at the sight of a visitor. Profits from the program help fund the village school, waste disposal and homestead farming, an alternative to previous slash-and-burn methods. Very expensive rates include transportation to the village, all meals and two tours. For information and reservations, contact the **Toledo Ecotourism Association** (P.O. Box 75, Punta Gorda; 7-22119).

If you do stay in Punta Gorda, you'll find just one first-rate establishment, which opened in 1992. The **Traveller's Inn** (José Maria Nunez Street, near the bus station; air conditioning; very expensive; 7-22568) offers roomy rooms, adorned with thick mauve carpets, vertical blinds and shiny wood dressers and armoires. There's also satellite television—generally unheard of in Punta Gorda.

Best of the low-end lodges, **Nature's Way Guest House** (83 Front Street, Punta Gorda; budget; 7-22119) gives the impression it's been here a very long time. Engulfed in flowering plants and vines, the funky seaside building has concrete floors of varying colors and a number of stoops and terraces. The rooms are one step up from a youth hostel, and have shared baths. The owners are an American-Belizean couple who also offer local tours.

The 11 rooms at the cinderblock **Miramar Hotel** (95 Front Street, Punta Gorda; budget for rooms without air conditioning; expensive for rooms with it; 7-22033) seem respectable enough, with their newish vinyl floors, tidy bathrooms and eccentric decor of paneled walls, butterfly-patterned shower curtains and terrycloth bedspreads. The concrete porches have views ranging from good to forget-it, and some rooms even have televisions, which you'll need to drown out the noise from the Chinese restaurant downstairs.

The **Saint Charles Inn** (23 King Street, Punta Gorda; budget; 2-22197) has rooms that are less run down than most in its price range. There are 13 units in all, spread between two buildings facing a grassy courtyard. All have private baths with hot water, pretty linoleum floors and walls painted a soothing cream.

RESTAURANTS If someone listed a few restaurants in Punta Gorda—Morning Glory Café, Sylvie's Country Paradise, the Miramar—you might begin to think you have culinary prospects, that this is what you have been waiting for in Belize. But these thoughts should be put to rest, since P.G. is not a culinary kind of place, but a town of stifling, bare-bones eateries serving strangely cooked food.

The single bright speck on the P.G. restaurant horizon is **Traveller's Inn** (José Maria Nunez Street; moderate; 7-22568), which opened in 1992 as part of a bright little motel near the bus station. Crisp linens and fresh flowers top the tables, and an air conditioner chases away the sweltering heat. Tender grilled steaks, saucy chicken and fresh seafood are the bill of fare, and the accompanying vegetables and salads are crisp and full of flavor.

For breakfast, the **Morning Glory Café** (59 Front Street, Punta Gorda; budget) serves fairly dependable fare if it decides to open. Eggs, bacon and papaya juice can be had for less than US$2. Later in the day, you can order fried chicken or fish, hamburgers or hot dogs, or smoked pork chops that have quite a good reputation around P.G. The venue isn't glorious, just a bottom floor of a well-worn building, with spidery plants covering the windows.

In a setting of painted concrete walls and doorways strung with glittering fake jewels, **Sylvie's Country Paradise** (45 Front Street, Punta Gorda; budget; 7-22102) will serve you fried chicken, hamburgers and rice and beans. If you'd like anything else, you'll have to move on down the road.

The menu's definitely not limited at the **Miramar** (95 Front Street, Punta Gorda; moderate; 7-22033), where you can order anything from beefsteak, pork chops and sweet-and-sour pork to baked pigeon, fried rice and seashell soup. P.G.'s best-known oriental restaurant comes with air conditioning and a vagabond motif of colored beads, tourist photos of China and folding metal chairs.

SHOPPING Other than Placencia, your only other shopping possibility is the Guatemalan market in downtown Punta Gorda. However, the clothing, radios, and beach towels sold here are better purchased across the border (see Chapter Eleven for more information).

GETTING THERE: By far the easiest way to reach Punta Gorda is by plane. Maya Airways has the most frequent service from Belize City, typically with stops in Dangriga and Big Creek on the way down. The trip by bus from Belize City, aboard the Z-Line, is a rough-and-tumble ten hours and borderline masochistic, especially considering the price of a round-trip air ticket from Belize City is only US$50.

By car Punta Gorda is another three to four hours south of Placencia, or nine to ten hours south of Belize City. No doubt about it—take the plane.

Side Trips from Belize

TIKAL

Western Hwy.

Belmopan

LAKE PETÉN ITZÁ

Melchor de Mencos

San Ignacio

Benque Viejo

Hummingbird Hwy.

13

Flores

Santa Elena

EL PETÉN

BELIZE

N

0   40 kilometers

40 miles

13

GUATEMALA

Punta Gorda

GULF OF HONDURAS

BAHÍA DE AMATIQUE

RÍO DULCE

Livingston

Biotopo Chacón Machaca

Livingston

Castillo San Felipe

EL GOLFETE

Río Dulce National Park

Puerto Barrios

Puerto Barrios

LAKE IZABAL

9

13

9

LAKE IZABAL

Río Dulce Area

QUIRIGUÁ

HONDURAS

9

COPÁN

ELEVEN

Side Trips from Belize

If you choose to venture beyond the western back of Belize, you'll find a badly beaten dirt road that punches into the ever-darkening well of Guatemala's vast northern jungle known as El Peten, past great guanacaste trees filled with the chatter of monkeys and sapodilla trees scarred by the machetes of *chicleros*, to Tikal, the most splendid of all cities in the Maya world. The lofty kingdom of Tikal rears up from the depths of North America's largest rainforest like some ferocious giant, its proud pyramids appearing to float above the dark green ceiling of the jungle. Anyone seeing Tikal for the first, or even the fifth, time will realize it is one of the true wonders of the world. No other Maya ruin boasts such majestic architecture and a setting that captures the imagination and won't let go. And if you want to experience primeval rainforest up close, Tikal is one of the best places on earth to do it.

On the southern fringes of Belize lies the threshold to a vastly different Guatemala, a paradox of paradisaic rivers and rainforests and villages virtually unchanged for 200 years, backing up to vast banana plantations, hot and dirty ports and squatters shacks—the fruits of 20th-century enterprise. From the locked-in-time Río Dulce River and village of Livingston, not far from the Belize coast, through the magical Parque National Río Dulce and mammoth Lake Izabal to the tough-and-tumble town of Puerto Barrios, this is a land of contrasts, and of extremely rewarding adventures.

Farther south into Guatemala, the little-known Maya city of Quiriguá beckons to those who would explore its grand plaza and storied stelae enveloped by banana plantations, and nearly obliterated by big banana business earlier this century. Quiriguá's rival, the fabulous Copán, looms four hours south off the beaten path, down a long, muscle-wrenching dirt road and across the Honduras border. It is so remote that fewer travelers go there than to the other great Maya sites, yet the unique stone sculptures of Copán are so striking—indeed, haunting—that visitors rank the city as one of the most thrilling destinations of Central America.

Whether you choose to take this southern side trip from Belize or the western foray into Tikal—or, best of all, both—you should allow several days in each region. For there is so much to see and absorb and ponder, and distances are deceivingly long, though travelers to these areas agree unanimously that they are well worth the effort.

WESTERN SIDE TRIPS

TIKAL NATIONAL PARK AND EL PETÉN   Tikal was the greatest capital of the ancient Maya world. Founded as early as 600 B.C., it reached a peak population of about 50,000 a thousand years later and was one of the two largest cities in the Western Hemisphere during the Classic Period, along with Teotíhuacan in central Mexico. Tikal was situated in the exact center of the Maya land, and had close cultural ties to all parts of the region. Many experts believe the knowledge and ideas that shaped the classic Maya civilization originated in Tikal around 250 A.D., and the abandonment of Tikal around 900 A.D. coincided with the collapse of high Maya civilization everywhere.

One aspect of Tikal's magic is that it is so hard to reach. What was once the wealthy and populous centerpiece of the ancient Maya world is now a remote frontier backwater surrounded by millions of acres of almost impenetrable rainforest called **El Petén**. There is no easy way to get there overland. But it is much faster to go there from Belize than from southern Guatemala. One reason is that more than a decade ago, Guatemala's military government at the time received international aid to widen and pave the road from southern Guatemala to El Petén, but the funds were diverted by corrupt leaders and the road never got built. More recently, in connection with the present Guatemalan government's agreement to set aside a large part of the Petén rainforest as a UNESCO Man and Biosphere Reserve, the World Bank pledged new funding to improve the road and stimulate tourism in El Petén—but the money will not be released until Guatemala convinces the bank that it will take all necessary measures to protect the Petén rainforest from pioneers flocking there to build new settlements and destroy the forest.

However, the road to Tikal from Benque Viejo, Belize, near the Guatemala border, is only about 40 miles. Still, it is a badly beaten dirt trail that promises a two-hour, battering, bone-jarring test of endurance for all who venture upon it. Plus, the hassle and delay of crossing the border, along with persistent reports of bandit activity along this road, make it a trip that's certainly not for the faint-hearted.

The easiest way to get to Tikal is by plane, a surprisingly short hop—only 45 minutes—from Belize City. Once you're in the plane, you'll be rewarded with a rich tapestry of smooth plateaus and dense rainforest. Notice the difference between the forests in Belize and Guatemala; in Belize, there are but a few tiny pockets of *milpa* farming, but flying over the Petén, you can see vividly the deforestation that is taking place in this environmentally delicate region. Thick rainforest still blankets the ridgelines and hilltops, but each valley is cleared for crops and livestock as fast as a narrow dirt jeep road can penetrate it.

Passenger planes land at the airport near **Santa Elena** on the south shore of Lake Petén Itzá, about an hour's trip by shuttle bus from Tikal National Park. Most of the Petén's 25,000 residents live in Santa Elena and the contiguous town of San Benito. Together, the two towns form a frontier boomtown sprawl laced with open sewers and rattling with gas-powered electrical generators. While a modest tourist trade provides income for some area residents, more of them harvest renewable forest products such as chicle gum and pepsin leaves or join crews for oil exploration, the newest threat to the rainforest.

The capital of El Petén, **Flores** (population 1500) is built on a small island in the lake and is reached by a long earthen causeway from Santa Elena. A quintessentially quaint little town with an Old World feel to its tangled, claustrophobic streets, Flores is built on the site of Tayasal, the last ancient Maya stronghold to fall to the Spanish Empire. Tayasal was visited by Hernán Cortés, conqueror of Mexico, in 1525, but endured unmolested for nearly two centuries before a military expedition captured and razed it in 1697. You can walk all over town in less than an hour. The La Ruta Maya Conservation Foundation and George Washington University's Institute of Urban Development

Research have developed plans that would encourage the cultivation of Flores as a tourist center complete with houseboat tourist accommodations on Lake Petén Itzá, a regional museum in the abandoned prison building facing the hilltop town square, and even a sewage treatment plant. All this is years in the future, though. For now, Flores is one of Central America's more low-key and isolated frontier towns.

Ask at any restaurant or hotel in the Flores-Santa Elena area and they can probably put you in touch with a guide who will take you on an inexpensive three-hour boat tour of the islands near Flores. Stops on the tour include a group of small temple mounds—all that remains of the old Maya fortress city of **Tayasal**—as well as a spot called **La Garrucha**, where you can climb a tall tower, hang from a cable and zip above the water to land on another island nearby, then climb another tower there and zip back. The final stop on most boat tours is **Petencito** (admission), a zoo occupied exclusively by animals native to the Petén rainforest, including many rare or elusive species—jaguars, cougars, marmosets, tepezcuintles—that visitors are unlikely to spot in the wild. If you thought the cable slide at La Garrucha was fun, give the very scary 300-foot concrete water slide at Petencito a try!

The 38-mile stretch of wide blacktop highway that runs between Santa Elena and Tikal National Park is, incredibly, the only pavement in the northern half of Guatemala. For much of the distance, the road runs past a huge but not very active army base left over from Guatemala's long civil war, during which rebel guerrillas are said to have operated within the national park and throughout El Petén. Midway along the highway, at the eastern tip of Lake Petén Itzá near the intersection with the road from Belize, a dirt road turns off and follows the north shore of the lake all the way back to San Benito. A few miles from the main highway on the north shore road brings you to the **Biotopo Cerro Cahui**, a 1600-acre reserve set aside to protect a last fragment of natural habitat for several endangered wetland species—the Petén turkey, the Petén crocodile and the tapir. Explore the network of trails through the luxuriant forest of the reserve. You'll spot bright tropical birds and maybe javelinas, armadillos and spider monkeys.

Tikal National Park (admission) is a different kind of experience from other major Maya ruins, in part because the archaeological site is so big. Most visitors find that trying to see everything at Tikal in a single day is too exhausting and that three days is just about right to fully appreciate the park.

There are two museums near the entrance to the ruins area. The **Tikal Museum**, located near the Jungle Lodge, contains many of the best small artifacts that have been found among the ruins, including pottery painted with elaborate scenes of ancient Maya life and polished bones etched with pictures of gods, demons and warriors. The highlight of the museum is a replica of the tomb of Lord Ah Cacau, the greatest ruler of Tikal, containing his bones, eight pounds of jade jewelry, incense pots and other treasures positioned as archaeologists originally discovered them in a vault below the Temple of the Great Jaguar. On the other side of the parking lot, a new building houses the **Visitor Center and Stelae Museum.** Although the Petén rainforest seems far removed from the industrial world, within the past few decades acid rain has seriously damaged many stelae, making it necessary to move the best ones indoors for protection. Outside the visitor center is a huge model, about ten meters square, showing what Tikal looked like 1100 years ago.

From the parking lot near the hotels and museums, a rocky causeway, or pedestrians-only road, built by the ancient Maya and restored by modern archaeologists, cuts through the dense forest for nearly a mile to the central Plaza Mayor, the heart of ancient Tikal. From there, a triangular loop trail takes you through the Mundo Perdido complex, to lofty Templo IV, then to clusters of nondescript structures, called simply Complex M, Complex P, Group H and Complex Q, before returning to the Plaza Mayor. A separate trail leads to the solitary Temple of the Inscriptions. Park rangers have placed small concrete water basins beside the causeways at several points to attract monkeys and birds. A full circuit of the main ruins involves a hot, fairly strenuous hike of some six miles through the rainforest.

At the center of the Tikal ruins area is the meticulously restored group of buildings flanking the four sides of the two-acre **Plaza Mayor** (Great Plaza). Now covered with neatly mown grass, the whole square was paved with stucco in ancient times and resurfaced about once every century-and-a-half. The plaza was in use as early as 150 B.C. The first layer of pavement has been dated to about 100 A.D. and the final layer to 700 A.D.—a generation before any of the temples that now surround the plaza were completed. All of the structures at Tikal were painted bright red, with colorful bas-relief murals on the huge roof combs.

Along the north side of the plaza stand two rows of tombstone-shaped **stelae** with round altars in front of them. Other, similar stelae are set near the stairways of the various structures around the plaza. Most of the stelae are carved with the images of Tikal's noblemen in ceremonial garb with elaborate plumed headdresses, and many have hieroglyphs carved along the sides. As you explore outlying parts of the ruins, you will see dozens of massive stone stelae like these scattered throughout the forest. On some, the relief carving has been obliterated by time; others were quarried but never carved or erected, or smashed on purpose as the leaders they glorified fell into disrepute; and the best-preserved still invite us to wonder about the meanings of the messages so painstakingly inscribed and dispatched across the centuries to us, the people of the future. The oldest dated stela at Tikal was erected in 292 A.D., and the most recent in 771 A.D.

At the east and west ends of the plaza stand two of the extremely tall, stepped pyramids unique to Tikal. On the east end, **Temple I,** sometimes called the "Temple of the Great Jaguar," is the taller. Towering 170 feet high with its lofty, crumbling roof comb, it is one of the few pyramids in the Maya world that the public is not allowed to climb. A sign on a chain across the narrow stairway says that it is closed temporarily for restoration, but tour guides claim that it has been closed indefinitely since a tourist fell down the steep stairs to his death in the early 1980s. The tomb of Ah Cacau, the most important of ancient Tikal's leaders, was discovered at the foot of this pyramid. He reigned during the early part of the 8th century A.D., and his name translates as "Lord Chocolate." His remains, along with artifacts from his tomb including priceless jade jewelry, can be seen in a replica of the burial vault at the Tikal Museum. Just to the south of Temple I is the main **ball court,** surprisingly small for such an important ceremonial center as Tikal.

Directly across the plaza, on the west side, is **Temple II,** also known as the "Temple of the Masks." It is squat and wider than Temple I, with three levels to Temple I's nine. The top level's broad walkway around all sides of the temple offers good views of the Plaza Mayor, the acropolises and the surrounding forest canopy. Temples I and II were built at the same time and are thought to represent the male and female principles. Carvings on the lintels and walls of the temple chambers on top suggest to some archaeologists that Temple II was a burial pyramid for the wife of Ah Cacau, who was buried under Temple I. This is mere theory, however, as her tomb has not been found.

While the **North Acropolis** may lack the dramatic architecture of the pyramids, it is by far the more interesting structure to explore. It is a broad mound with a number of separate temples, apparently dedicated to different gods, and a tricky labyrinth of stairways and passages to reach them. Eight temples made up the acropolis in the 8th century, when Tikal's great pyramids were built. Archaeological digs have revealed that the mound on which the temples stand contains older temples built upon the ruins of yet older ones, dating back to 400 B.C. One excavation of the facade of a buried temple contains a huge stucco mask, taller than a person, of a fierce-eyed rain god with a bulbous, warty nose, perfectly preserved by earth and rubble while the stucco sculptures on the exposed buildings of Tikal were being obliterated by the rainforest climate. To the right of the giant mask, a dark, vaulted passageway leads into the pyramid. Feel your way through the darkness to the end, then strike a match and you'll find yourself face-to-face with another gargantuan god mask.

The **Central Acropolis** sprawls across four acres. It is believed to have been the royal palace of Tikal, a complex of spacious multistory residences built around six separate courtyards. Only the front part of the palace, facing the plaza, has been completely excavated; the back part blends gracefully into the forest. The stupendous roof comb that breaks the skyline behind the Central Acropolis is the top of **Temple V,** the second-tallest pyramid at Tikal at 185 feet in height. Still unexcavated and shrouded by trees, it shows what all five of the great temple pyramids at Tikal must have looked like when early archaeologists came to explore and photograph the site at the end of the 19th century. A narrow foot trail from the east end of the Central Acropolis leads into the rainforest to Temple V, then returns to the main trail near Mundo Perdido.

The **Mundo Perdido** ("Lost World") complex, which lies southwest of the Plaza Mayor, presents a sharp contrast to the central ruins area. The massive **Main Pyramid** at the center of a group of 38 structures was built at least 500 years before the pyramids of the Plaza Mayor, suggesting that this area may have been the main ceremonial center for much of Tikal's history. Unlike the main plaza with its formal, landscaped feel, the Mundo Perdido complex has been excavated with an eye toward minimizing the impact on the surrounding forest, so the lower structures are nestled among the roots and trunks of forest giants. From the top of the great pyramid, you can see the summits of Temples I and II on the Plaza Mayor, just the roof combs rising face-to-face, sun-and-moon, he-and-she through the canopy of a rainforest that rolls unbroken, astonishing in its vastness, all the way to the distant horizon. East of the pyramid and north of a small plaza with seven temples, is a **triple ball court** thought to be the only one of its kind in the Maya world.

At the westernmost end of the ruins area, **Temple IV**, known as the Temple of the Double-Headed Serpent, is the tallest manmade structure at Tikal. At 228 feet high, this pyramid was also the second-tallest structure in the ancient

Maya world. It was believed to be the tallest until one pyramid at El Mirador, 42 miles straight-line distance to the north across the roadless depths of the Petén rainforest and presently inaccessible to sightseers, was measured at about a meter taller. Temple IV has been cleared but not excavated, so instead of a very steep stairway to the top, there's a very steep foot trail. As you reach the summit, a metal ladder affixed to the temple wall lets you climb all the way up to the roof comb. Near Temple IV are a parking lot, reached by a road that circles around the archaeological zone, and a group picnic area, so it is common to find busloads of school children swarming up and down the pyramid.

On the other side of the main ruins area, the Méndez Causeway branches away from the main trail and leads in a straight line through the forest for half a mile to the **Temple of the Inscriptions**, a large, solitary temple on the outskirts of the ancient city. Covering the entire surface of the roof comb, you can still make out the only major hieroglyphic inscription found at Tikal. The temple is so far removed from the main ruins of Tikal that it was not discovered until 1951. Why this unusual and impressive temple should be set apart by both distance and architecture from the rest of the city is unknown. The stela that stands in front of the temple was intentionally smashed, probably by the people of ancient Tikal.

Visitors are not allowed to spend the night in the ruins area. Rangers check to see that everybody is out before dark. They explain that jaguars and other

Spider monkeys

dangerous beasts roam the forest at night, and if pressed ("But I thought jaguars were almost extinct. . . .") admit that it is other, supernatural beings that make the ruins a place to be avoided at night. Outsiders doubt it, they say, but everybody around there knows it is true.

No night watchman will stop you from walking to the ruins after midnight. Dawn as experienced from the ruins at Tikal is an ultimate travel experience, absolutely worth the inconvenience of rising before first light. Early-to-bed, early-to-rise is less of a hardship here than it would be most places because the electricity shuts off at 9:30 p.m. in the national park hotels.

A mist as thick as ocean fog shrouds Tikal in the hours before dawn. As the sun rises, the mist glows first pink and then golden. For a moment, you can glimpse the glory of Tikal in ancient times. Then the ancient temples, shadows at first, turn to stone as the mist burns away. The forest comes alive suddenly with the cries of monkeys and birds and the throbbing drone of insects, and the heat of the day begins. A dawn tour led by freelancing off-duty park rangers is well worth the small fee. The rangers, many of whom were born and raised on the edge of the Petén rainforest, are amazingly knowledgeable about the diversity of plant and animal species found in the park. You can also walk into the park on your own as early as you like, and young travelers staying at the campground organize informal 4:00 a.m. expeditions to the pyramids most mornings.

At any time of day you choose to walk among the various outlying ruins of Tikal, they quickly become a mere excuse for venturing deeper into the rainforest. At every turn, a smaller trail beckons you off into the deep jungle for a spontaneous visit to some half-buried temple or hidden forest glade. Monkeys create dins of excitement as you enter their territory. Colorful toucans scatter from the trees in front of you. The diversity of plant and animal life in the Petén jungle means that around every bend in the trail you discover something new—a tree full of orchids, a strange fruit, a kaleidoscopic butterfly swarm, a line of leafcutter ants marching in single file for as far as you can see. The Petén rainforest supports the richest array of wildlife to be found anywhere on the North American continent.

Mammals that live in the Petén forest include several species of predatory cats—margays, jaguarundis, ocelots, cougars and jaguars—as well as other uncommon species such as anteaters, kinkajous and tapirs. Visitors are unlikely to see any of these rare, elusive animals in the wild, but there are other jungle creatures you can expect to see. Foremost among them are spider monkeys, easy to spot because of the rattling, crashing noises they make as they leap from branch to branch. Black howler monkeys, common in Belize and reportedly common throughout the Petén just a few years ago, are still spotted once in a while. Armadillos, tepezcuintles and coatimundis may be seen in the underbrush toward dusk, as are javelinas (called peccaries in Belize), a small piglike beast. Visitors often catch glimpses of silver foxes, known to the locals as "gatos de la selva" ("forest cats"), gliding through the ruins of Tikal. Other forest denizens include weasels, opossums, porcupines and deer.

The abundance of wildlife is particularly astonishing considering much of its habitat is almost certainly less than a thousand years old. Using satellite mapping to reveal the outlines of ancient farmers' fields, archaeologists have determined that virtually all the land within a 60-mile radius of Tikal had been cleared for cultivation 1100 years ago. Here, peasants grew maize, beans and tomatoes on small suburban farms, supplying food for themselves as well as the priests and rulers who lived in the great city center. After the abandonment of the city began, around 900 A.D., it is difficult to estimate how long it took for the lofty ceiba, mahogany and sapodilla trees to take root among the ruins. The jungle existed in something like its present form when Spanish conquistador Hernán Cortés visited the region in 1525.

Anywhere you go in the backcountry of Tikal National Park, you will find low mounds and tumbled-down stone walls that remain from those ancient homesteads—even in places that are almost inaccessible today. Archaeologists will probably never excavate all of the sites in the jungle of Tikal National Park, and visitors will always be able to wonder what undiscovered treasures may lie hidden there. Whenever you explore and wherever you wander, use good judgment. Jungle trails have a way of tempting people onward. Remember that there is a risk of getting lost in this terrain.

Despite its size, the 222-acre Tikal National Park protects less than two percent of El Petén, the largest contiguous expanse of rainforest on the North American continent. The northern third of the Petén rainforest—all the land north of Tikal to the northern, eastern and western borders of Guatemala, has been designated as the Maya Biosphere Reserve, a unit of the UNESCO Man and Biosphere program that protects inhabited wilderness areas, allowing some economic use of the forest in a buffer zone around a protected core area. The Maya Biosphere Reserve, encompassing an area of 5400 square miles, is one of the most ambitious efforts to save the rainforest anywhere in the world. La Ruta Maya Conservation Foundation, armed with a large grant from the MacArthur Foundation, hopes to go one step further, merging Guatemala's Maya Biosphere Reserve with Belize's Río Bravo Conservation Area and Mexico's Calakmul Biosphere Reserve to form the Maya Peace Park, a huge international park that would span the three nations' often-troubled borders and allow cooperative ecotourism development in the region.

At least 25 other major ceremonial centers have been found in the Maya Biosphere Reserve and another dozen along the Río Pasión in the southwestern part of the department of Petén. Of those in the biosphere reserve, most are accessible only by very primitive four-wheel-drive tracks that can only be used during the dry season, and several are located in terrain so impassable that archaeologists can only reach them by helicopter. None are currently open to the public, though proponents of the Maya Peace Park plan hope that El

Mirador, site of a large ceremonial center whose temples include the tallest known Maya pyramid, will someday be opened to tourists by shuttle bus or even monorail.

At present, the only ruin in the Maya Biosphere Reserve that casual visitors can get to from Tikal is **Uaxactún,** located 12 miles north of the Tikal ruins and just a short distance outside the north boundary of the national park. For centuries, Uaxactún was a rival city to Tikal. Nothing about these partially excavated but unrestored ruins suggests that this ceremonial site even came close to achieving the grandeur of Tikal, but inscriptions on Tikal's temples and stelae reveal that the two cities fought bloody wars and that, at least once, the army of Uaxactún conquered Tikal. Backpackers may chose to hike from Tikal to Uaxactún. Camping equipment is a must, since even strong hikers find it impossible to walk there and back the same day. Or a local guide can take you in a four-wheel-drive vehicle, a rough one-hour trip each way.

One Maya ruin site that you may want to visit is **El Ceibal** (see "Getting there" section later in this chapter for details), noted by archaeologists as having the only circular temple in the entire Maya world. It also has 56 carved stone stelae, including one that certainly seems to depict a Maya warrior talking on the telephone! The stelae, altars and stone walls at El Ceibal are covered with a bright orange lichen, creating a dramatic contrast to the amazingly lush rainforest that constantly threatens to swallow the ancient city once more.

LODGING   Staying at Tikal National Park is best because there is too much in the park to experience in a single day, and the shuttle trip between Flores/ Santa Elena and Tikal, an hour each way, costs more than a hotel room does. Staying in the park also lets you spend the night surrounded by the sounds of the jungle and visit the ruins in the eerie dawn mist.

There are three hotels in Tikal National Park, totalling 49 rooms between them. Because of development restrictions imposed by the Guatemalan government when the Maya Biosphere Reserve was created, no new hotels can be built. Sometimes, tour groups fill them to capacity and other times they are almost empty. You don't know until you go there, because it's not easy to make advance reservations and none of the hotels has a telephone. The men who drive shuttle vans between the airport at Santa Elena and the national park may know about room availability. Otherwise, the best plan for travelers arriving on the morning plane is just to go to the park by noon and see whether you can find lodging. If you can't get a room, you'll have time to return to Flores by midafternoon and find one there.

The most comfortable, and most interesting, place to stay inside the national park is the 15-room **Tikal Inn** (moderate), a classic jungle lodge that consists of an attractively rustic main building, where you'll find the dining room, lobby and four rather elegantly decorated guest rooms with four-poster beds, as well as a row of thatched-roof cabanas along one side of a broad expanse of lawn with a swimming pool in the center and dense rainforest around the perimeter of the grounds. The cabanas have complete modern conveniences, including electric light from 6:00 to 9:30 p.m. and private bathrooms with running water that is warm late in the day. The hotel's mascot ocelot lives in a large enclosure in the jungle nearby, screams hauntingly in the night, and sometimes is let loose on the grounds to romp with cat-loving guests. Reservations can only be made by sending a letter to "Tikal Inn, Tikal, Petén, Guatemala" telling what dates you want, then sending payment in full after you receive confirmation. Modified American plan available.

The largest hotel at Tikal is the 32-room **Jungle Lodge** (moderate; send reservation requests to 29 Calle No. 18-01, Zona 12, Guatemala City or call 76-02-94 in Guatemala City). It was originally built in the 1930s to house archaeological teams working at Tikal. A recent remodeling has converted the rustic old cabins into spacious, pleasant cabanas with tin roofs that are noisy in the rain and private baths with reliable hot water. The rates are higher than at the Tikal Inn.

The third option, the **Jaguar Inn** (moderate), next door to the Tikal Museum, has just two guest rooms in simple thatched-roof cottages with private baths. During the dry season, several large, furnished tents are also rented out as guest accommodations. The food here is not very good, so it is better to opt for a room only, without meals, and eat across the road at the campground.

The most luxurious accommodations in the Petén are at the **Hotel Camino Real Tikal** (El Remate; air conditioning; very expensive; for reservations call 33-46-33 in Guatemala City), outside the national park near the intersection where the road from Belize intersects the highway between Santa Elena and Tikal. All 120 rooms have private baths and satellite television complete with remote control—self-indulgent amenities in a region where most of the local people live without running water or indoor plumbing. Guest facilities include a swimming pool, a lakefront beach, tennis courts, restaurants, a bar and a disco.

In Santa Elena, one of the better hotels is the **Hotel Maya Internacional** (moderate; 81-12-76; for reservations write 2 Avenida No. 7-78, Zona 10, Guatemala City, or call 36-39-09). This compound of 20 rustic rooms in duplex bungalows on stilts over Lake Petén Itzá used to be the top of the line in the Petén region, but has lost most of its formerly landscaped grounds to the rising water lever of the lake over the past few years. Nature lovers can watch from the bungalow porch as multitudes of egrets, herons and other wading birds fish among the water lilies just a few feet away. Rooms have private baths. Be careful of the electric water-heating shower heads, common in hotels around Santa Elena and Flores, but said to be dangerous because of the possibility of electrocution.

Of numerous small lodgings in the island town of Flores, the modern **Savanna Hotel** (moderate; 81-12-48) is a favorite simply because of the view. Unlike most of the other hotels, which are located near the causeway, this one is on the far side of the island overlooking the full expanse of Lake Petén Itzá. Of the 23 rooms, the ones at the back have the best lake views. The four-story hotel has nothing in the way of decor to spruce up its plain, concrete block architecture, but the grand panorama from the second-story patio makes up for it.

RESTAURANTS   At Tikal, each of the hotels has its own small restaurant serving a set menu at set hours, with the price of breakfast and dinner included in the "modified American plan" room rate. The only alternatives are a series of *comedores* situated down the road from the campground, serving basic food at budget prices. The restaurant at the campground itself is the largest in the area and serves a low-priced selection of soups, sandwiches and spaghetti.

Flores has a number of rustic-but-nice restaurants that offer entrées of local game from the Petén rainforest, typically including alligator, venison, tepez-cuintle, armadillo, wild turkey, pheasant and rabbit. This is the traditional food of the region, and travelers who feel queasy about dining on freshly killed jungle animals may have to subsist on fruit salads. More conventional meats such as chicken and pork are only found in the dining rooms of better hotels. The town's best restaurants are in a cluster along Calle Centroamérica, the main street one block north of the island end of the causeway.

The tastiest meals in Flores are found at **La Mesa de los Maya** (Calle Centroamérica; budget; 81-12-40). The servings are generous and the cuisine is out of this world. Handwoven tablecloths and wall hangings brighten the two cozy, plain-but-honest little dining rooms, as does the friendly pet toucan. There is a full bar on the premises, though a drink costs much more than a dinner does.

A block down the street, **Restaurant La Jungla** (Calle Centroamérica; budget) is overgrown with jungle plants like a fern bar run amok—strange but tolerable. What's not tolerable are the boa constrictor skins, jaguar heads, stuffed birds and other wall trophies that not only shriek of anti-ecotourism but make you feel as if your dinner entrée were watching over your shoulder. Beyond this, the food and service are okay.

Around the block, facing the waterfront about a block west of the causeway, **El Faisan** (Flores; budget) is another small restaurant and bar serving a similar selection of grilled wild animal meats. Rough wood paneling decorated from floor to ceiling with photos, drawings and maps of Tikal create an archaeology ambience that sets it apart from the other restaurants nearby. It is open later in the evening than most of the others, too.

SHOPPING   The souvenir industry in Flores and Tikal is in its infancy. A cluster of four shops near the Tikal Museum and the entrance to the ruins area has a high-priced selection of native *típica* clothing from other parts of Guatemala that is worth looking at only if you are not planning to visit the highlands on your trip. It also has lots and lots of Tikal T-shirts. Other makeshift shops along the narrow streets of Flores also stock limited selections of *típica*. The best souvenirs of Tikal are the videotapes with aerial footage of the rainforest and the ruins and audio tapes of jungle sounds recorded at Tikal.

GETTING THERE   The best way to travel overland to Tikal is with a tour arranged through one of the many lodges in Belize's Cayo District (see Chapter Nine). A package tour eliminates potential problems of going it on your own—changing buses at the border, being denied entry if you're in a rental car (which are rarely allowed across the border), being denied a tourist card (or having to pay a generous *mordida* for one), trusting taxi drivers to take you all the way to Tikal on the agreed fee, or dealing with Guatemala military officials (and rebel guerillas impersonating military officials) who stop you en route to Tikal to check your passport. If you do decide to cross the border on your own, make sure you obtain a Guatemala visa in advance, either in the United States or Mexico, as there is no Guatemalan consulate in Belize.

By far the simplest way to get to Tikal is by plane, a surprisingly short hop—only 45 minutes—from Belize City. **Tropic Air** (2-45671 in Belize City or 800-422-3435 in the United States) offers two flights daily on most weekdays, and the fare is only about US$96 round-trip. Be aware, however, that flights are frequently delayed or canceled altogether, especially if there aren't enough passengers, so stay flexible.

The biggest problem facing visitors who would like to explore more remote areas of El Petén is lack of transportation. Very few travelers come to Tikal in their own vehicles, and public transportation is quite limited. A few enterprising guides, who don't advertise but can be found by word of mouth through any hotel or restaurant operator or shuttle van driver, run tours from Flores and Tikal to other Maya ruins in the Petén—especially El Ceibal, which can also be reached by public transportation. The trip involves traveling 36 miles by car or bus on a good dirt road to the jungle village of Sayaxché and hiring a boat there to take you 11 miles down the Río Pasión to the ruins. The ruins can also be reached by a new four-wheel-drive track, but the jungle boat trip is more fun.

SOUTHERN SIDE TRIPS

RÍO DULCE AND QUIRIGUÁ AREA   From Punta Gorda in southern Belize, it's a short, scenic ride across the Gulf of Honduras to the Guatemala coast, stopping first at Puerto Barrios and then Livingston. To cross into this southern area of Guatemala, you will need only your passport and a visa, issued in advance from a Guatemalan consulate in the United States or Mexico. If you plan to continue on to Copán in Honduras—a highly recommended side trip—a passport will suffice.

One of Guatemala's most unusual little towns, **Livingston** is perched at the mouth of the Río Dulce River, where the gorge spills into the Gulf of Honduras, an outcropping of a village in the southwesternmost corner of the Caribbean Sea. Isolated by unbridged river, roadless forest and the Belizean border just up the coast, Livingston is Guatemala's only Garifuna community. It's a small community of 3000 people, most of whom are multilingual, speaking Spanish and English as well as the African-based Garifuna patois.

Livingston's brightly painted wooden houses and storefronts run uphill from the docks along a single main street, which is paved, although there is not a single motor vehicle in town—a fact to which the town owes its timeless tropical charm. In a few hours, you can stroll every street in town, visit the simple Catholic church with its ebony-skinned Jesus and Virgin of Guadalupe, then walk over the hill and up the narrow, hard, brown beach where Livingston's dreadlocked youth can usually be found savoring reggae and ganja, to the far end, where a trail leads up to **Siete Altares**, a series of waterfalls and pools just right for bathing. *Note*: Hire a local to guide you there; a few tourists have been robbed at the falls.

Beyond that, there's not much for either visitors or locals to do in Livingston. For both, people-watching is a major pastime, and the most rewarding time to do it is on weekends, when settlers paddle to town from fishing camps up the coast and emerge from the jungle via foot trails to attend church services. No cars, no televisions, no soldiers or armed guards, and nothing to do at all. If you do spend a night or two, you may find Livingston one of the most relaxed and relaxing places on the continent.

Once you feel rejuvenated, you won't want to miss a trip up the **Río Dulce**. This truly rewarding excursion up the "Sweet River" will undoubtedly be one of the highlights of your southern side trip from Belize. You can hire a boat in Livingston to take you the 18 winding, hill-studded miles into the gorge and to the crossroads of Castillo San Felipe. (Conversely, you can cruise *down* river from Puerto Barrios to Livingston, after disembarking in Puerto Barrios from Punta Gorda, Belize). Paddling down the Río Dulce, spectacular scenery presents itself at virtually every turn, from the sheer silver cliffs that soar above the riverbanks to the colossal trees upholstered in emerald greenery. The remote tropical paradise feel of the Río Dulce is in part illusory, for just beyond the top rim of the gorge are endless banana fields and the shacks and villages of some of the poorest country people in Guatemala. Yet the river still allows glimpses of one of the last fragments of primeval America, much of it practically unchanged since the days of Columbus.

The river narrows abruptly into a steep canyon whose walls, dripping with lush vegetation, reach hundreds of feet above the water. Egrets peer from every tree, pelicans glide by just inches above the water, turtles sun themselves along the riverbank. Here and there a cluster of thatch-roofed huts nestles between the cliffs and the water. People who live along the Río Dulce—mothers with infants and bundles of groceries from Livingston, even unaccompanied young children—paddle their hand-hewn dugout canoes called *cayucas* up and down the river in a kind of uncomplicated purity that daydreams are made of.

After the steep canyon, the Río Dulce opens into a broad expanse of open water called **El Golfete**, where local fishermen cast their nests. Much of the north shore of El Golfete is protected as the **Biotopo Chacón Machaca**, a wildlife sanctuary for the endangered West Indian Manatee. Guides claim that jaguars and tapirs also still roam the deep forest along the north shore.

Upriver from El Golfete is a scattering of expensive vacation homes and several marinas mostly full of American yachts and sailboats. Then there is **Lake Izabal**, the largest lake in Guatemala, stretching some 12 miles wide and 27 miles long. Its waters reach a depth of 60 feet. The lake's shoreline, dotted with more than a dozen fishing villages, is virtually inaccessible by land. The largest village, El Estor, can be reached by a grueling 84-mile unpaved road that leaves the highway midway between the Biotopo Mario Dary Rivera quetzal sanctuary and Cobán, and takes all day to drive. The other villages can only be reached by boat. Fishing is the main pastime on the lake, and motor launches with pilot can be hired at the Castillo San Felipe bridge or any of the resort hotels nearby.

Presiding over the lake is **Castillo San Felipe** (admission), a small stone fort complete with lookout towers, a drawbridge and cannons on the ramparts. It was built in 1686 to guard the mouth of Lake Izabal from British privateers like Sir Francis Drake. The fort has a shady picnic area and a swimming beach.

The castillo marks the end of the line for the Río Dulce River. Which means you can spend a night here and then head back to Livingston, or continue your side trip to southern Guatemala. From Castillo San Felipe, you can hire a guide or possibly even a car to take you to the ruins at Quiriguá. You can get to Quiriguá via Route 13 to Route 9. At Route 9, you can head west to Quiriguá. Or, if you haven't already been there on the ferry from Punta Gorda, Belize, head east 31 miles for a look at the rugged banana republic town of **Puerto Barrios**. A hot, charmless place full of railroad tracks, Puerto Barrios is home to 25,000 people. It's formerly the shipping port for United Fruit Company, and though today bananas still travel by boat, most set sail from the giant new dock complex at Santo Tomás de Castilla on the southern tip of the bay. Puerto Barrios has an evil reputation as a town of tough waterfront dives, drugs and prostitutes. Except for those seeking cheap and potentially dangerous thrills, there is not really much to attract visitors.

From Puerto Barrios, travel west on Route 9, until the highway descends along the Río Montagua from its steep-flanked valley into the broad, hot, moist delta that is Guatemala's major banana-growing region. In the midst of the bananas lie the ruins of **Quiriguá** (admission). The Classic city was Copán's major rival for several centuries, from about 600 to 900 A.D., and archaeologists have devoted much energy to unraveling the true relationship between the two cities. Hieroglyphic records seem to suggest that the royal families of Quiriguá and Copán were related by marriage. An inscription at Copán reveals that one of its greatest rulers, Lord 18-Rabbit, was captured by soldiers from Quiriguá and later beheaded. Some experts also think that Copán captured Quiriguá earlier in 18-Rabbit's reign. While most of the stelae at Quiriguá were done in a style much different from that of Copán, the first stela erected there—**Monument 8**, which bears an inscription dating it to 751 A.D.—is so similar in style to those at Copán that many archaeologists believe the lords of Quiriguá hired artists from Copán to create it.

Quiriguá is situated in the middle of a vast banana plantation formerly owned by the United Fruit Company. Although Quiriguá was a small city, it covered a much larger area than the restored site would suggest today. Most of the city's temple mounds were razed and obliterated to plant banana trees. But the Great Plaza, with its huge, unique stelae and zoomorphic altars, was so remarkable that United Fruit hired a team of archaeologists in 1934 to restore it and set aside a tiny parcel of the once-magnificent jungle surrounding it. On the road in to the ruins you'll pass huge trucks carrying away unimaginable quantities of still-green bananas in a virtually nonstop tropical harvest. A quick look at a working plantation may change the way you look at bananas in the supermarket back home.

The original layout of Quiriguá, much of it now concealed by a thousand-year overgrowth of rainforest, was a lot like that of Copán. The only structures that have been cleared and excavated at Quiriguá, however, are the small, plain temples surrounding the **Acropolis**, a sunken ceremonial plaza flanked all around by stone steps like the antithesis of a pyramid. Even more than Copán, Quiriguá is architecturally unimpressive but redeemed by its artwork. Towering stelae statues, the tallest in the Maya world by far, line the **Great Plaza**. The zoomorphic altars are also the largest found anywhere. The free-flowing, abstracted features, symbols and hieroglyphs of these imaginative giant frog and cockroach figures create a counterpoint to the rigid, formal statues.

Each of the statues and altars was carved from a single large slab or boulder of a peculiar reddish sandstone. It came out of the quarry, soft, damp and easy to carve, but dried harder than concrete, so tough that statues made from it have survived a thousand years of abandonment and neglect in surprisingly

Tapir

good condition. Bringing the massive stones from the quarry three miles away was a remarkable feat. No one knows for sure how it was done. The tallest of the sculptures, **Monument 5**, stands 35 feet high and was carved from a single 43-foot stone monolith that weighed 65 tons.

All of the Quiriguá stelae were erected during the 64-year period from 746 to 810 A.D. For half of that period, Quiriguá was ruled by a single leader, Cauac Sky. Hieroglyphs on one stela record that earlier in his reign, in 737, Lord Cauac Sky waged war against Copán and put its leader to death. Although little is known of the history of Quiriguá before Cauac Sky ascended the throne, most experts believe that Quiriguá's independence from Copán was won in this war, and that the giant stelae were erected at Quiriguá after independence in order to establish that the city was every bit as magnificent as its rival to the south. Fully half of the stelae in Quiriguá's Great Plaza portray Lord Cauac Sky at different times during his reign. They include, in chronological order, **Monuments 8, 10, 6, 4, 5, 1** and **3**. (The stelae zoomorphs are numbered according to their positions around the plaza, not in the order in which they were made). Hieroglyphs on **Monument 11** record his death. After his death, the statues of subsequent rulers were smaller and more modest, and most of the creative energy of Quiriguá's sculptors went into fantastic zoomorphic altars instead. At Quiriguá, as at Copán, many of the men portrayed on the statues have beards. Lord Cauac sky apparently introduced the fashion around 761 A.D., when Monument 6 was erected, and the style continued for 12 years after his death. The long goatee-style beards look remarkably like the ornamented chinpieces of ancient Egyptian pharaohs, and we can only speculate whether the lords of Quiriguá and Copán grew real beards or donned artificial ones.

It is best to visit Quiriguá late in the day or when the weather is overcast, since in bright sunlight the thatched roofs that protect the huge stelae and zoomorphic altars cast shadows that make photographing them almost impossible.

LODGING   An anomalous 45-room resort hotel tucked off the main street about a block above the docks in Livingston, the **Hotel Tucán Dugú** (moderate to expensive; 48-15-88) offers bright, modern rooms and suites in a huge thatch-roofed building with a swimming pool. Prices are moderate for regular rooms in the main building and expensive for the more private bungalows along the walkway that leads down to the hotel's private beach.

Practically across the street from the Tucán Dugú, you'll find a completely different kind of Caribbean charm at the **Hotel Río Dulce** (budget; 48-10-59), a plain but picture-perfect little blue two-story inn with a white picket fence, flower gardens, a big front porch perfectly situated for main-street people-watching, and basic shared-bath rooms at a very low budget price. Youthful backpackers find their way here from all over the world.

If you choose to stay in Puerto Barrios (as you might on the way to or from Punta Gorda, Belize), the town's best accommodations are found at the **Hotel**

Puerto Libre (Carretera Atlántica Km. 292; air conditioning; moderate; 48-04-47), an American-style motel with a swimming pool and satellite television. Located out of town at the junction with the road to Santo Tomás de Castillo, the Puerto Libre can present a problem for those who are traveling by public transportation. In town, the **Hotel Del Norte** (7 Calle at 1 Avenida; budget; 48-00-87) is a partly renovated, Caribbean-style wooden inn on the waterfront. Shuttered doorways open out onto private balconies with views of the bay. Only two of the bright, simply furnished rooms have private baths.

The closest comfortable lodging to Quiriguá is to be found at the upper end of the Río Dulce near the Castillo San Felipe Bridge. Here you'll find the **Hotel Catamaran** (moderate; 32-48-29), a complex of bungalows on an island downriver from the bridge. There is an inexpensive guarded parking lot under the bridge, and motor launches—often the same ones that go downriver to Livingston in the morning—wait nearby to take you across to the hotel. Guest accommodations, set along the shore and around grounds bursting with colorful flowers with a cage of parrots and a swimming pool in the middle, are rustic and simply furnished but quite large and airy, with private baths, screens to keep the mosquitoes out and balconies overlooking the water. The river gently lapping outside the window assures guests a sound night's sleep.

Another resort complex in the best sense of the word, the **Hotel Izabal Tropical** (ceiling fans; moderate; 47-84-01) is situated on the shore of Lake Izabal about two-and-a-half miles down a dirt road from Castillo San Felipe. Fourteen thatch-roofed bamboo-and-stucco guest cabanas are scattered across a hillside along the lake. Each has a private bathroom with shower. The hotel has both a children's and an adult's swimming pool and luxuriant gardens that blossom year-round. It also has its own dock, and you can usually find boats for hire there with or without a captain.

RESTAURANTS   Livingston has several modest restaurants that cater to the low-key lunchtime tourist trade, since the locals generally catch their own meals. The **Restaurante Tiburongato** (budget), a clean place with checkered plastic tablecloths and an open-air latticework facade that looks out on the town's main street, is typical. Menu items include ceviche and a local seafood stew called *tapado*, made with coconuts and plantains.

If you're spending the night in Livingston, your best dinner bet is the amazing **African Place** (moderate). Designed and built by an immigrant from Spain, it is an authentic Moorish-style stone castle in miniature, patterned after those of southern Spain, with archways, ornate tilework and wrought-iron grillwork accenting windows that peer out into the jungle. On the menu are wonderfully imaginative seafood dishes such as shrimp in garlic sauce and curried fish.

Puerto Barrios has no restaurants special enough to search out. The restaurant at **Hotel Del Norte** (7 Calle at 1 Avenida; 48-00-87) with its no-nonsense ambience and predictable menu of fish and chicken dishes, is reputed to be the best in town.

Aside from a few small food stands along Route 9, there are no restaurants in the vicinity of Quiriguá. Boys often hang around the parking lot at the ruins selling big bunches of small, sweet bananas to visitors for a few pennies.

In the Río Dulce resort area around the bridge at Castillo San Felipe, the best meals are served in restaurants at the various hotels along the river. The **Hotel Catamaran** (moderate; 32-48-29) has a thatch-roofed open-air restaurant built out over the water. The menu includes most of the standard Guatemalan restaurant items—fruit salads, *desayuno chapín*, roast chicken, spaghetti, local fish—and you can watch the big luxury sailboats with American names glide past as you eat. Hours of service are limited. Accessible by a dirt road instead of by boat, the **Hotel Izabal Tropical** (moderate; 47-84-01) also has a restaurant built over the water, with a range of menu choices and prices similar to those at the Catamaran.

Budget-priced food stands clustered around the Castillo San Felipe bridge sell fish—most likely perch or tarpon—freshly caught from the lake, grilled with spices and served with tortillas and rice on the side. Try **Mary's** (budget), a tiny place at the end of a dock just east of the bridge.

SHOPPING   Many of the storefronts that line the main street of Livingston offer various handcrafted goods. Prices are high for clothing brought in from other parts of Guatemala, but locally made gift items such as coconut carvings and Afro-Caribbean paintings may bring a smile to your face as they tug at your billfold.

A few roadside stalls near the Castillo San Felipe bridge offer limited selections of native *típica* clothing. A hut near the pool at the **Hotel Catamaran** houses a small gallery where members of a cooperative network of American artists—who live on boats nearby—show their work.

GETTING THERE   From Punta Gorda, in southern Belize, it's a short boat ride across the Gulf of Honduras to the Guatemala coast, stopping first at Puerto Barrios and then Livingston. You can catch a boat at the **Punta Gorda Wharf** (Front Street on the sea), where there is service twice a week, usually on Tuesday and Friday afternoons. Or, walk over to the **Toledo Visitors Information Center** (next to the wharf; 7-22470), which can arrange excursions ranging from one to several days, taking in Livingston and Guatemala's Río Dulce River.

From Castillo San Felipe, you can hire a guide or possibly even a car to take you to the ruins at Quiriguá. The way to Quiriguá is via Route 13, which stretches 21 miles to Route 9. At Route 9, you can head west to Quiriguá or head east 31 miles to Puerto Barrios. From Puerto Barrios, travel 55 five miles west on Route 9. To get to Quiriguá from the main highway, you need to go about two miles south on a wide unpaved road frequented by huge trucks carrying bananas.

COPÁN   The straight-line distance from Quiriguá to **Copán** (admission) is a mere 29 miles. Traveling as the macaw flies between the region's two great ancient city sites would carry you above a formidable mountain ridge, skimming the canopy of luxuriant, impenetrable rainforest as you glided over the international border. By road, however, the distance is more like 102 miles, which, including the formalities of crossing the Guatemala-Honduras border, takes half a day. And if you are coming from the Río Dulce area, where you can hire a taxi or join an overnight tour to Copán, add at least another two hours to that.

It is more than worth the trouble of getting there. Indeed, after visitors set eyes on Copán and its unique, haunting stone sculptures, most agree that it is one of the most exciting Maya sites of the world. You can still feel the magic that inspired American explorer John Lloyd Stephens to write in 1841, "The beauty of the sculpture, the solemn stillness of the woods, disturbed only by the scrambling of monkeys and the chattering of parrots, the desolation of the city, and the mystery that hung over it, all created an interest higher, if possible, than I had ever felt among the ruins of the Old World."

Copán lies just six-and-a-half miles across the Honduras border, so close it is often regarded as a Guatemala travel destination. The border crossing is a tiny place called El Florida. There are shuttle vans from the border that go both to the village of Ruinas Copán and to the ruins a half-mile away. It is an easy and pleasant walk between the village and the ruins visitors center on a pretty forest trail that parallels the road and leads directly to the **Great Plaza** of ancient Copán. Also known as the Plaza of Red Plaster, this broad ceremonial courtyard now covered with lawn was entirely paved during

Copán Ruins

East Court

Hieroglyphic
Stairway

Stela H
Altar G
Stela C
ball court
Great Plaza

Acropolis

West Court

Copán's days of glory. It contains the most remarkable sculptures found anywhere in the Maya world. While the major features of Copán—the great statues and the hieroglyphic stairway—are right on the plaza, visitors who walk
from the village to the ruins soon realize that the ancient city covered a large
area and that impressive stelae and unexcavated temple mounds can be found
along a number of trails through the forest.

Set on the bank of the Río Amarillo, Copán dominated a vast series of valleys
upriver to the east. Though it is one of the most remote and undeveloped parts
of Honduras today, the valleys and forests around Copán were a densely populated region in ancient times. The city itself had a population of about 10,000,
and most of the jungle in the valley had been cleared for agriculture. Today,
the area has grown back in a wild tangle of hardwoods and vines, out of which
archaeologists have reclaimed the ancient city's central plazas. Beautifully
carved stelae, which may mark astronomical alignments, stand on several hilltops reached by foot trails from the main center, and if you take time to walk
up to one of them, particularly **Stela 12,** you will be rewarded with a stupendous view of the ruins and the river valley over which the lords of Copán
reigned. Carved on the stela is the most complete genealogy anywhere of a
Maya royal family.

Archaeologists know a lot about the history of Copán because of the detailed
records carved on the city's famous monuments. Copán was ruled by a single,
unbroken dynasty of lords for four centuries, from the ascension of the legendary god-king Yax-Kuk-Mo' in 426 A.D., through 17 generations of lords,
to the death of U-Cit-Tok (whose mother was a princess of the royal family
at Palenque) on February 10, 822. The city thrived all through the 8th century,
but civilization began to collapse at Copán around the year 800 and the city
was gradually abandoned. During its heyday, Copán produced the greatest
sculptural accomplishments of the ancient Maya world, as well as the most
ambitious hieroglyphic records.

Carved from massive blocks of a fine-textured stone called andesite, the stelae
of Copán stand about ten feet tall. Unlike the relief stelae sculptures of human
forms seen at other Maya sites, the stelae of Copán are carved almost completely in the round. There are a dozen stelae in the Great Plaza. All portray
rulers of Copán, and each statue is decorated with hieroglyphs that record
the lineage, birth, death and marriage dates, and major accomplishments of
the lord it represents. The headdresses, too, bear amazingly detailed ornamen-
tation of stylized human and animal forms with symbolic meanings.

Facial hair was apparently in fashion for rulers of Copán. Art found elsewhere
in the Maya world suggests that beards were very rare in ancient times, as
they are among Maya Indians today, leading some to speculate that the lords
who reigned over the Motagua River Basin may have been of a different race
from another part of the world. At Copán, the personage on the west side
of **Stela C** has a full beard. Those on **Stelae B** and **D** have goatees, and **Stela**

F has one with a moustache. Archaeologists have theorized that the figure on **Stela H** may have been a woman. If so, she would be the only known woman ruler in the ancient Maya world. Gender, however, was not part of the information carved on the stelae in hieroglyphs, and some contemporary experts assert that Stela H shows a king wearing unisex clothing.

The stelae were originally painted bright red. **Stela C,** the only one in the plaza with faces on both sides, had fallen over and lain with one side protected from the weather for centuries, and so still shows traces of paint. Each of the stelae has a cross-shaped underground vault at its base. Some of the vaults have been excavated to reveal objects such as knife blades, pottery, animal bones and even, in the vault below **Stela H,** pieces of gold imported from South America. The vaults are unique to Copán, and their exact meaning remains a mystery.

In front of several stelae are strange zoomorphic altars carved in highly stylized animal shapes—frogs, jaguars, giant snakes and more fanciful forms— patterned with hieroglyphs and sacred signs. The altars were used for religious offerings, including animal sacrifices. They may also have been used as thrones for priests. Near Stela H are two altars in the shape of plumed serpents and a third showing men's faces peering from the open jaws of a two-headed snake. The two-headed snake, **Altar G,** bears the latest date hieroglyph found at Copán—800 A.D.

On the south side of the Great Plaza, just past the largest and most impressively decorated of ancient Copán's several ball courts, a group of low, broad stepped pyramids and ceremonial platforms surrounds two smaller plazas designated the **East Court** and the **West Court.** By the entrance from the Great Plaza into this complex stands the most spectacular structure in Copán, Building 26, home to the **Hieroglyphic Stairway.** Rising between two balustrades decorated with serpent motifs, the stairway is made from 2500 blocks of stone— each carved with hieroglyphs. The longest inscription found anywhere in the Maya world, it appears to be a comprehensive history of Copán up to the stairway's dedication date, 763 A.D. On this masterpiece, as John Lloyd Stephens mused a century and a half ago, the rulers of Copán "published a record of themselves, through which we might one day hold conference with a perished race." More than a few archaeologists have dedicated their whole lives to deciphering the message of the Hieroglyphic Stairway and, today, with the aid of computers, they have translated roughly a third of it.

In 1989, members of the Copán Acropolis Archaeological Project tunneled 56 feet in from an entrance beside the Hieroglyphic Stairway to discover a large burial vault containing the remains of a noble personage believed to be a son of Copán's greatest king, Smoke-Imix, and brother of the next king, 18-Rabbit. Buried with him were some of the most exquisite jade carvings and jewelry that archaeologists have ever found at a Maya site.

Many of the artifacts found during excavations of the ancient city are exhibited at the **Museo Regional de Arqueología,** facing the central plaza in the village of Ruinas Copán. In ancient times, the finest pottery in the Maya world—notably polychrome pieces decorated with elaborate ceremonial scenes—was made at Copán, and some of the finest examples are on display in the museum along with jade masks and jewelry, tools and sculptures in clay and stone. Some hieroglyph panels have been moved to the museum for protection from wear and erosion, while replicas have been installed at the ruins. Included among the exhibits are the complete contents of the tomb of a priest or sorcerer, found in a section of the archaeological zone now called Las Sepulturas ("The Tombs") and dated to about 450 A.D.

LODGING   Spending the night on the Honduras side of the border affords you the opportunity to visit the ruins in the cool, misty hours just after dawn, when you may find that you have the mystery-laden site all to yourself. There are several small hotels in the village of Ruinas Copán. Electricity at the better hotels, which comes from gasoline generators, is turned on at 6 p.m. and stays on until about 9:30 p.m. Advance reservations are unheard of, but travelers arriving by early afternoon usually have no problem finding a room.

The best is **Hotel Maya Copantl** (budget), on the town square. Behind its flashy multihued pastel paint job, the hotel offers decent rooms with modern furnishings and private baths, as well as a courtyard so overgrown with flora that guests feel like they are staying in the jungle, not in town.

Nearby, also on the main plaza, the **Hotel Marina** (budget) has guest rooms with private baths. It may be more old-fashioned and a bit threadbare and musty, but the laid-back tropical ambience—screened porch and colorful bird mascots—makes it a reasonable choice in its price range. The Hotel Marina also has an annex around the corner that offers very inexpensive rooms with shared baths down the hall, and several other little places around town offer similar rudimentary accommodations.

RESTAURANTS   The best place to eat in Ruinas Copán is the plain-looking dining room at the **Hotel Maya Copantl** (budget), where generous multi-course set meals are served. You can get a good, basic *comida chapín*, a workingman's meal of beans, rice, fried plantains and fat little corn tortillas along with a tiny chunk of meat or chicken, at the **Mini-Hotel Paty** (budget), a short walk from the plaza on the way to the ruins, or a plate of spaghetti at the nearby **Tunkul Restaurant** (budget). The village also has a small public market with food stalls, and you'll find a **cafeteria** at the ruins.

GETTING THERE   From the Río Dulce area, you can hire a taxi or join an overnight tour to Copán, which lies just six-and-a-half miles across the Honduras border. The border crossing is a tiny place called El Florida. The border is open from 7:00 a.m. to 6:00 p.m. You must clear both Guatemalan and Honduran authorities each direction and pay fees in the US$5 to $10 range each time. Telling the border guards of both countries that you are only visiting the ruins saves time and trouble. The Honduran authorities will issue a frontier pass that eliminates the need to apply for a visa in advance. The Guatemalans will save your tourist card (the paper stapled to your passport), cancel the exit stamp when you return and let you back into the country on the same document, avoiding the technicality that would otherwise bar travelers without multiple-entry visas from reentering Guatemala for 72 hours. Minibuses putt back and forth frequently along the road from the border to both the ruins and the nearby village of Ruinas Copán.

Spiny anteater

RECOMMENDED READING

Baudez, Claude and Sydney Picasso. *Lost Cities of the Maya*. New York, Harry Abrams, 1992. An excellent account of recent discoveries and revelations in the Maya World.

Chaplin, Gordon. *Fever Coast Log*. New York, Simon & Shuster, 1992. A telling sailboat journey through the ports of Belize and Central America, related with biting wit and an eye for the offbeat.

Ellis, Zoila. *On Heroes, Lizards and Passion*. Benque Viejo del Carmen, Belize, Cubola Productions, 1988. A collection of seven short, warmly told stories by young Belizean writer Zoila Ellis.

Foster, Bryan. *The Baymen's Legacy*. Benque Viejo del Carmen, Belize, 1992. A history of Belize City, spanning the 18th to the 20th centuries, it's packed with interesting anecdotes.

Horwich, Robert H. and Jonathon Lyon. *A Belizean Rain Forest: The Community Baboon Sanctuary*. Gay Mills, Wisconsin, Orangutan Press, 1990. How a group of Belize farmers joined together to create one of the world's most unusual sanctuaries.

Kricher, John C. *A Neotropical Companion*. Princeton University Press, 1989. A fascinating and comprehensive handbook to the plants and animals of the rainforest.

Rabinowitz, Alan. *Jaguar: Struggle and Triumph in the Jungles of Belize*. New York, Doubleday, 1986. The highly entertaining story of a New York zoologist who befriended the local Maya and survived plane crashes, drug dealers and ruthless poachers in his quest to establish the world's only jaguar preserve. An excellent insight into Belize's Maya culture.

Rauscher, Freya. *Cruising Guide to Belize and Mexico's Caribbean Coast*. Westcott Cove Publishing Company, 1991. The most comprehensive guide to Belize's offshore, weaving navigation and description with local color and anecdotal history. Sailors will find it indispensable.

Schele, Linda and David Freidel. *A Forest of Kings: The Untold Story of the Ancient Maya*. William Morrow, 1990. The authors decode Maya hieroglyphs to unlock an astonishingly complex world of rulers and kingdoms. With detailed diagrams and splendid color photos.

Stephens, John L. *Incidents of Travel in Central America, Chiapas and Yucatan*. New York, Dover Publications, 1969 (two volumes). Originally published in 1841, this book covers Stephens' groundbreaking discoveries of the Maya world in Belize, Copán and Quiriguá.

Stephens, Katie. *Jungle Walk: Birds and Beasts of Belize*. Belize, Angelus Press, 1989. An amusing, informative guide to Belize's wild animals.

Wright, Ronald. *Time Among the Maya*. Weidenfeld & Nicolson, 1989. Told with passion, wit and cynicism, this follows the author's eventful journey through the Maya world.

Snakes of Belize. Belize City, Belize Audubon Society. A handy guide for anyone headed into the jungle.

GLOSSARY

CUISINE

ariba—Garifuna flatbread made with cassava

bamboo chicken—iguana

Belikin—Belize's ubiquitous national beer

boil up—a stew, usually made with fish

Caribbean Rum—Belize's best rum

cassava—ruddy white tuber and a staple of the Garifuna diet

ceviche—raw white fish cured in lime juice with diced onions, chilies, seasonings and tomatoes

gibnut—a large, nocturnal rodent whose white meat is considered a delicacy (also called paca).

habañero—an extremely hot pepper, and the primary ingredient in Marie Sharp's Hot Pepper Sauce

heart of palm—tender, snow white core of the cohune palm, considered a delicacy since the time of the Maya

Marie Sharp's Hot Pepper Sauce—addictive habañero pepper sauce, brewed in southern Belize and found on most Belizean tables

MISCELLANEOUS DEFINITIONS

baboon—black howler monkey

Belize breeze—marijuana

biosphere reserve—a nature preserve where human activity is controlled but not prohibited

biotope—areas within a biosphere reserve that have a uniform environment of plants and animals

brukdown—rhythmic island music, originating in 19th-century Belizean logging camps

cayo—Spanish for caye, or island. San Ignacio was named Cayo because from the air it appears as an island surrounded by rivers

chicle—the sap from the sapodilla tree, used during the early 1900s to make chewing gum

chiclero—Maya bush man who gathered *chicle*, mainly for the Wrigley's chewing gum and Life Savers companies

coatimundi—also called a quash; a forest dweller, similar in appearance to a raccoon, that is easily spotted around Maya ruins and on back roads

dory—dugout canoe

garifuna—also *garinagu*; person of African and West Indian blood who immigrated from the island of St. Vincent

glyph—hieroglyph, as in those found in Maya cities

high bush—thick jungle

Kekchi—a distinct Belizean Maya group with its own Maya dialect

kinkajou—also called honey bear; a member of the raccoon family, with soft fur and a gregarious, endearing personality

Kukulcán—Maya sun god

Mestizo—person of mixed Spanish and Indian blood

milpa—corn field; often a slash-and-burn field

Mopan—a distinct Belizean Maya group with its own Maya dialect

peccary—a bristle-haired, snouted mammal that looks like a cross between a porcupine and a pig

pit-pan—wooden boat that plies the Belize rivers. Just 50 years ago, pit-pans were a primary transporation in Belize

pok-ta-pok—a basketball-style Maya sport using a small rubber ball

punta rock—Caribbean-style music that sounds part reggae, part disco and part rock 'n roll

sacbé—a Maya causeway that was paved with limestone in ancient times

sleeping policeman—speed bump

tapir—also called mountain cow, the shy, portly, long-snouted forest dweller is Belize's national animal

tayra—also called bushdog, it is a weasel-like animal that's extremely territorial

tiger—local term for jaguar

tiger cat—local word for ocelot; a "small tiger cat" is a margay

Yucatec—a distinct Belizean Maya group with its own Maya dialect

wee-wees—leaf-cutter ants

wowla or *woala*—boa constrictor

Notes from the Publisher

An alert, adventurous reader is as important as a travel writer in keeping a guidebook up-to-date and accurate. So if you happen upon a great restaurant, discover a special locale, or (heaven forbid) find an error in the text, we'd appreciate hearing from you. Just write to:

Ulysses Press
P.O. Box 3440
Berkeley, CA 94703

* * *

It is our desire as publishers to create guidebooks that are responsible as well as informative.

We hope that our guidebooks treat the people, country and land we visit with respect. We ask that our readers do the same. The hiker's motto, "Walk softly on the Earth," applies to travelers everywhere . . . in the desert, on the beach, and in town.

* * *

Index

Admiral Burnaby's Art Gallery and Coffee House, 106
Agoutis, 17
Air travel, 48
Airlines, 30
Airport transit, 46
Airports, 48
Altun Ha, 118–20, 122; map, 119
Ambergris Caye, 83–89
Animals, 14–21
Anteaters, 16
Archaeological preserves, 66–68. *See also specific archaeological preserves*
Archaeology Department, 132
Atolls, 72, 96–99
Augustine, 141

Banks, 46
Baron Bliss Memorial, 104–105
Beaches, 82. *See also specific towns or areas*
Beans and rice, 61–62
Beer, 35, 63
Belize, origin of name, 4–5
Belize City, 102–11; map, 102
Belize City Market, 59, 105
Belize City Municipal Airport, 48
Belize Commercial Center, 105–106
Belize Philatelic Bureau, 105
Belize Post Office, 105
Belize Tourist Board (Belize), 39
Belize Tourist Board (U.S.), 39
Belize Zoo, 129–31
Belmopan, 104, 132–34
Benque Viejo, 149, 151, 172
Bermudian Landing, 115
Bicycling, 77–78
Big Creek, 163–64, 165, 166
Biotopes, 66–68; map, 66. *See also specific biotopes*
Biotopo Cerro Cahui, 174
Biotopo Chacón Machaca, 185
Bird Caye Bird Sanctuary, 159
Birds, 19–20, 117–18
Birdwatching, 75–76
Blackbird Caye Village, 97
Bliss Institute, 106
Blue Creek, 167

Blue Hole (ocean sinkhole), 71–72, 97
Blue Hole and St. Herman's Cave National Park, 134
Bluefield Range, 100, 101
Boats, 48
Books, 34, 52
Border crossings: El Salvador, 28; Guatemala, 28, 29, 149, 184, 191, 194–95; Honduras, 28, 191, 194–95; Mexico, 126–27; United States, 29
Botflies, 56
Bottlass, 56
Bowen, Barry, 151–52
Brodies Department Store, 106
Bull's Point, 142
Burrell Boom, 115
Buses, 47–48
Business hours, 50
Butterflies, 125–26
Butterfly Falls, 142

Cahal Pech, 135
Calakmul Biosphere Reserve, 180
Calendar of events, 26–27
Camping, 68
Canoeing, 77
Car, bringing in to Belize, 31
Car insurance, 31
Car rentals, 49–50
Car travel: in Belize, 48–50; to Belize, 30–31
Caracol, 142–47, 151; map, 145
Carrie Bow Caye, 100–101
Cars for hire, 47
Castillo San Felipe (fort), 186
Castillo San Felipe (village) (Guatemala), 186, 189, 190
Caye Caulker, 89–94
Caye Chapel, 94
Cayes, 80–101; map, 80
Cayo Country, 134–41
Central Park, 106
Cerro Maya, 126
Chan Chich, 151–53
Chan Chich's Spicy Refried Bean Dip, 62
Chase, Arlen and Diane, 143, 144, 146–47
Chetumal (Mexico), 126–27
Children, traveling with, 37–38

202

St. John's Cathedral, 106
San Antonio (Western Belize), 136
San Antonio (Southern Belize), 167
San Benito (Guatemala), 173
San Ignacio, 135, 137–41
San Luis Rey Church, 167
San Pedro, 83–84, 85–89
San Pedro Airstrip, 84
Sandflies, 55
Santa Elena (Guatemala), 173, 182
Santa Rita, 126
Scuba diving. *See* Diving
Sea lice, 56
Sea thimbles, 56
Sea-ing is Belizing, 90–91
Seasons, 25–26
Senior travelers, 38
Sergeants Caye, 100, 101
Shipstern Nature Reserve and Butterfly
  Breeding Centre, 125–126
Shuttle boats, 48
Side trips from Belize, 170–95; map, 170
Siete Altares, 185
Snake Cayes, 167
Snakes, 18–19
Snorkeling, 75
South Water Caye, 100, 101, 158
Southern Belize, 154–69; map, 154
Southern Highway, 49
Spanish Lookout, 134–35
Spanish Lookout Caye, 100, 101
Specialty tours, 41–43
Stelae Museum, 175
Stingrays, 56
Student travelers, 39
Supreme Court, 106
Swimming, 75
Swing Bridge, 105

Tanah Mayan Art Museum, 136–37
Tapirs, 15

Taxis, 46–47
Tayasal, 173, 174
Teas, herbal, 22
Telephones, 51
Temperature, 25–26
Thousand Foot Falls, 142
Tiampiha, 162–63
Tikal Museum, 174–75
Tikal National Park, 172, 174–80, 181–
  82, 183–84; map, 177
Time zones, 50
Tipping, 46
Tobacco Caye, 158
Tours, specialty, 41–43
Transportation, local, 46–48; to Belize,
  30–31
Traveling expenses, 34–35
Turista, 53–55
Turneffe Islands, 72, 96–97, 98–99
Turtles, 17
Tzimin Che, 162–63

Uaxactún, 181
United States: border crossings, 29
United States Embassy, 104

Vegetables, 59–61
Victoria Peak, 155
Visas, 28
Visitor information, 39–40

Water Caye, 100, 101
Weather, 25–26
Western Belize, 128–53; map, 128
Western Highway, 49
Wildlife refuges, 66–68; map, 66. *See
  also specific wildlife refuges*
Women travelers, 36–37

Xunantunich, 147–48, 151; map, 147

Also Available From Ulysses Press

HIDDEN GUIDES

Adventure travel or a relaxing vacation?—"Hidden" guidebooks are the only travel books in the business to provide detailed information on both. Aimed at environmentally aware travelers, our motto is "Adventure Travel Plus." These books combine details on unique hotels, restaurants and sightseeing with information on camping, sports and hiking for the outdoor enthusiast.

HIDDEN BOSTON AND CAPE COD *228 pages. $7.95*
HIDDEN COAST OF CALIFORNIA *480 pages. $14.95*
HIDDEN FLORIDA *528 pages. $14.95*
HIDDEN FLORIDA KEYS & EVERGLADES *168 pages. $9.95*
HIDDEN HAWAII *468 pages. $14.95*
HIDDEN MEXICO *444 pages. $13.95*
HIDDEN NEW ENGLAND *564 pages. $14.95*
HIDDEN PACIFIC NORTHWEST *528 pages. $14.95*
HIDDEN SAN FRANCISCO
  AND NORTHERN CALIFORNIA *456 pages. $14.95*
HIDDEN SOUTHERN CALIFORNIA *516 pages. $14.95*
HIDDEN SOUTHWEST *504 pages. $14.95*

VIRAGO WOMAN'S TRAVEL GUIDES

Written through a woman's eye and steeped in the grand tradition of travel literature, these guides speak directly to the special interests of solo female travelers, businesswomen and women traveling with children. Each title offers a fascinating blend of practical information and cultural insights. History, art and contemporary society are examined from a woman's point of view with fascinating results.

NEW YORK *360 pages. $13.95*
PARIS *276 pages. $13.95*
ROME *360 pages. $13.95*

THE NEW KEY GUIDES

Critically acclaimed as the best resource to Costa Rica in print, *The New Key to Costa Rica* has captured the imagination of travelers everywhere. This edition is completely updated with hundreds of details on tropical rainforests, endangered species and awesome volcanoes.

THE NEW KEY TO COSTA RICA *312 pages. $13.95*

ULTIMATE GUIDES

These innovative guides present the best and most unique features of a destination. Quality is the keynote. They are as likely to cover a mom 'n pop café as a gourmet restaurant, a quaint bed and breakfast as a five-star tennis resort. In addition to thoroughly covering each destination, they feature short articles and one-line "teasers" that are both fun and informative.

ULTIMATE ARIZONA *324 pages. $11.95*

ULTIMATE CALIFORNIA *528 pages. $14.95*

ULTIMATE MAUI *192 pages. $11.95*

ULTIMATE SANTA FE *228 pages. $11.95*

ULTIMATE WASHINGTON *324 pages. $11.95*

DISNEY WORLD AND BEYOND:
The Ultimate Family Guidebook *300 pages. $10.95*

DISNEY WORLD AND BEYOND:
Family Fun Cards *90 cards. $7.95*

DISNEYLAND AND BEYOND:
The Ultimate Family Guidebook *240 pages. $9.95*

FLORIDA'S GOLD COAST:
The Ultimate Guidebook *192 pages. $8.95*

LAS VEGAS AND BEYOND:
The Ultimate Guidebook *240 pages. $9.95*

THE MAYA ROUTE: The Ultimate Guidebook *432 pages. $14.95*

ABOUT THE AUTHOR

Stacy Ritz, co-author of *The Maya Route: The Ultimate Guidebook*, wrote the best-selling *Disney World and Beyond: The Ultimate Family Guidebook* and co-authored *Hidden Florida*, *Florida's Gold Coast* and *Hidden New England*. Formerly a staff writer for *The Tampa Tribune*, she has written for *Parents Magazine*, the *Washington Post*, the *Miami Herald*, *Caribbean Travel & Life*, *Glamour* and *Bride's*.

ABOUT THE PHOTOGRAPHER

Doug Perrine has had a varied career as an English teacher, a marine biologist, a scuba diving instructor and a photojournalist. His photographs have been published in numerous books and magazines, including *National Geographic Traveler*, *Smithsonian*, *Elle*, *Newsweek*, *U.S. News and World Report*, *Geo*, *National Wildlife*, *International Wildlife*, *Ocean Realm* and *Wildlife Conservation*. Perrine is a contirbuting editor of *Scuba Times* magazine.

ABOUT THE ILLUSTRATOR

Glenn Kim is a freelance illustrator residing in San Francisco. His work appears in numerous Ulysses Press titles, including *Hidden Southwest*, *Ultimate Washington* and *Disneyland and Beyond: The Ultimate Family Guidebook*. He has also done illustrations for the National Forest Service, a variety of magazines, book covers and greeting cards.